HOME BEFORE MORNING

HOME BEFORE MORNING

With a new afterword by the author

Lynda Van Devanter

The Story of an Army Nurse in Vietnam

UNIVERSITY OF MASSACHUSETTS PRESS Amherst

Although the people and events described in this book are real, names and other identifying characteristics relating to certain nonpublic figures have been changed to protect their privacy.

Printed in the United States of America
Printed and bound by Sheridan Books, Inc.

LC 2001027636
ISBN 1-55849-298-4 (pbk. : alk. paper)

This book is published with the support and cooperation of the University of Massachusetts Boston.

Library of Congress Cataloging-in-Publication Data

Van Devanter, Lynda.
Home before morning : the story of an army nurse in Vietnam / Lynda Van Devanter.
p. cm.
Originally published: New York : Beaufort Books, 1983.
ISBN 1-55849-298-4 (pbk. : alk. paper)
1. Van Devanter, Lynda. 2. Vietnamese Conflict, 1961–1975—Personal narratives, American. 3. Vietnamese Conflict, 1961–1975—Medical care. 4. Nurses—Vietnam—Biography. 5. Nurses—United States—Biography. I. Title.
DS559.5 . V36 2001
959.704′37—dc21 2001027636

British Library Cataloguing in Publication data are available.

TO
LIEUTENANT SHARON A. LANE
AND ALL OF THE UNKNOWN WOMEN
WHO SERVED
FORGOTTEN
IN THEIR WARS

CONTENTS

FOREWORD

I began this book as a form of therapy in early 1979. I was hoping somehow to exorcise the Vietnam war from my mind and heart. What I learned in the intervening years of writing and reliving the pain of that war is that my feelings about the war will never go away. I don't want them to. For if I forget entirely, I may be passively willing to see it happen again. I did learn, however, that the war doesn't have to own me; I can own it.

When the book was finished, I wanted to share it with others. My story is only my own, but many other women and men shared similar experiences both during and after the war. I hope to let them know that they are not alone, and that they, too, can find the way back home.

For many years, I longed to speak to the families of those many casualties who did not survive. I wanted the parents, children, brothers, and sisters to know how hard we tried to save the lives, and how awful we felt when we couldn't. I wanted to tell Katie, and Gene's parents, that someone held his hand while he died, and that I, too, cried for him for years.

I have not said it all. If I tried to, this book would never be finished, and there is so much of that year in Vietnam and the long years after that I cannot remember. I needed to forget during those early years, and now that I want it back I have to struggle to regain it. But it is coming back, and I'm learning to live with it.

In most forewords, authors want to thank those who have helped make their books possible. There are those for me, but more than that, are those who have helped make my life possible.

Foremost is Bill Blackton. As the cancer patient is eaten away by a strange malignant cell, so was I being destroyed by an unknown thing when I met him. He helped me through the most destructive times of the cancer—the Vietnam war's aftermath. I am alive because of Bill, and I will be forever grateful to him.

In addition, there are some others who were a part of my rebirth and growth. The first is Shad Meshad. He walked me through Vietnam emotionally for the first time. When I silently called "medic," he was there, doing what he did best, and I thank him.

Next is not a person, but a concept: Antioch University, Los Angeles. Antioch's process forced me to learn to examine and evaluate my life and what had happened to me, and it was a major step toward resolution of my life experiences. Al Erdynast and the Developmental Group helped me learn to open many doors and look inside.

To many others I owe a debt of thanks. Rose Sandecki, Lily Adams, Chuck Figley, John Wilson, Wellbourne Jacks, Jr., Wayne Felde, Graves Thomas, Art Blank, Harold Bryant, Jack Smith, Mary Lane, Rick Weidman, Bob Muller, Judy Kolarik, Sara McVicker, Joan Furrey, Jane Thomson, Donna and Jessica Blank and especially the "Back in the world" group, and Ken Harbert have each had a significant impact on my survival.

To Gloria Emerson goes my gratitude for continually encouraging me to keep writing. I also thank Chris Morgan for forcing me to remember and dredge up things I thought best forgotten and for putting my story on paper. I often hated him for it, but I know it had to be done. I am grateful to Susan Suffes, and the rest of the folks at Beaufort, for their belief and help and to my sister Jean for her suggestions and criticism of the manuscript.

I want to thank my family for their support and encouragement, especially my parents and my sister Mary. I know it must have been terribly confusing for them to have their child and sister return so totally changed after only one year in Vietnam. It was a long year.

1

Just Another Warm Summer Night

Three A.M. Sometimes, when the nights are not easy, I can lie here alone in this big bed for hours, listening to the ticking clock or the sound of the crickets in the bushes beneath my window, part of me wanting desperately to get back to sleep, knowing that if I don't, tomorrow's meetings will be filled, for me, with little more than exhaustion.

I hate dragging myself through the deadening days that follow these long nights. I hate that sick morning feeling in my stomach that comes from being too tired. I hate the thought that, in my half-awake state, I will lose some of tomorrow.

But more than all that, I hate what I might face were I to once again allow myself the mixed blessing of sleep. It's not that I don't want to sleep, only that I'm afraid of tonight's kind of sleep, afraid of what it often brings.

In part, this night is my own fault. Lately, these difficult times have been almost nonexistent and, if I hadn't spent so many hours this afternoon reliving Vietnam with another troubled woman veteran, I would now be resting quietly. But at a 3 A.M. like this one, that thought offers little consolation.

They flew him in by chopper and there were streaks of dirt along his face. His sandy brown hair was uneven, with patches pressed down where the sweat-soaked straps of his helmet had been. With his eyes closed, he might have been just another tired soldier resting. However, the bloody mess that was once his body told a different story.

Maybe, if there were time, he could be saved. But there were too many others.

In some ways, the bad nights must have been easier when Bill was here. He used to tell me that I ground my teeth in my sleep. He would touch my cheek and I'd stop for a while, only to start again later. He told me about the talking in my sleep and the moaning sounds I would make before waking in fear.

I would put my arms around him and hold myself tightly against his body, trying to draw enough strength to make him understand all that I had seen. It was useless. He could listen to me, yet I hadn't figured out how to say all that was inside, and probably, like the others, he wouldn't want to know anyway.

What did he do to help me on nights like this one? Did he hold me, return my frantic hugs with reassurance? Did he tuck my head into the hollow formed by his shoulder and tell me it would be all right? Did he make me feel protected? Did he take away any of the pain? Could he? Could anyone?

Maybe the nights are worse since we separated. Or were they just as bad when he was here?

I don't remember.

The boy couldn't have been more than ten years old, the kind of kid who would have been sitting down by a stream, dangling his feet in the water, holding the end of a fishing line, enjoying a lazy summer day—if he hadn't stepped on the land mine. When his mother carried him onto the compound, there were two bloody stumps where his legs had been.

Any shrink worth his ninety dollars an hour would probably say I should "face the pain and deal with it." In fact, I've heard those words more than once. They even sound like something I might say to the women who come to me for counseling, looking for someone to take away their pain, their voices breaking as they recount the horrors of their own personal hells while I sit there listening, trying to assure them that they are not crazy.

"I understand," I say. "You're not alone. Many of us have seen the same things. Together, we can get past the problems. It's hard work, but it can be done."

Occasionally, the words work. But it's on nights like this that they and I must face the realization that we are alone, that ours is a solitary pain, to be felt in hundreds of 3 A.M.s when those around us are sleeping peacefully.

There was a time when I didn't understand that, when I didn't know how alone I was, how alone we all were. It was a time when I thought I would be able to talk about—exorcise—all the memories of hours spent in the operating rooms of Pleiku and Qui Nhon, working with surgeons as we tried to save the lives of boys who would never again be whole. I wanted to tell someone I loved—my parents, a friend, a relative, anyone—about the rocket attacks and all the nights I slept under my bunk; about the weeks we had more casualties than we could handle and how hard we worked even when we knew it was hopeless; about the tiny children with their arms and legs blown off; about the terrible oppression of the monsoon and the nights we knew we would die. Vietnam was the worst time of my life, yet it was also, in many ways, the most important and the most intense. For years, I tried to talk about it. Nobody listened.

Who would have wanted to listen? Mine were not nice, neat stories. There was love, but no cute little love stories; heroes, but no grand, heroic war stories; winners, but you had to look hard to tell them from the losers. On our battlefields, there were no knights in shining armor rescuing damsels in distress. The stories, even the funny ones, were all dirty. They were rotten and they stank. The moments, good and bad, were permeated with the stench of death and napalm.

And when that year was over, when the "Freedom Bird" took me back to "the world," I learned that my war was just beginning.

They wheeled her in on a gurney. She'd already gone into labor. With the bullet wound in her belly, a normal childbirth would be out of the question. So we cut into her, and found a perfectly formed live baby boy. He had a gunshot wound in his belly.

There are beads of sweat on my forehead. A few roll down the side of my face. With the back of my hand, I wipe them away, but not before a single drop rolls into my left eye and burns. These Virginia summers are unbearably hot. I can remember nights like this in Vietnam, nights when I couldn't escape the all-encompassing steam bath, my sweat-stained jungle fatigues clinging to my body while the heat slowly drained every ounce of life from me, making me far too miserable to cry. It was the kind of heat that goes all the way to your soul, a heat that makes you wonder if the prophets hadn't experienced their visions of hell on one of these stifling nights.

For some reason, tonight's heat seems worse than any I remember from Vietnam. Or is it? Have I been spoiled by all those years in southern California, where the ocean breezes helped to make the nights more comfortable?

I should call the air-conditioning contractor in the morning and ask him to finish the system. What person with any sense would try to get through these hot, humid Virginia summers without air-conditioning? Or maybe I should just forget the air conditioner and try to sell the house, move into an apartment like Bill did. Do I really need all this room? Probably not.

We were going to remodel the place, take the paint off all the molding and bring it back to the way it must have looked a hundred years ago. We probably saw fifty houses before finding this one, and as soon as I walked in the front door, I knew this was it. At first Bill was reluctant to buy something needing so much work, but later he felt differently.

It's a special place. The floors are all hardwood, and there's the most interesting squeak when you walk in the upstairs hallway. We planned to strip the wood and refinish it. The cracks in the plaster were going to be fixed and the painted kitchen cabinets would be replaced with natural oak, oiled to a warm luster. I wanted hanging plants in the large windows. In the daytime, they let plenty of light in. A healthy Boston fern would look nice in the front hallway; maybe a couple of coleus plants in the living room, or a wandering Jew, or some baby's breath. We were going to fill our lives with growing things, maybe even a baby after we learned more about the dangers of my exposure to Agent Orange.

I remember the afternoon more than a year ago, after the spring thaw, when we dug holes in the side yard so we could plant fruit trees. We joked that day about spending our old age in rocking chairs under the trees, reaching up from time to time and grabbing another peach. Bill had said that sixty years from now, when we were long gone, there would be a young family in the house and they would make occasional references to "the old couple who planted the fruit trees."

That day was a happy one. For at least a few hours, I partly believed in our future and in my future. But I didn't have to wait sixty years to be the old woman who had lived in the big house on the corner. In my mid-thirties, I already felt far older than any chronological age I might ever reach.

It wasn't something that had developed recently, with the marital problems. I had felt like an old woman long before I'd ever met Bill. The feeling had been there at twenty-two, that bone-tired weariness that makes daily living an extreme test of will. Maybe I thought that Bill could help turn back my emotional clock. It was too much to ask of anyone.

We never got around to buying those fruit trees. For a while, I left the empty holes, which served no function other than to create hazards when I tried to mow the lawn. Then, I filled them in.

About a hundred feet past the former holes, just beyond the hedges, two people are walking silently in the softness of the night. It's a man and a woman, both in shorts and T-shirts, probably other unfortunates without benefit of air-conditioning. As they turn the corner, the woman speaks quietly and her muffled words rise to my window. The man answers her. They seem comfortable together, happy to be alive in spite of this godforsaken heat. I envy their three o'clock in the morning intimacy and feel a dull ache inside as I wipe more sweat from my face.

When they disappear back into the shadows, I sit up and put my feet over the side of the bed. The sheets are soaked with sweat, partly from the heat and partly from the night. My T-shirt looks as if it just came out of the wash. I grab another from the dresser and remove the soaked one, throwing it into a corner.

He was only eighteen years old. I put his hand in mine. "I'm a nurse," I said. "You are in an American hospital. We're going to make you as comfortable as possible." It was what we said to all the ones we classified as expectants, those we expected to die. It was simply a matter of time.

Against my better judgment, I decide to try once more for sleep, hopefully a peaceful one this time. I crawl over to the dry empty side of the bed—Bill's side—and lie down. Eyes closed, breathing slowly, I attempt to calm myself. It works. I am drifting, resting normally, this time possibly until morning. It is peaceful, so peaceful.

The dreams come slowly. I can hear birds and the sound of water lapping against my air mattress as I lie in the middle of a pool. The sun is setting, casting long shadows. Some men and women are sitting on the grass nearby. They are laughing and talking. Behind them, the top of a makeshift chapel rises above a wooden fence. The building is dwarfed by twin radar screens on the hill to the right. Near the screens, a soldier sits in a guard tower. I can hear the tanks rolling across the compound. Suddenly, it's all interrupted by a rocket attack and mud is oozing through the walls of the operating room, while we work frantically to put some soldier's leg back together. There's an explosion.

Everything goes black.

After a few moments in the darkness, I hear the insistent ring of a telephone outside my door. It's 3 A.M. in Pleiku. The fighting in the Central Highlands is heavy, with the continuous sound of rifles, mortars, and artillery off in the distance. I've been sleeping under my cot, having been awakened an hour earlier by a rocket attack. In my exhaustion, not even the concussion of explosions nearby could keep me awake. But the telephone sets me in motion.

Still half asleep, I hold the receiver to my ear. "Incoming wounded! Get everyone down here on the double." The adrenalin flows as I run through the hooch, waking the other nurses—"Mickie, get up!" "Oh, no! Not again!" Banging on their doors—"Coretta, casualties." "Don't those V.C. ever rest?" Racing against time, while the sound of the med-evac choppers grows louder—"Jill." "Leave me alone, Van. I'm tired." "Let's go, kiddo, we're on!" A groan, and I hear her moving.

Back in my room, I can hear running footsteps on the hall floor as I remove my nightgown and hustle into fatigues. *Bastards! Won't they ever let us sleep?* I throw my flak jacket over one shoulder, my helmet onto my head, and race to the doorway of the hooch, my untied bootlaces dragging on the floor. By the time I reach the outside steps, my fatigue shirt is buttoned and the flak jacket is hoisted onto my other shoulder, one snap fastened to keep it from flapping. Others are running ahead of me toward the emergency room, their silhouettes sharply outlined by the flashing light of flares, exploding artillery rounds, and rockets. My heart is beating wildly. Miles away, red tracers rain down from Cobra gunships. The ARVN tanks are moving around the edges of our compound. Overhead, a helicopter begins its descent with more wounded as doctors, nurses, and medics push gurneys to the landing pad. The roar of the rotor blades becomes deafening.

I run to the ER, grab a gurney, and wheel it out. The first dust-off is already lifting off, heading back into combat for more casualties, while a second chopper comes in quickly to take its place. As soon as the bird touches down, the medical personnel and flight crew work frantically to unload the damaged human cargo. The pilot is a twenty-one-year-old kid nicknamed Shortstop, because he's barely five foot six. He has an oversized baby face that is usually dominated by his cute, puffy red cheeks. Those cheeks are now a pasty white as he yells from his seat, "Get those fuckers moving. We gotta get back there quick!" There's blood down the left side of Shortstop's flight suit. I notice it as I'm helping another nurse drag a litter from the chopper onto a gurney.

"Come on, assholes, we don't have all day!" Shortstop screams.

I jump back on the chopper and grab his left shoulder. I have to yell to be heard above the engine. "You're hit."

"No shit, Dick Tracy."

"Let someone look at it."

"Later, Van. It's a fucking mess out there right now. Get the fuck off my goddamned machine so I can go back to work." Although he protests, I quickly wrap a pressure dressing around his arm to stop the bleeding. It takes only a few extra seconds.

With all the wounded cleared out, I jump to the ground. Shortstop's chopper is lifting off even before my feet have touched the earth. It is the last time I will ever see him alive.

I run to catch up with a corpsman pushing the last gurney as another chopper lands behind me. More medical personnel start off-loading new wounded, but by now my full attention is on the soldier at my side. As we roll through the doors of the ER, I am using my scissors to cut his uniform off so we can examine his sucking chest wound. The corpsman pushes the soldier's litter against a wall and I hang his IV bottle. In the light, it quickly becomes apparent that this guy has more than just a chest wound. There's a through and through gunshot wound in his left shoulder and hundreds of smaller wounds—multiple frag wounds—covering his entire body. They probably came from a rocket, mine, or grenade. Although he doesn't say a word, I can see the fear in his eyes. I give him a shot of morphine and try to offer some reassurance before moving along to another case. This one will survive. "Don't worry," I say. "We've got the best doctors in the world here. You'll be better before you know it." My words don't ease the pain, but I know the morphine soon will.

One of the ER doctors comes up behind me with a clipboard as I'm drawing some blood to be typed and crossmatched for later transfusion. "What do we have here, Van?"

"A sucking chest wound," I answer. "GSW T and T in the left shoulder and MFWs front and back. Blood pressure eighty over fifty, pulse one fifty."

"Okay, we'll send him in as soon as he's stabilized."

I begin moving through the seemingly endless flow of wounded soldiers, working with the doctors, making quick, superficial examinations to determine which will be first into the operating rooms, which ones can wait for treatment, and which ones will be left to die because we lack the time or resources to save them. The emergency room is filled with the moaning and screaming of boys and men who have been rudely confronted with their own mortality, their mangled and twisted bodies contorted by more than physical pain. Mixed among their cries are the urgent, but professional voices of the medical people.

"Get another IV into this one, he's shocky."

"Somebody help me!"

"They're only MFWs of the legs. He can wait."

"I want my mother."

"Type and cross this one for fifteen units."

"Don't let me die."

"Wheel that one over to the expectant room."

To the average person, the scene in the ER might appear to be one of absolute chaos. But the actual precision of this system is amazing, especially for the Army. Everyone knows exactly what to do and does it without question, giving the best possible care in the shortest amount of time, to keep as many people alive as possible.

As I finish one soldier's examination, a weak hand grabs my arm. "Hey, Van?"

I turn to find Bennie Dickenson, a twenty-year-old field medic from the 4th Division lying on a gurney. Almost every man in his platoon has been killed or wounded tonight. Bennie has a gaping hole in his left side, exposing half of his chest, another in his belly, and a bloody stump where his left leg used to be. Around the stump is a tourniquet that he probably applied by himself. He might make it, but he'd need to get to an operating room quickly.

In spite of his pain, Bennie's voice is calm and well modulated, sounding like that of a precise and highly trained medic, and not that of a man with half his body blown away.

"I apologize for the unexpected visit," he says. "I wanted to surprise you guys to see if you really work as hard as you say."

I am speechless—I've partied with Bennie, compared stories about our respective childhoods, and more than once, I've considered saying yes to his half-joking requests for a date. His best friend, Phil Conklin, is an OR technician here, and Bennie frequently spends his free time at our hospital, playing cards and chess with Phil or conning us out of extra medical supplies that he can take to the field. Phil and Bennie have gone through grammar school, high school, and basic training together. They even worked it so they arrived in Vietnam on the same day. But their different medical specialties landed them in different assignments, a problem that Phil had wanted to correct by having Bennie apply for a transfer to our hospital. By the time the skids were greased, Bennie was so worried about "his boys" in the platoon that he refused to budge. Like most field medics, he's been their mother hen almost since the day he arrived. He worries that no one can care for them as well as he can.

I wipe the sweat from his forehead. "Van, could you please do me a big favor?" he asks.

"Sure, Bennie. You need some morphine?"

"No, thanks. It's Petrocelli over there." He lifts his arm weakly and points to a brawny, dark-haired kid about five feet away. "I ran out of plasma before he got hit and he's lost at least three or four units of blood. He looks like he's going into shock. Could you get an extra IV into him?"

"Sure thing."

As soon as I take care of Petrocelli, I come back to Bennie. It's difficult to keep my hands from shaking as I cut away his uniform and examine his open belly. I've worked on friends before, but it's never easy.

"Don't waste your time on me, Van. Take care of my guys first."

I ignore his suggestion and continue the exam, trying to see him as merely another case, and not as a person who was telling me jokes only four days earlier.

"When you get to Spezak, you better turn him over," Bennie says. "He's got some frags in his back. And I think he might have something going on in his belly, because it was rigid. Better get a surgeon to open him up quick."

He continues, "When you get Mitchell into the OR, tell the gas passer to be careful putting him under. The crazy fucker just finished eating six cans of beans and dicks before we got hit."

I cut away what's left of Bennie's fatigue pants and can see a long deep wound down to the bone in the back of his "good" leg. I cover it and him with a clean sheet. I touch his cheek before moving on to another casualty. He smiles weakly. He knows that his chances are not good. He probably knew it from the moment he was hit.

Five minutes later, with the choppers still bringing in wounded, I am called to scrub for surgery. On my way to the operating room, I walk past Phil Conklin as he pushes a dead body toward the morgue. He's muttering to himself and trying to hold back tears. "Stupid fucking hero."

I glance down and see Bennie's face. I too want to cry; to mourn not only Bennie, but the thousands like him who have come through this hospital. But tonight, neither Phil Conklin nor I, nor any of the other personnel at the 71st Evacuation Hospital will shed a tear for Bennie Dickenson. There isn't enough time to cry while so many others are depending on us to keep them alive.

When I wake again, my body is shaking and the sheets under me are saturated with sweat. I stare at the bedroom ceiling and try to tell myself that it's all over, that Vietnam is behind me. In spite of my best efforts, a single word keeps screaming inside my head:

Why?

There are hours left until daybreak. The sun is half a lifetime away. In a moment, when the tears stop, I will climb out of bed, head downstairs for a drink, and try, once more, to figure out where it all began.

2

The All-American Girl

"We're never going to fit all this junk, Lynda." Barbara Kaplan sat on the curb next to her huge, ridiculous hair dryer, a bright red dome that looked like a canister-style vacuum cleaner. A few strands of her shoulder-length red hair were out of place. They fell across her sweat-dampened forehead and hung in front of her green eyes. She lazily brushed the hair aside and leaned back on her elbows, yawning as she stretched her long, willowy body. We'd been up since 4 A.M., hoping to get an early start. Now, four hours later, she looked as tired as I felt. And the trip hadn't even begun.

"I don't see why you have to bring that monster anyway," I snapped. In spite of the cool September morning air, I could feel the beads of sweat rolling down my back. We had spent three of the last four hours trying to pack everything we needed into the old black convertible, a '62 Chevy II Nova, I had bought from my older sister, Nancy, for three hundred dollars. Barbara's hair dryer was the only thing we couldn't fit. "Leave it behind," I said.

"How am I going to dry my hair?" she asked.

"You can use mine every morning after I'm done with it."

She sat forward and brought her knees to her chest. "I've got a better idea," she said. "Let's leave *yours* behind and you can use *mine* when *I'm* finished."

I was beginning to get annoyed. We had planned to be on the road by six thirty. "All right. I get the point. We'll take the hair dryer, but we have to get rid of these." I lifted a big heavy box from the car's trunk and dropped it on the ground. Then I placed her hair dryer into the empty space.

"Hey!" she said. "Those are my nursing textbooks."

"You don't need them."

"Says who?"

"We already passed the state board exams," I replied.

"I might want to review some things."

"You can use the books in the library."

"I want my books."

"Then you'll have to get rid of something else," I said.

"Fair enough." As I watched in disbelief, Barbara stood up, grabbed *my* television from the other side of the trunk, and put it on the curb where her hair dryer had been. She lifted her books back into the trunk.

"You can't do that," I said.

"I just did." She smiled triumphantly. "Besides, if you spend too much time in front of that boob tube, it'll fry your brain."

The nerve! I reached into the backseat, shoved aside two garment bags, a Coleman lantern, and a box of kitchen utensils, then lifted out her stereo. "If my television stays behind, so does this piece of trash." I set it on the road next to the car and stood defiantly, with my hands on my hips, glaring up at her, trying to look as menacing as possible. I was almost ready for a fight. She may have been six inches taller than me, but I had her by ten pounds.

"Fine," she said smugly. She walked to the other side of the car, dug down under a couple of sleeping bags, suitcases, and a pup tent, and lifted out another box, slightly larger than her box of books. "I guess if we can't bring my stereo, there's no sense in bringing these."

My records! I was beginning to doubt whether this friendship, which had survived nursing school and a summer of weekends at the beach, would last out the morning. In my anger, I grabbed her garment bag and tossed it onto the road. "Then maybe you won't need these party dresses either."

She threw my garment bag on top of it. Next went the suitcases, one at a time, first hers, then mine. Then came the sleeping bags, the pup tent, the box of utensils, the bag of canned goods, the portable radio, the case of beer, my four bottles of Blondsilk hair bleach, both makeup kits, the Coleman stove, the fuel can for the stove, a lantern, and everything else. Each of us was determined not to quit this lunacy until the other admitted she was wrong. Ten minutes later, the car was empty and all our gear was scattered around it—all except that ugly hair dryer, which still sat in the trunk. Barbara and I reached for it at the same time, tugged it between us for a few seconds, and finally, out of sheer frustration, we both started laughing. The two of us sat on the curb, surveying the mess that was half in the street and half on the sidewalk, laughing so hard there were tears in our eyes.

"Now what do we do?" I asked.

"We start again," she said between laughs. "It should be easier now that we know where everything fits."

"Everything except your hair dryer."

"I never liked that ugly thing anyway."

Two hours later, after saying good-bye to my parents, we were on our way. The problem hair dryer was resting snugly in the trunk, under a couple of blankets. We had compromised—Barbara had agreed to take only the most essential textbooks and I had agreed to leave some of my records behind. We were beginning a journey that had been planned for more than a half year, ever since we had signed the contracts with the Army recruiting sergeant while we were still in nursing school. It was a journey that would give us, in Barbara's words, "probably the only chance we'll ever have to be as free as the wind." We didn't want to miss the opportunity.

It was to be a time without any obligations. Our only requirement was to be in San Francisco by October 31, the date on our orders, so that Barbara's father, an Army colonel stationed at the Presidio, could commission us as second lieutenants in the Army Nurse Corps. The week after that, we would be due at Fort Sam Houston, Texas, to begin our basic training, which we fully expected to be the start of the most challenging period of our lives. Until then, September and October of 1968 were going to be all ours, to travel wherever my rattletrap of a car and our limited funds would take us, and to do whatever we pleased. We were filled with anticipation as we left my parents' house on Edison Street and drove through Arlington toward the Capitol Beltway, knowing inside that when we returned, we would no longer be the same.

To Barbara, leaving those Washington, D.C., suburbs probably seemed less significant than it did to me. As the only child of a West Point–trained Signal Corps officer and his high school sweetheart wife, she had spent most of her formative years traveling to places like

Europe, Japan, Turkey, the Philippines, and Korea. Although her family always returned to their house in Arlington between overseas assignments, or when her father was sent on unaccompanied hardship tours, northern Virginia was merely a second home for them. Like most Army brats, Barbara's real home wasn't a geographical location; it was the Army. From that point of view, after three years of nursing school, she wasn't leaving home, she was going back to it—back to the Army—at least for the next two years and perhaps for a lifetime.

Unlike my best friend, I saw Arlington as my only home. I'd spent almost my entire life in the house my father built on Edison Street. Although I'd actually left three years earlier to go to nursing school in Baltimore, this would be the first time I was ever going to be living more than a short distance from my parents. While I drove along the familiar streets, my mind filled with the images of my childhood. I could remember those Sunday afternoons spent sitting on the living room couch watching baseball with my father and Uncle Joe, feeling special as Uncle Joe let me take my first sips of beer, which he poured into my little glass, an empty jar that had once contained Cheez Whiz. I could almost feel the cool, fresh air from the fall evenings spent camping on a piece of property my parents owned in the Shenandoah mountains, my father chopping wood and my mother cooking dinner, while my four sisters and I warmed ourselves around an open fire; I could hear the shouts of neighborhood boys on those bright Saturday afternoons when we played tackle football and I threatened to take my football home if they didn't play by my rules. There were dozens of quick images: going to Mass with my father; laughing with my younger sister, Mary; watching the sunset from the upstairs bedroom window; singing Christmas carols during the holidays; eating my mother's lasagna.

As we passed the softball field, I could hear the voice of my father from an earlier time, yelling encouragement to me and my sister Jean, two years younger than I am, as we gave those games everything we had. We wanted the coach—our father—to be proud of us. "Good hit, Lynda. Way to go. Come on, Jean, get another hit and bring her around." My father used to call me the talking catcher and he swore that with my constant chatter behind the plate, I could talk even the most confident batter into striking out. I was as good as most boys, but in those days, girls weren't allowed to play Little League—I guess because they were considered too delicate. So we did our hitting, fielding, and baserunning in the Pigtail and Ponytail Leagues, on teams coached by men like my father who found themselves without sons.

My father never told any of us he wanted a son. On the contrary, he always said that his girls made him the happiest guy in the world, that any man in his right mind would be more than content with our love and that he could never love any son more than he loved his daughters. It wasn't the Van Devanter name that was important, he said, it was the family pride. He wanted all of us to know that we were special. He and my mother encouraged us to be independent and to believe ourselves the equals of anyone. But shortly after my youngest sister, Sue, was born, my father received a cartoon from one of his friends. It showed a mother and father walking down the street, pushing a baby carriage, with four little girls, each wearing frilly little dresses and ribbons in their hair. The husband was talking with another man and he said, "We wanted a boy, but Helen goofed." My mother's name was Helen and the cartoon was stuck in my father's dresser mirror for a long time. That was around the time I learned that I had an older brother who died at birth.

I was born two years later.

In some inexplicable way, kids usually know what their parents want and, perhaps to compensate, I became one of the boys. When did it begin? Most likely the first time I picked up a football and saw my father smile.

However, being without other males in the family was something my father was accustomed to long before we came along. Rodney Van Devanter was an only child whose father died early in the Depression years. Brought up by his mother and an aunt, the boy's major masculine influences came from the Xaverian Brothers who ran Mount Saint Joseph's in Baltimore, and who gave him a classical education that developed speaking and writing skills that made him sound like an authority even when he was addressing us on a mundane topic. He had the verbal precision and mental acuity of a good lawyer, although he spent almost all of his adult years as a bureaucrat. I've always thought that there was a part of my father, especially when he was going to commit his words to paper, that saw those words as something that might live forever. They had to be the best words possible. When he attempted to make a point to us, he always tried to make it in a way that would be memorable and would encourage us to move to a higher level of thought. Unfortunately, he was not always successful. We probably disappointed him many times.

He also tried to instill in us as deep a feeling for Catholicism as he held, and during my childhood and early adolescence, I faithfully followed his example, going to Mass with him on early weekday mornings when it wasn't required. Often, we would be the only two people in the chapel other than the priest. My father would serve as the acolyte while I sat in the first pew. Each night I knelt and prayed the Our Father, the Hail Mary, and the God Bless with Mom or Dad. The God Bless was a made-up prayer for anybody we wanted to encourage special blessings for; however, it was usually: "God Bless Mom and Daddy, Nancy and Jean, Mary and Sue, Aunt Betty Ann, and all my aunts and uncles and cousins, and please make me a good girl. Amen."

Those were the days when I had no other desire than to grow up to be a martyr, although I'm sure that if I'd ever talked about it with my father, he would have discouraged me. Of course, at the time, there was no way to talk me out of the notion. While good Catholic boys usually fantasize about becoming major league baseball players or professional basketball stars, good Catholic girls usually harbor, at least once in their lives, a secret desire to become martyrs. If I couldn't make it to martyrdom, there was always sainthood, which was kind of like being on the second string of an athletic team; you were good enough to make the squad and maybe even play once in a while, but the martyrs were the real heroes. I wasn't sure exactly what had to be done to become one, but I knew it had something to do with being burned at the stake or pilloried, although I wasn't quite sure what being pilloried meant. My hero was Catherine of Sienna, who had been a young girl living in Sienna, Italy, when she started having these visions that let her know she was supposed to be a Catholic. Her parents used to beat her and do mean things to keep her from converting, but good old Cat hung in there. She finally ended up being killed for the faith, which was the Catholic girl's equivalent of growing up to be Babe Ruth.

My father's hero was probably Saint Paul. From the time we were old enough to understand, he told us the story of the Roman tax collector Saul, who had been rotten to the Jews, until he was struck down by a bolt of lightning from God, causing him to change his sinful ways and to become Paul. I probably heard that story at least ten times when I was a child. Whenever I wanted, I could close my eyes and see the picture from the religion book, showing Saul kneeling on the ground, with the bolt of lightning coming out of the sky, accompanied by the words, "Saul, Saul, why do you persecute me?" Beating up Jews and taking their money was Saint Paul's indiscretion, for which he repented, and from which he went on to lead an admirable life. Like Paul, my father also had committed an indiscretion early in life, although his was far more modest. He had flunked out of college in his freshman year.

He told us he had spent his time at the University of Maryland majoring in fraternities. But after leaving the university, he, like Paul, got a jolt, and saw the error in his ways. He never told us whether the jolt was lightning from God or a good old-fashioned hickory-stick licking from his mother. Whatever it was, it led him back to college, this time under the tutelage of the Jesuits at Georgetown University, where he graduated near the top of his class in 1938.

Three years later, shortly before the United States entered World War II, he married my mother, whom he had known since childhood. The oldest of six girls, my mother claimed her diploma from the University of Hard Knocks. She had lived in Arlington from the time she was four and had also attended Catholic schools. At the time she married, she was a clerk-typist for the Washington Gas Company and my father was an investigator for the Civil Service Commission.

After Pearl Harbor, Dad promptly did what every normal healthy American man was expected to do: He volunteered for the military. Three times he tried and three times he was rejected. When he got to the point of appealing his case before the draft board, he was told he would be more valuable working as a civilian in places like Boston, Washington, and Rhode Island, rather than as a soldier in Normandy, Iwo Jima, or Anzio. Instead of winning medals and battle ribbons like other men of his generation, my father found himself, in 1944 with the birth of my sister, Nancy, starting a family. He rarely talked to any of us about his attempts to join the military, but when he did speak, it was obvious that he always regretted having been denied the opportunity that had been given to so many others of his generation—the chance to fight for "freedom and democracy." As we were growing up, both he and my mother emphasized the obligation we all had to be of service not only to our family, community, church, and country, but to all of mankind.

Their words were not empty ones. They practiced their beliefs. Although my father had to moonlight fixing televisions in the basement to support his growing family on a tight budget, he always found a way to give money and time to those who were in need.

But all was not hard work and sacrifice. He had something of the ham in him and, in his spare time, had played in amateur stage productions and the Knights of Columbus minstrel shows presented for charitable causes. I also developed a taste for the footlights. Encouraged by Dad, I made my first appearance at age two in a benefit for the March of Dimes, singing "Me and My Shadow" with a woman who looked and sang like Kate Smith. I played the shadow. The next year, after I had fallen and knocked out my front teeth, the logical tune was "All I Want for Christmas Is My Two Front Teeth," and the year after that it was "Oh, You Beautiful Doll," which I sang to an oversized doll that was bigger than I. Although all these efforts were hits with the audience, the highlight of my short singing career came at age five, when my father and I did a duet on the Lyons Village Community House stage. He sang "I'm the Last of the Red Hot Papas," in a tux, while I played a pint-sized vamp dressed in a red taffeta spaghetti strap evening gown, silver high heels, and my mother's makeup, and chimed in with "I'm the Last of the Red Hot Mamas." It brought the house down.

For a few years after that, I imagined myself growing up to be an actress and a singer. But not many middle-class suburban kids were encouraged to enter those professions. Instead, I channeled my dreams toward a more accessible career—nursing. The inclination started when I was four and running around the house with kitchen towels, tying slings around everyone's arms. It continued while I was nursing injured birds back to health. I read all the books about nurses I could find and by the time I was twelve, I was already working as a volunteer "pink angel," running errands and emptying bedpans at Georgetown Hospital, along with my older sister, Nancy. Later, when I was seventeen and working part-time at a geriatric home, I began to understand why some nurses called their profession a "shitty" one. I realized that they were probably speaking literally. During those days, I spent almost 90 percent of my working hours either passing bedpans or giving enemas. Before I even had a chance to see the inside of a nursing school, I became an expert at enemas. I gave them in beds, in chairs, over the tops of johns, in shower stalls, and in bathtubs. Some of those old people had to have an enema every day of their lives. It drove me nuts. But for some reason, I continued liking medicine.

Another major factor that undoubtedly influenced my leanings toward nursing was my mother's illnesses. When I was seven and she was pregnant with Sue, my mother was too sick to care for us. After Sue was born my mother was ill for some time.

A year after Sue's birth I made my first meal—dry meat loaf, lumpy mashed potatoes, and thick gravy. With a broad grin on his face, my father told me it was some of the best cooking he'd ever eaten. As we passed the food around, Dad asked, "Would you like a slice of gravy, Lynda? It's terrific." That backhanded compliment made my day.

When I was a teenager and Mom had developed a chronic middle ear infection, I became very proficient at running the household. I was a natural caretaker. Nursing seemed only logical.

But even more than that, nursing was the way I was going to make my contribution to society. I was part of a generation of Americans who were "chosen" to change the world. We were sure of that. It was only a matter of waiting until we all grew up.

By 1968, I felt that I had waited long enough. Now was my time. And on that fall day of my twenty-first year, as I turned off the Capitol Beltway and onto I-95 South, I eagerly anticipated my work as an Army nurse. I saw it as one of the best ways to help those in need. While Barbara and I passed the cars and trucks, I could feel a surge of pride. I was a citizen of the greatest country in the world and was about to give part of myself to keep America great. It was a feeling that had taken root during talks with my father and had started to sprout on January 20, 1961, when another Catholic, a young, vigorous man, told us that no dream was unattainable.

He said, "The world is very different now. For man holds in his mortal hands the power to abolish all forms of human life. And, yet, the same revolutionary beliefs for which our forbearers fought are still at issue around the globe—the belief that the rights of man come not from the generosity of the state but from the hand of God."

I had listened to that speech from the couch, sitting with my parents and Nancy and Jean, while Mary and Sue played on the floor in front of the television.

"Let every nation know," the man said, "whether it wish us well or ill, that we shall pay any price, bear any burden, meet any hardship, support any friend, or oppose any foe in order to assure the survival and success of liberty."

Not knowing where these words would eventually lead our country and believing in this new President, we were carried along by the noble sentiments of John Fitzgerald Kennedy. We all felt ourselves part of a just and honorable nation when he said, "To those people in the huts and villages of half the globe struggling to break the bonds of mass misery, we pledge our best efforts to help them help themselves, for whatever period is required—not because the communists are doing it, not because we seek their votes, but because it is right."

At the time, none of us realized that there were American military advisors in a small country ten thousand miles away, a country where the French had fought a colonial war during the fifties. That war had bitterly divided all Frenchmen. Yet, we couldn't see that the experience of the French was but a preview of what faced the United States; that decisions made by this new President and his successors would lead to the deaths of thousands of Americans in a land that most of us, in 1961, could not even locate on a map. As John Kennedy spoke, we never even thought about Vietnam. We only thought about how inspirational he was and how he would lead us into a new era.

He continued, "In the long history of the world, only a few generations have been granted the role of defending freedom in its hour of maximum danger. I do not shrink from this responsibility—I welcome it. I do not believe that any of us would exchange places with any other people or any other generation. The energy, the faith, and the devotion, which we bring to this endeavor will light our country and all who serve it—and the glow from that fire can truly light the world."

I could see from my father's face that he, too, shared Mr. Kennedy's principles. They were the same ones he had been trying to impart to all his daughters. I touched his arm as we heard our new President confidently issue those climactic words that would become the touchstone of an entire generation: "And so, my fellow Americans: Ask not what your country can do for you—ask what you can do for your country."

Seven years later, as those glorious words echoed in my head and I fantasized about my own glorious future, my thoughts were interrupted by the sound of thumping and the pull of the steering wheel. The Nova veered to the right and into the path of a truck that narrowly missed us. I eased the car into the right lane and then onto the shoulder of the road. Barbara and I got out.

''A flat,'' she said. ''Great way to start a trip.''

I shrugged.

''Well,'' she continued, ''we can play damsels in distress and try to get someone to stop and fix it for us, or we can do it ourselves.''

''Shall we get started?'' I asked.

''Where's the spare?''

I pointed to the trunk. The tire was under the television, a half dozen other items, and Barbara's hair dryer.

''And the lug wrench and jack?'' she asked.

I thought for a moment and then pointed to the backseat. ''It's on the floor,'' I said. ''Under all the other junk.''

3

Mercy

Barbara and I spent our first night on a beach in a North Carolina park, both of us exhausted after having fixed not one, but two flats. The second came about four miles from the first. Since we hadn't found a gas station to fix the first one, we were stranded. I had tried driving on the deflated tire for about a half mile, hoping to find a station, but was unsuccessful. When we finally got some help, we learned that the two tires were so bad that they both had to be replaced, along with the wheel I had bent by driving on the flat. We hadn't planned on the extra expense. The money would have to come out of our entertainment budget.

However, we were undeterred. We told ourselves that we had to expect some drawbacks. So, in true pioneer style, we set up camp. Barbara gathered the wood for a fire, while I worked on the pup tent, putting the ridgepoles together and anchoring the stakes. Because we had forgotten to bring something to drive the stakes, I had to search for a heavy rock to do the job. The tent went up without a hitch. Before I was finished, Barbara already had the fire going and was cooking the hot dogs and beans. I lit the lantern and set out the paper plates.

Barbara handed me a cold beer. "To our first day of freedom," she said. "May the others be just a little more sweet."

We hadn't planned on the mosquitoes being so bad. In fact, we had forgotten to plan for any mosquitoes at all. We were forced to spend the night slapping at what seemed like swarms of the little bloodsuckers.

As the night wore on, the mosquitoes got more and more cruel.

We were certain that every mosquito in North Carolina had heard we were coming and had fasted for a week while waiting for us. When we realized that smacking our clothes offered little protection, we decided, in spite of the heat, to try zipping up the sleeping bags all the way. After a few minutes of roasting we were both drenched with sweat. That was no way to get to sleep, either.

By three in the morning, we were at the point of pleading with the mosquitoes. That didn't work. We next tried pleading with God. He was our only hope.

Apparently, he didn't care about our plight.

Or maybe he was in cahoots with the mosquitoes.

It must have been four thirty before I fell asleep. Most of the mosquitoes seemed to have had their fill of my blood, except for a few piggish fellows who didn't want the feast to end. I was awakened at dawn by a scream. Before opening my eyes I got a faceful of dirt. Barbara was frantically brushing her face, body, and the sleeping bag.

"What's going on?" I demanded.

"A spider," she screamed. "A creepy, hairy thing that crawled right across my face."

I jumped up and immediately brushed myself off. "Don't put it on me!"

She cried out again and smacked at her right hand. "Another bug! I can't take this anymore." She bolted out of the tent, knocking down the ridgepole and collapsing the canvas on top of me. I crawled out of the mess to see her running into the water still wearing her clothes. The sun was rising. I ran to the edge of the water and jumped in after her. We scrubbed the night out of our hair and off our faces. I scratched a mosquito bite on my arm until it bled. Then we started splashing each other and laughing like five-year-olds.

"Those mosquitoes sure did a job on your face," Barbara said.

"My face? I think you better look in the mirror."

We broke camp early that day and immediately headed for the nearest town to buy two air mattresses, some mosquito netting, and a couple of large cans of insect repellent—more expenses that weren't in the original budget.

When we came out of the store, I heard a loud hissing sound from the car. When I located the source, Barbara looked like she was going to cry. "Not another flat," she said.

I leaned against the Nova and scratched a bite. "At least there's a bright side," I said.

"What's that?"

"We don't have to dig into the trunk for the spare." After yesterday's flats, we had put the spare in the backseat in case we needed it again.

"Good," Barbara said. "We'll be able to fix it and be on our way in a half hour." She put her purse on the front seat. "We might as well get started."

We moved a few items from the back seat and lifted the spare out. I leaned it against the side of the car. "That was easy enough," I said. "Now, where did you put the jack?"

She looked at me sheepishly. "Uh oh," she said. "I thought you put the jack away."

I was incredulous. "You mean—"

"Yup," she said. "It's somewhere in Virginia on I-95."

As we walked to the nearest auto parts store to buy a new jack, I stayed at least five steps ahead of Barbara in spite of her longer stride. When we reached the store, the teenager who worked behind the counter practically ignored me while he fawned all over her. Men had always been attracted to Barbara. It was something I usually accepted. She was tall, thin, and beautiful. Next to her, with my 140 pounds on a five-foot-three-inch frame, I felt the ugly duckling without any hope of ever becoming a swan. But that morning I was already aggravated past my limit and in no mood to waste time watching some idiot try to impress her. "Listen sonny," I said brashly. "Would you put your tongue back in your mouth and get me that jack?" I must have scared him, because he practically ran to the back room to find a jack. He called me "ma'am" all the way out of the store.

On the way back, Barbara grabbed my arm. "Are you mad at me?" she asked.

"Is the Pope Catholic?" I pushed her hand away and walked ahead, carrying the jack under my arm.

She tried again. "Come on, Lynda. Don't be mad."

"Who, me mad?"

"It's not my fault," she said.

"You're the one who forgot to put the jack away."

"I wasn't the only one. You forgot, too."

I was stunned. ''Me?'' I turned and stared at her in disbelief.

''That's right,'' she said. ''Why didn't *you* remember to put the jack away?''

''Am I supposed to remember everything?''

''Of course not,'' she said. ''But it's as much your fault as it is mine, so don't just blame me.''

''You're crazy.'' I started walking again.

She followed. ''I'm crazy?'' she said. ''Look who's talking. If you had any brains, you would have at least checked the tires before we left home.''

''If you're so smart, why didn't you check them?''

''It's not my car,'' she said. ''I wouldn't own a piece of junk like that.''

''Excuse me!'' I huffed. How dare she insult my automobile. ''Maybe you wouldn't want to be seen in a car like that. A piece of junk might be beneath your dignity.''

''Maybe you're right,'' she said.

''Then maybe you should find another way to get to California.''

''Maybe I will.''

''There's a bus station in town,'' I said. ''I'll give you a ride.''

''I don't need any ride from you,'' she replied. ''I'll walk.''

''Fine.''

We trudged back to the car in silence, each of us steaming. We had taken our positions and neither one wanted to back down. While I jacked the car and removed the hub cap and lug nuts, Barbara started going through our stuff to separate her things. It would be impossible for her to carry that load on foot.

I was struggling with a lug nut that was frozen in place. Sweat ran down the sides of my face. I cursed under my breath. I even tried standing one foot on the wrench and bearing down with all my weight. It wouldn't budge.

By this time, Barbara had started to find my dilemma interesting.

I heaved and grunted. The lug nut didn't move. I tried again. Still no luck. Once more. My head pounded and my eyes bulged as I gave everything I had. Nothing. I kicked the tire.

''There's an easier way,'' Barbara said.

''If you can do any better, you're welcome to try.''

She brushed her hair back and smiled mischievously. ''Bet you a dollar I can get it off.''

Her cockiness annoyed me. "Let's make it five dollars."

"You're on."

Instead of reaching for the lug wrench, she reached for her compact and a comb. Two minutes later, she was across the street talking to one of the biggest men God had ever created. "Excuse me, sir, but we seem to be having a little bit of trouble getting our car fixed."

Within three seconds after that oversized lug picked up the wrench, he had the nut loose. He even put the spare on. After he left, Barbara held her hands over her head in the pose of a boxer who had just won the championship. "You owe me five dollars," she said.

"You cheated."

She chuckled. "I didn't cheat. I just used my brain to locate a little brawn. No sense in getting your hands dirty when somebody else is so anxious to do the work for you."

"But—"

"Lynda, be reasonable. If God hadn't wanted women to use their superior intelligence, he wouldn't have made us smarter than men." She mimicked the voice she had used five minutes earlier: "Oh, mister, would you please help us poor defenseless little girls?"

I had to laugh at her impudence. "I'm sorry for yelling at you," I said.

"Me, too."

"I never expected the trip to be so—"

"So miserable?" she volunteered.

"Right."

"It's bound to get better," she said.

"You're right," I replied. "Nothing could be worse than these last two days."

She smiled. "I don't want to disagree with you again, Lynda, but there is one thing that could be a whole lot worse."

"What's that?"

"Being back at Mercy."

I probably should have taken my first visit to Mercy Hospital School of Nursing three years earlier as an omen. On the trip up, I got a speeding ticket. While I was in the pre-admission interview, I got a parking ticket. And the interview didn't go so hot, either.

I had decided to attend Mercy for what I thought an excellent reason—it was the only nursing school that would have me.

Actually, that's not entirely true. I had originally applied and been accepted by a small Catholic nursing school in Florida. I had visions of basking in the sun and having parties on the beach. Three months before high school graduation, I got a surprise in the mail:

> *Dear Miss Van Devanter:*
> We regret to inform you that our school of nursing will no longer be in operation after the end of this term. We are returning your fees. Please apply elsewhere.

Elsewhere was Mercy, after thirteen fast applications and twelve rejections. If I ever thought their quick acceptance meant an easy training program, I was about to be sorely disappointed. Little did I know how tough those three years would be.

I hadn't spent my high school years tearing up the academic track, although my grades had been average and would probably have been good enough to get me into other schools if it hadn't been for my earlier expulsion. As unlikely as it might sound today, I was thrown out of Holy Trinity High School in Washington in the ninth grade because I had been caught—by a tenth grader—smoking in the ladies room of a department store thirty miles from the school. Smoking was a definite no-no for good Catholic girls. "If you don't report yourself," she said, "I'm going to report you." I surrendered myself to a nun who was a stickler for the rules. Honesty didn't count for any brownie points. She taught me that the Catholic notion of forgiveness didn't extend to transgressions against school law. I was banished to the public school with all the other "heathen savages."

"You've broken your mother's heart," my father said. What he didn't say was that I had broken his heart, also. I couldn't have felt worse. However, it wasn't the last time I would disappoint him in high school. My later participation in civil rights demonstrations was just as upsetting.

As a high school junior and senior, I became involved in the Congress on Racial Equality and the Student Nonviolent Coordinating Committee. It wasn't that Dad objected to racial equality. He was concerned that by belonging to organizations that were led by people like Stokeley Carmichael and H. Rap Brown, I would jeopardize my future. He had lived in Washington during the McCarthy era and didn't want to see his daughter hurt by good faith participation in groups that might be viewed as communist fronts. "With those things on your record, you'll never be able to get a government job," he said.

"Maybe I don't want to work for a government that practices discrimination."

It was an argument repeated in thousands of households throughout the United States during the sixties. I was forbidden to do work for either of these groups, to attend demonstrations, or to have friends who did. Rather than accept my father's terms, I ran away from home.

It took a week for him to find me and send one of our parish priests to talk to me. After I went back home, I still participated in civil rights demonstrations while my father and I tried to maintain an uneasy truce.

We were on better terms when I went to Mercy. I'm sure he was happy to see his daughter once more in a Catholic environment under "better influences." I was back in the fold.

Mercy was the kind of place where you went in as a freshman and knew exactly what you would be doing every day until graduation—if you weren't either thrown out or dead by then. We spent full days in the classroom, worked eight-hour shifts on the wards, and then found time to study. All the while as the nuns were trying to kill us with work, we'd hear the same words: "Someday you'll appreciate this." Even if they were right, we promised ourselves we'd never tell them. But they were right. It was the best possible training we could have received. Mercy was a completely isolated environment where the only thing that mattered was nursing. There was little time for other concerns.

According to my friend Gina, a raven-haired Italian girl from New York who had the somewhat dubious distinction of being four inches shorter than I am, we were to be "indentured servants" for three years. I was sitting next to Gina at our orientation on the first day when one of our class advisors, Sister Gregorius—also known as the Nazi, because of her heavy German accent and pronounced dictatorial tendencies—told us, in no uncertain terms, that she intended to work our buns off. There would be no summer vacations, few free weekends, seven o'clock curfews during the week, mandatory study periods every evening, and at six fifty-five every morning a military-style roll call.

"Didn't anybody ever tell that broad that Lincoln freed the slaves?" Gina whispered to me before we had been introduced. "I suppose she expects us to polish her shoes and swagger stick, too." Gina should have been Irish, because she had the distinct sparkle of a mischievous leprechaun in those deep green eyes. She also had a knack for raising Cain, and a fiancé who was six years older than she was. Gina was incorrigible. I immediately liked her.

Our daily roll calls weren't merely for taking attendance. There was a higher purpose. The Sisters of Mercy were petitioning to have Mother Catherine McAuley, their founder, declared a saint and they needed all the help they could get. Every morning we were required to kneel in the chapel in precise ranks and say: "O most merciful Father, who hast given us in Thy servant, Catherine McAuley, a wonderful example of love of Thee, of zeal for Thy glory in the care of the poor, sick and ignorant, grant, we beseech Thee, if it be pleasing to Thy holy will, that she may soon be glorified here below. We implore this favor through the intercession of Our Lady of Mercy and the infinite merits of Thy Son, our Lord Jesus Christ. Amen. Mother of Mercy, pray for us."

"The prayer isn't gonna work," Gina would say. "God doesn't like people brown-nosing Him when He's looking for another saint."

One of the first things we learned was that there were no electives in nursing school, none of the lighter courses that make it possible to devote most of your energy to the more difficult subjects. They were all killers. During that initial year, in addition to working on the wards, we took courses at Baltimore Junior College and at the hospital. Along with the more academically oriented subjects like English, sociology, psychology, anatomy, physiology, chemistry, and biology, we learned basic nursing procedures like bathing the sick, changing beds, giving bedpans, and keeping records. We studied and practiced things in those years that we needed to know to work in different areas of nursing, rotating through such wards as pediatrics, obstetrics, psychiatry, neurology, surgery, and urology. We spent many of our free hours in the anatomy lab with boxes of bones, blindfolding each other so we could become accustomed to identifying each one by touch. Our anatomy instructor required us not only to be able to blindly identify each bone, but also to distinguish between the left bones and the right ones. The hardest was the patella, the kneecap. It was the one she always caught us on.

As we studied different diseases, we encountered a unique syndrome that afflicts medical and nursing students—psychosomatic illness. We developed the symptoms of almost all the medical conditions we were exposed to. We all thought we had cancer, and gall bladder problems, and tonsilitis, and chronic ulcerative colitis, and arthritis, and renal failure, and kidney stones. About the only condition we didn't develop was pregnancy. That was because we knew for a fact that you had to do the dirty deed to become pregnant. Most of us, including me, had never even come close to doing it. Of those few who had, no one was crazy enough to admit it.

With all our course requirements, the pace was murder. We barely had enough time to get things done before we were piled with more work. Sixty girls had started school that first year. By June, forty were left.

In spite of the rigorous demands, we managed to find time for mischief. The Fundamentals of Nursing classroom was downstairs in our dormitory, an old four-story structure that was rumored to have been condemned in 1850. In the Fundamentals classroom, we had the infamous Chase family—Mr. Chase, Mrs. Chase, and Baby Chase—anatomically correct life-size rubber dolls meant to be instructional tools. We occasionally used them for other purposes.

One night we hung Mrs. Chase outside a third-floor window and pleaded with her not to jump, while a crowd of onlookers gathered on the street. That was a difficult trick to pull off, since we had to cart Mrs. Chase up four flights of stairs, past the eagle eye of our house mother, a dour old maid who delighted in reporting erring students to the Nazi.

Another time, we took Mr. Chase to the hospital chapel and hung him on the crucifix. But the one that really got the nuns upset was the time we moved the seven-foot-tall statue of Joan of Arc from its pedestal on the third floor into the Nazi's bed. She went nuts and started an investigation to find the instigator of these incidents. Gina was walking on eggshells for a while. Although the ideas hadn't actually been hers, she was usually our leader in these crazy stunts. Fortunately, nobody talked. The investigation was dropped.

Gina also knew how to lead us into the party spirit and she had the perfect room for it. While most of our windows faced on a street, Gina's faced the alley. Her windowsill was the ideal place to keep contraband beer cold during the winter. If you lined the cans up right, it was big enough to hold a full case. Sometimes, on weekends when we were feeling particularly adventurous, one of us would sneak past the night house mother while she slept and race to the Calvert Bar across the street. The bar was strictly off limits and getting caught would have meant immediate expulsion. The danger made those nighttime missions more exciting. Eventually, I got good enough to make the complete circuit from my room, downstairs, past the house mother, across the street, and back again in less than five tension-filled minutes.

Barbara didn't arrive at Mercy until our second year, coming in on the same day as the new freshmen. She was only two years older than the rest of us, but seemed to possess a great deal more maturity. Yet it wasn't only her age that made her different. She had a quality that was hard to define. It wasn't that she walked around telling us she was different, or that she went out of her way not to be one of us; it was just that we knew she was somebody we should look up to.

However, Barbara was far from being a saint. She could party with the best and she knew how to raise hell as well as Gina. She got blitzed with us more than once and even made a few successful Saturday night runs to the Calvert Bar. But it took awhile for her to warm up to us. Initially, she seemed to be holding so much inside.

Although Barbara had completed her first year of nursing school in Indiana two years before, while her father was stationed at Fort Benjamin Harrison, she was only now entering her second year of training. During her time in Indiana, her mother had died and her father developed cancer. Soon after Barbara had finished that first school year, she returned to Washington with Colonel Kaplan. He had been assigned to the Pentagon so he could get treatments at Walter Reed. Instead of returning to school, Barbara spent the next two years nursing him and trying to replace her mother. Fortunately, the cancer went into remission and the colonel got well enough to return to full duty.

Rather than return to Indiana, Barbara decided to attend Mercy to remain close to her father. She was an outstanding nurse and was a take-charge kind of person. The first time I saw her in action was when a guy came into the ER after a knife fight with a stab wound in his thigh, the knife handle still sticking out. He collapsed on the floor. Barbara was on top of him in a flash, doing closed chest massage and mouth to mouth resuscitation while yelling, "Somebody call a code. Get a crash cart. He needs blood. Somebody get an IV and a tourniquet." She brought him around moments before a doctor arrived. It would have been a solid performance from an experienced nurse. It was more impressive coming from a second-year student. She was the most competent person in our class. When others tried to praise her after it was over, she shrugged them off. To her, it was only part of the job.

A few months after she arrived, Barbara helped me through one of my biggest crises. It was the first time I lost a patient for whom I was responsible. Marty Galloway was on the eleventh floor with a chronic heart condition. He was forty-seven and in many ways seemed almost like a father to me. However, we discussed things that were more personal than I had discussed with my own father for fear of disappointing him. Some evenings after my shift would end, I would return to Marty's room and talk with him for hours. At the time, he was going through some deep philosophical and theological questioning. He was Catholic and legally divorced from his wife, with whom he had been miserable for more than twelve years of marriage. After nine years of being single and lonely, he had fallen in love with a widow who had three children. The problem: Divorce was not recognized by the Church; it would be a mortal sin for him to marry again. He felt so strongly about the teachings of his Catholic faith that he did not know if he could bear to leave it, even for love. Religion had given him strength.

Marty's dilemma was finally solved by God. One evening Marty's heart arrested. Nobody was able to revive him.

I had been in the ER when I heard the code. I immediately knew it was him. That night, as I lay crying in my bed, someone slipped a letter under my door:

Dear Lynda,

Tonight you lost, through loving, a part of you. It was a precious part, and it will not grow back. It will hurt for a while, but it was worth it. You'll always have a special place in your heart for Marty Galloway.

You have loved. It hurts now, but you did it. And wasn't it beautiful? You have accomplished what each of us here, as students, tries to attain. You have recognized Marty as the individual he is. You saw good in Marty and you loved him. That is the whole basis of the Christian life. He needed you, Lynda. You helped to fulfill him. He taught you the real meaning of love—to leave yourself and go to the needs of another person. To give of your whole being and to see the goodness in your fellow man. To love someone is to bid him to live, invite him to grow, motivate him, show him that you care.

Marty saw that in you, Lynda, and he responded through his simplicity and childlike being. He desperately longed for someone to love him and to give to him and this is what you have done. He relied on you and he appreciated you.

Maybe this sounds like a lot of bull right now, but it isn't. You gave to Marty and he to you and now you're both better persons for it. You were a part of that beautiful world of love.

None of us knows why Marty died tonight, but maybe he has already found that love which he so thirsted for down here—the love which we were able to supply only in spirit in the form of substitution.

You're probably mulling over all that you could have given to Marty which you didn't. Granted there probably was a hell of a lot more to be given, but since we're all human and blind, we don't see this point until it's too late. The only consolation lies in the fact that we will be given another chance, another Marty, and maybe this time we'll be capable of giving a little bit more of ourselves. There will be another patient who will need this love, the gift of self. If you're lucky, Lynda, maybe he's on the eleventh right now.

Love,
Barbara

By the time we were near the end of our junior year, we had more practical experience than the medical students who had spent college and med school mostly in the books. They didn't get to work as closely with patients as we did until their internships. However, for many who felt they had to live up to the image of the all-knowing doctor, their egos wouldn't allow them to take advice from mere nursing students, regardless of the consequences.

Stanley Witkowski, a fourth-year med student from one of the nearby schools, was a perfect example of this syndrome. To call Stanley a nerd was probably an understatement and a kindness, since he was light years behind being a simple nerd. He had an ego that was large enough to fill the state of Texas with plenty left over for a few counties in Oklahoma. Stanley was also anally retentive. His affliction was not of the figurative type that Freud described. Stanley was literally always constipated—or at least that's what he usually grumbled to us when he'd disappear to the bathroom. We preferred to think that he was full of crap.

One day when he was working on the pediatrics ward, Barbara finally taught Stanley that nursing students might be worth listening to after all. He was told that day by one of the doctors to take some blood from a small baby. Unlike an adult's blood vessels, most of a baby's veins are too small to be adequately used to draw blood. It's necessary to take blood from the baby's femoral vein, a big vessel that runs down through the groin. Because the vein can't be seen, the person drawing blood has to feel for the femoral artery, then move a centimeter medially to make the puncture. It's a simple process with only one complication—it hurts. And when little boy babies are hurt, they will almost inevitably pee.

That was something we learned in the first month of nursing school. We were also taught to keep a diaper over the baby's private area unless we wanted to change our clothes every few hours.

Barbara and I were in the room when Stanley was about to make his initial unassisted femoral puncture. He started by removing the baby's diaper. "Excuse me," Barbara said. "I think you might want to cover him."

Stanley let loose with one of his arrogant laughs. "What's the matter, ladies? Haven't you girls ever seen a boy's penis before?"

I could have strangled the obstinate idiot, but Barbara tried again,

"Look, Stanley, I'm trying to tell you for your own good that you should—"

"Oh, the cute little nursie is going to tell me something for my own good," he said.

"Stanley, listen—"

"Barbara, shut up."

She looked at me and shrugged. We smiled as we watched Stanley go through the procedure. His fingers located the femoral artery. When he could feel the pulse, he moved medially and located the vein. Then he made the puncture.

Immediatley, the baby's little penis stood straight up and started its shower, hitting Stanley right in the middle of his forehead. He was stunned. He stood there in shock and as the baby's pain lessened, the penis started going down, spraying Stanley's shirt, tie, and pants.

Stanley pulled the needle out and took a step back. He looked down at his clothes in disbelief. "Clean shirt," he said. "New tie. Fresh pants." Then he turned hopelessly to us for sympathy. We were laughing hysterically.

Unable to regain any semblance of a professional bearing, Stanley stormed out of the room. Another med student finished drawing the blood—the right way.

One of the things we liked best about Mercy was getting away from it. That's why we especially appreciated our rotations to other institutions during our second and third years. Probably the most relaxing time we had was at Mount Wilson, the state tuberculosis institute. Because of limited space, four students had to share the available apartments. Gina and I were teamed with, of all people, two nuns who hadn't yet taken their final vows. "Just what we need," Gina said. "A couple of prayer pushers to ruin every party." I'm not sure what we expected, other than to be stuck with two sexless automatons who spent all their free time praying for the redemption of lost souls like ours. One of the biggest shocks of my life came one day when I came back to the apartment and found a nun sitting in the living room in a bathrobe watching television with nothing covering her hair. They actually had hair under those habits! It was the answer to a question that had plagued me since grammar school. And they not only had hair like normal women, they also talked and acted like regular people, except for a few extra references to God. Even Gina started to like them. In fact, she had such a good time with them that I worried she might go off the deep end and join a convent. When she failed to talk them into a secret beer blast, I realized that my fears were groundless.

We got our experience with chronic psychiatric patients at another institution away from Mercy—Saint Agnes Psychiatric Hospital near Hershey, Pennsylvania. It was run by the Daughters of Charity of Saint Vincent DePaul and was one of only a few Catholic psychiatric institutions on the East Coast. We especially liked it because it was in the country, and it gave us a chance to get away from the dinginess of Baltimore. In many ways, it was almost a vacation. We lived in nice apartments with six girls to each one; our hours were more reasonable; curfews were not strictly enforced; and the food was a big improvement over the Mercy cafeteria. But we didn't relax completely or sneak in past curfew too many times. We were scared. We had heard too many stories about people who had got through their time at Saint Agnes thinking that all was well, and then when they got back to Mercy, the Nazi had them kicked out because she had been aware of their transgressions from the start. Whether the stories were true or not was irrelevant. We believed them.

At Saint Agnes we were not dealing with illnesses caused by germs and microbes; we were dealing with the fragility of the human psyche.

On one ward, Barbara and I had a patient in his mid-twenties who was always trying to commit suicide. When he first came in, he had no self-image at all. He had been heavily involved in hard drugs before we got him.

He was put in a padded room for his own protection. He used to smear excrement against the glass observation window in the door. "The sad thing," Barbara said, "is that we never cure these people. We just warehouse them. If I felt myself going crazy, I'd rather be dead than to spend my life like this."

When the guy finally came out of the dangerous phase of his illness, his case got even more interesting. He started to become other people for days at a time, and he had an uncanny knack for taking on the proficiency of that person in any field of endeavor. For instance, we used to play a lot of bridge with the patients. Before this guy had arrived, he had never been a card player. But he picked up a book titled *Goren on Bridge,* riffled through it for a few minutes, and then decided he was Charles Goren. By the next day, he was unbeatable. Another time, he decided he was the Russian chess master, Boris Spassky. No one was able to survive a game with him beyond six moves. Sometimes he'd even get us into checkmate in only three moves. "Can you imagine what this guy might be capable of if he hadn't burned himself out on drugs?" Barbara would ask.

Perhaps the two most famous patients in that hospital were Melanie and Father Bob. Father Bob was a sweet, meek little man who had been admitted shortly after his ordination. At St. A's for fifteen years since then, he had never been able to function in normal life. He had spent his whole childhood and young adulthood in the protected environments of Catholic schools and the seminary. When it was time for him to leave and face the real world, he simply cracked.

Melanie was loud, obnoxious, and crazy as a loon. She had a permanent spot on the women's ward for the craziest of crazies and spent at least half her time in the padded room. Whenever she was in that room, she would scream through the barred window that looked out on the yard. I first heard her in the middle of the night. She howled at the moon like a wounded wolf. It sounded like she was being tortured.

Her specialty was tormenting poor Father Bob. When she saw him in the yard, she used to scream at the top of her lungs, "Come on, Father. Please. I need you inside me." If Father Bob couldn't tolerate the real world, he certainly wasn't ready to handle the worst of Melanie's language, which was enough to make even the male attendants blush. For a long time, he refused to go outside for recreation periods. When the burly orderlies finally forced him to get some fresh air, he tried hiding behind them. That didn't work. Melanie could still see him and she continued her taunts. Once, he even tried going on a diet, hoping that he would become invisible. He was unsuccessful.

The saddest case of my experience was in the adolescent ward. Stevie was sixteen, with his whole future ahead of him. His moderately long brown hair and crystal blue eyes that seemed to look right through you made him one of the most attractive sixteen-year-olds I'd ever known. If we all hadn't been five or six years older than he was, there would have been a lot of nursing students with incurable crushes.

The doctors were calling Stevie an adolescent adjustment reaction instead of a sociopath, because the thinking at the time was that if you labeled somebody a sociopath, you were saying there was no hope of change, regardless of the therapy. His problems, they believed, stemmed from his father. After Stevie's mother had died when the boy was still a preschooler, the father had remarried immediately. It was the beginning of a string of marriages that numbered seven by the time Stevie was admitted to the hospital. After his last mother had left, Stevie became violent and tore the house apart. When I met him, he was spending his days sitting in one place doing sketches on a pad and never talking to anyone. I tried to befriend him and finally got him into a few brief conversations, but he seemed totally uninterested in anything. However, shortly before I was to return to Mercy, Stevie gave me a pen and ink drawing. It depicted a bare, black tree that was hanging off the edge of a desolate cliff. There was the sense that if somebody even blew on it, the tree would go crashing down to the bottom of the canyon. Under the drawing he wrote, "As you look at this tree, think of Life and the hardships within it, but also look at the grass and beauty within it as it overcomes them with its strength and becomes stronger, and think of me."

I wanted, more than anything, to see Stevie get better. When I returned to Mercy, wiser for having known him, I had to learn to accept the idea that he might, like the others, spend his entire life there. If there was a God, it was hard to understand why he allowed such waste.

Although our three nursing school years were spent totally immersed in the medical world, by the time I reached my senior year, I began to realize again that there was a different kind of world outside the walls of Mercy Hospital, a world where all was not clean sheets and morning roll calls. The images from the seven o'clock news in the dorm's first-floor lounge began my return to consciousness. One night Walter Cronkite talked about body counts while sweating soldiers ran across the screen firing rifles. Another night, Huntley and Brinkley talked about American victories while wounded soldiers were being carried into a helicopter. I started to pay closer attention to the stories and found the images intruding into my life more and more frequently. Every evening, at seven and eleven, human destruction was brought into the homes of millions by television.

''Those guys look so young,'' I said one night.

Barbara nodded. ''Most of them are no more than eighteen or nineteen,'' she replied. ''My father said half of them learn about death before they even learn to shave.''

''Was your father over there?''

''In '62, as an advisor,'' she said. ''He was there before the troop buildup. He says if he were healthier, he'd be back there right now.''

Although I had hardly paid any attention to the news of Vietnam before, I now began to search out information. From my naïve perspective, I saw the United States pursuing a course that President Kennedy had talked about in his inaugural address: we were saving a country from communism. There were brave boys fighting and dying for democracy, I thought. And if our boys were being blown apart, then somebody better be over there putting them back together again. I started to think that maybe that somebody should be me.

By January of 1968, when an Army sergeant arrived at Mercy to talk to us about opportunities in the military, it didn't take much convincing for me to sign up. Shortly after that, Barbara joined, too.

''Are you crazy?'' Gina said. ''You go in the Army, they'll send you to Vietnam. It's dangerous over there.''

''I want to go to Vietnam,'' I told her.

''But what if you get killed?''

Barbara provided the answer to that one. ''The sergeant told us that nurses don't get killed,'' she said. ''They're all in rear areas. The hospitals are perfectly safe.''

Gina was unconvinced. ''I think you're both nuts. If you had any brains, you'd do exactly what I'm going to do: Find a decent job, get married, and have a house full of kids. Leave the wars to the men.''

When I told my parents of my decision, my mother had a similar response, although she wasn't as outspoken as Gina. My father said very little. He mostly listened as I gave him the same talk the recruiter had given me. I mentioned the benefits, the pay, the extra training, the free travel, the excitement, and the challenge.

''It's a job that somebody has to do,'' I said.

''I understand,'' he replied. ''But I'm worried about my little girl.'' In spite of those words, I thought I saw a gleam in his eyes. He was proud of me.

4

Dunes 'til Dawn

By the end of the second week of our cross-country trip, my Chevy II had four new tires, a new radiator and hoses, and a new rear main seal. The fourth tire was from Georgia, the hoses from Alabama, the radiator from Florida, and the rear main seal from Tennessee. We also found ourselves quickly headed for a cash crunch.

But the trip was more than a series of car repairs. We saw the tourist sights, the old southern mansions, and the squalid shacks of the back country. We danced in Underground Atlanta, swam in the Chatahoochee River, and hiked in the Okeefenokee Swamps. Barbara had an old friend living in Columbus, Georgia, outside of Fort Benning. We drove into town on a Sunday afternoon, picked up the phone and called her as if we were neighbors who wanted to drop in for a casual visit. When we were in Nashville visiting the Grand Old Opry, I wondered how an old guitar-playing high school friend was doing. So we made a side trip to Memphis to track him down. Every day, we did whatever struck our fancy. We didn't worry about plans or tomorrow. If we wanted to sleep late, we stayed in our sleeping bags until the afternoon. If we wanted to celebrate, we went to nightclubs and drank beer until dawn. And if we wanted to swim in the middle of the night, we found a lake.

On the highways and back roads, Barbara and I talked a lot about how much promise the future held. Mostly, we daydreamed. Our dreams were of two entirely different types. One minute, we would envision ourselves as world travelers, hopping jets to take us from London, to Rome, to Hong Kong, to Waikiki. We would summer in the south of France, spend our winters in Switzerland, and buy our clothes in Paris. "I've always wanted to see the Himalayas," Barbara said.

"I want to see Tripoli," I added.

"And Pakistan."

"And the polar icecaps."

"And the Amazon."

The next minute, we would be off in the other direction, seeing ourselves as happily married to ordinary guys who worked in the city and commuted to their homes in the suburbs. I was going to have a big old house that my husband and I would renovate. It would have a white picket fence around it. And there would be three kids—a couple of boys and a girl—and two cars, one of which would be a Ford station wagon with wood on the side.

"Maybe Gina has the right idea," Barbara said. "Get married and retire. Sit home all day, eat candy, and watch soap operas."

"Chocolate-covered cherries and *The Edge of Night,*" I added.

"No, it has to be something real gooey, like milk chocolate caramels."

I licked my lips. "Sounds great."

"And we'll bake cakes for the PTA bake sales," she said.

"And become class mothers so we can go on all the trips with the little buggers."

"And have husbands who look like Omar Sharif."

"No way," I protested. "I want mine to look like Tab Hunter or Troy Donahue."

"You have no taste in men, Lynda."

"I beg your pardon," I said with joking indignance. "What about J.J.?"

She laughed. "Maybe he's the exception."

Everyone who met J.J.—Jonathon James Smith—agreed that he was exceptionally handsome. My mother called him a "pretty boy," and at the beach, I would notice my friends stealing glances at him when they thought I wasn't looking. With his short dirty blond hair and a face that looked boyish and yet rugged at the same time, J.J. bore a certain resemblance to Troy Donahue if you looked at him from a distance. Close up, he was even more attractive. He had these cute little laugh lines around the edges of his mouth and a cleft in his chin.

The thing that made J.J. most exceptional, however, was that he wanted to marry me, a girl who wore Clearasil to bed every night and who still could live up to the nickname my sisters had given me when I was ten. They called me Crisco. It was short for "fat in the can."

He said he loved me that night in August when he gave me the ring, a third-of-a-carat oval-shaped diamond. We had been lying on the beach, looking up at the stars, and holding hands. It had been the first time a boy spoke to me of love. I thought I was dreaming. But it wasn't a dream. He wanted to marry me. And I said yes. Now, I was wearing that diamond.

J.J. and I had met two weeks after my graduation from nursing school, when he came up to me at Bayshores, a nightclub in Somers Point, New Jersey, and asked me to dance. He was one of the two best dancers I knew. The other was Barbara. Maybe it was fortunate for me that she wasn't there that night.

I had gone to Ocean City with five other girls who also graduated from Mercy. Together, we got a house near the beach and jobs at a local hospital in Somers Point, where I worked the seven-to-three shift in the emergency room. Our plan was to spend all our free time during June helping each other to study for the Maryland state boards, which would be given at the end of the month. When the exams were finished, we would spend the remainder of our summer celebrating and waiting for the exam results. It was a good plan. Each day, as soon as we were through at the hospital, we would grab our bathing suits and books and head down to the beach where we worked on our tans and our nursing fundamentals, quizzing each other on everything that had been covered in the previous three years. Although Barbara came up to visit on weekends, she spent the summer with her father, who had orders transferring him from the Pentagon to the Presidio of San Francisco in September. Gina was in Philadelphia, where she and her fiancé were making final plans for their wedding, which was to take place in July. "I'll give him about one year of fun," she said. "Then we're gonna start making a whole bunch of babies. None of this birth control crap. I'm going back to being a good Catholic girl."

That first night with J.J., we danced until we were both ready to drop. Then we danced some more. When the band played the slow songs and he gently eased my head onto his shoulder, I had new and unfamiliar stirrings inside. I could smell a musky scent from his sweat and I felt both protected and afraid when his strong arms encircled me.

His parents had a house nearby in Tuckahoe, but he was only

visiting. J.J. was a soldier, a buck sergeant, who had returned that week from a year as an infantryman in Vietnam.

"What was it like?" I asked.

"It sucked."

During the next few weeks, I saw him every day. He would join us for our study sessions at the beach and he sometimes served as our quizmaster, firing questions at us as quickly as his machine gun must have fired rounds at the Viet Cong.

"What did you do in Vietnam?"

"I sweated all the time, took a lot of crap from people, and dreamed about the kind of car I would buy when I got back to the world."

"No, really. What was your job like?"

"I humped the boonies and got shot at too many times."

"But what was it like?"

"I told you: It sucked."

We went out to dinner together, walked the beach in our bare feet, and laughed at the silliest things. On weekends, we would party with my friends and their newly acquired boyfriends. We'd start out at the Anchorage, a neighborhood bar that offered seven beers for a dollar, and leave there about ten o'clock to go dancing at Bayshores. When Bayshores closed around two, we'd head for a place called the Dunes, on the peninsula in Somers Point. It was open until six and the theme was "Dunes 'til Dawn." Those words were on the black T-shirts J.J. and I were given the night we won the dance contest.

"Isn't your father proud that his son fought in the war?" I asked.

"I don't know."

"As soon as I finish my training, I'm going to ask them to send me to Vietnam."

"Don't do it."

"Why not?"

"Because it sucks."

He had a way of dancing that was wild and flamboyant, yet somehow controlled. He seemed to be not just moving to the music, but a part of it, his body another instrument being played by the band. He would laugh in the middle of a song, get a faraway look in his eyes and then release an energy that would automatically draw everyone's attention. Curiously, I found myself keeping up with him. It was fun. And exciting.

"What are you laughing at, J.J.?"

"Myself. I never knew I could feel this way about a girl."

"What way?"

"You ask too many questions."

We made out on the dining room floor while my girlfriends slept in their beds. We used to kiss until it felt like my lips might fall off. I wanted to crawl up into his arms and spend my whole life there. My heart would beat so fast that I thought it was going to pound its way right out of my chest.

"I can't breathe."

"I don't care."

"But I'm afraid."

"Don't be."

When Barbara came up two weeks after I'd met J.J., I couldn't wait to let her in on the good news. She listened with amusement and then grabbed my wrist. "Three hundred and twenty-eight," she said. "Fastest pulse I've ever seen. Let's see if I have all the symptoms right: heart palpitations, rapid pulse, chills and sweats, clammy palms, loss of appetite, and an overwhelming desire to jump someone's bones."

"I didn't say anything about wanting to jump someone's bones."

"But you do. Don't you?"

"Maybe."

"Ah, ha," she said. "Just as I thought."

"Well, nurse," I said, "what is it?"

She furrowed her brow and paced the floor with her hands behind her back. "In my professional opinion, after three years at the best medical facility in the world, studying under the sharpest minds God ever created, I would unequivocably diagnose this rare affliction as a case of love."

"Oh, no," I said in mock horror. "Do you think it's curable?"

"Curable? No," she said. "In your case it's probably chronic. However, there is one possible way to keep it under control."

"Please, nurse, please tell me."

"You must jump his bones."

I was genuinely horrified. "What?"

"I can see that the patient doesn't quite accept my professional recommendation."

I was too shocked to respond.

"There is also another possible way to help this case," she offered. "Perhaps a method that would be more acceptable."

"What is it?"

"Have him jump your bones," she said, "and make him think it's all his idea. Of course, this is the more difficult method, because it will call for you to have a strong resolve while he spends some time whining, wheedling, and cajoling. Those elements are absolutely required so that he's convinced it's his idea and you're only going along with it to please him."

"But I'm a virgin," I said.

"Ah, yes, that rare species: Americanus Catholicus Virginus. Probably of the type that believes in saving oneself for marriage."

"That's right," I answered firmly.

Although I may have been sexually naïve that summer, I had the misfortune to become known as "the penis expert" at the hospital. The unofficial title didn't have anything to do with my virtue, or lack of it. I just happened to be in the wrong place at the wrong time.

It seemed that whenever I worked the ER, I always ended up with the males who had problems with their genitalia. One day I got this guy whose wife had put a wedding ring on his penis. He became hard and the ring wouldn't come off. With the blood supply blocked, the penis wouldn't go down, either. Although it may sound funny, any man who has been through anything like it probably doesn't think of it as a laughing matter.

We tried a couple of different methods to remove the ring, including soap and grease. None of them worked. There was only one solution. I called the hospital's engineering department. When we walked into the guy's cubicle a few minutes later with a long-handled tool that looked like oversized cutting pliers, he looked like he would have a heart attack. "What are you going to do with that?" he asked.

"We're going to cut it off," the doctor answered.

The guy put his hands in front of his private area. "No!"

"Not the penis, dummy. The ring."

Another time, I took care of a kid who had been surfing when he got hit in the groin after falling off his board. The injury had stimulated his artery to shoot blood into his penis, which had become engorged. The bruise from the hematoma had blocked the blood from returning through the vein, so he was in a state of priapism. "Jesus, Van Devanter," the doctor said. "If that's the way you affect all men, spare me."

There was another guy who came stumbling in near the end of my shift one day when I was writing some reports. He leaned over the counter. "I need to see a doctor," he whispered.

"What is it about?" I asked.

"I just need to see him."

"Can't you tell me what it's about?"

"Please let me see a doctor."

I tried reasoning with him. "Sir," I said. "I would be glad to let you see a doctor, but if you don't tell me what's wrong, I won't know which doctor to call."

He lowered his head. "It's my—you-know."

"I'm not sure what you mean by 'you know.' "

"It's my thing."

"What about your thing?"

He looked like a little boy who was about to get the beating of his life. "Well, I, uh, sort of cut it in the vacuum cleaner."

When I looked over the counter, his pants were bloody. I rushed him into the back where a doctor helped him. The blood had made it seem worse than it actually was. "That's carrying it a little too far, Van Devanter," the doctor said. "I know you're a vamp, but go easy on these guys, will you?"

The people making the jokes may have thought they were funny, but I began to feel that the real joke was on me. Here I was, a twenty-one-year-old girl who had probably seen hundreds of penises in nursing school and the emergency room, and I hadn't yet seen a single one being used for its intended purpose. I began to feel like my virginity was an albatross. I had to get rid of it.

However, there was the problem of finding the right situation. When it happened the first time, I didn't want it to be on the dining room floor while my girlfriends were asleep. On the other hand, I was afraid that if I waited for the perfect circumstances, I would end up being a fifty-year-old virgin, still anticipating "the night." Even at that, I still had to convince myself that the person I was going to make love with for the first time was the person I would marry.

J.J. came to Ocean City every weekend and some weeknights after he started working at Indiantown Gap. I began to notice how different he was from the boyfriends the other girls had. Once, when he fell asleep on the dining room floor, he woke up in the middle of the night screaming. When I mentioned it in the morning, he shrugged it off. Another time, he yelled something about "slopes" and "gooks" in his sleep. When I touched him to wake him out of the nightmare, he was covered with sweat. As soon as he felt my hand, he jumped on top of me, put one hand at my throat and drew back the other hand to smash my face. Then he woke up.

I was terrified. "Is something wrong?" I asked.

"Don't touch me right now."

"Okay, but what's the matter?"

"Just a bad dream," he said. "Go back to sleep." He rolled to his side away from me and I thought I heard him crying softly.

He had periods when he was moody and they could come at any time. He'd go into depressions for a few hours and wouldn't talk to anyone. Maybe I should have questioned these things more than I did, but I figured him for the strong silent type. In a sense, his dark moods made him more intriguing.

Once, when a gas station attendant didn't have any hi-test for J.J.'s Barracuda, J.J. got this wild look in his eyes and acted like he was going to kill the guy. He screamed obscenities, smacked his hand against the dashboard, and then floored the accelerator, leaving a patch of burning rubber and a perplexed pump jockey. He would sometimes come out of his depressions with a bang and immediately begin partying like there was no tomorrow. He could be a wild bronco—unruly, loud, and full of fire.

But he was always gentle with me. I was sure I loved him, which was why, a few weeks after I got the engagement ring, I told him that I was ready to make love with him.

It was Labor Day weekend.

As soon as J.J. got over the shock, we began the search for a nice place. Unfortunately, trying to find an open room at the Jersey shore on Labor Day weekend is about as difficult as locating the Holy Grail. We started in Ocean City at seven o'clock. Next was Somers Point. Then Longport, then Margate City, then Ventnor City and all the way past Atlantic City to Brigantine. It was all the same—NO VACANCY. We drove out to the parkway and headed south. By midnight, we had tried motels all the way down to North Wildwood and the only thing we had to show for it was frustration.

"Lynda, please, let's go back to your house."

"I want more privacy."

"All right, then I know a great spot where we can park and—"

"No! Not in the car."

"Well, I guess we're out of luck."

"I guess so."

We headed back to the Anchorage to drown our frustrations at seven beers for a dollar. J.J. had such a sad expression on his face that he looked like a little boy who had just seen his puppy run over by a train. We sat in silence, both of use staring into our beers until around two in the morning. Suddenly, J.J. snapped out of his mood. He grabbed my arm, swung me around on the stool, kissed me, and laughed, "How could I have been so stupid?" he asked. "We've got a place we can use right under our noses, or should I say right over our heads."

"What are you talking about?"

"This place," he said. "There's an old room upstairs. They used to rent it out. What do you say?"

"Well—"

He took that for a yes, because he was off the stool in a flash. A few seconds later I saw him standing in a corner, talking to the owner and nodding his head. He came back to his seat with a key in his hand and a broad grin on his face. "Shall we?"

"Are you positive it's all right?" I asked.

"Come on, Lynda."

We walked up the back steps to what must have been one of the all-time sleaziest rooms in the world. It had boxes piled all around, a dirty mattress without any sheets, and a single exposed bulb hanging directly over the bed. Outside the window was a neon sign that kept blinking on and off. "It's not much," J.J. said.

"You can say that again."

"At least it's private, Lynda."

"Does it have bugs?"

"Bugs?" J.J. repeated. "Don't be ridiculous. Let's get comfortable."

I've waited twenty-one years for this, I thought only moments before I felt the quick sharp pain that marked the end of my virginity. I think it happened when the neon sign was off. Or maybe it was on. It was hard to tell because the damned thing flashed so quickly. I guess I must have been in love.

By the time Barbara and I reached Louisiana, I was already thinking that my love for J.J. might be curable. I was beginning to wonder if I hadn't used him as an excuse so I could make what I thought would be the transition from girlhood to womanhood. So many of my girlfriends were getting engaged and married that summer. Perhaps I didn't want to be the only one left.

It wasn't that there was anything wrong with J.J. In many ways, he made me feel like I'd never felt before. He told me I was special and sometimes made me believe that I was more than a short, slightly overweight, average girl who still had a long way to go before growing up. But when the summer ended, I found myself wondering if we had anything else in common besides dancing and my deflowering. His main concern was cars and I knew nothing about them. Mine was medicine, a topic in which he had no interest. He wanted a traditional kind of woman who would make his dinners and wash his socks. In spite of my romantic fantasies, I didn't know if I wanted that kind of life. There were so many other things to do first.

I guess my parents' lukewarm attitude to him also caused me to take another look. They were smart enough never to say anything against him, but when they suggested we wait awhile before rushing into marriage, it was obvious that they doubted he and I would be happy together.

Now, as Barbara and I drove toward New Orleans, we had concerns that were far more pressing than my future with or without J.J.: muffler trouble, a dying battery, and a burned-out voltage regulator. Also, we were almost broke. When we reached the city limits, we immediately started calling registries to see if we could get temporary jobs doing private duty nursing. Everyone told us the same thing: without Louisiana licenses, we couldn't do any nursing at all; it could take as long as six months before we could get a license. We spent half our remaning cash on a couple of hamburgers to bolster our spirits as we considered the options. They actually boiled down to one—calling home for help. Neither of us cared for that course of action. We were too proud to admit to our parents that we couldn't survive on our own.

"New Orleans is a swinging town," Barbara said ironically as she finished the last of her Pepsi. "We could always try prostitution. If we put our experience together we can probably earn at least a dollar ninety-eight a week."

"Two dollars if we're lucky," I added.

"Can you see the headlines when we get thrown in jail? 'Mercy Grads Forced into Prostitution by Cruel Chevy.' "

A light bulb went off in my head. "That's it," I said.

She gave me a funny look. "Lynda, there is absolutely no way I'm going to prostitute myself for that junk pile you call a car."

"Not prostitution," I said. "Mercy. There's a Mercy hospital in New Orleans. Maybe they can help us."

We told our story to the hospital's director of nursing, who by coincidence was a recently retired Army nurse. She was almost as excited about our trip as Barbara and I had been before the car problems. She also had a best friend who was an executive for the State Board of Nursing Examiners. Within a few hours, she got verbal approval for us to work. Because we had passed Maryland's tough exams and the nursing director vouched for the quality of our training, her friend offered us reciprocal privileges to practice in Louisiana. We went through orientation, and, the following day, Barbara and I were each running wards by ourselves. The hospital was painfully understaffed.

For the next two weeks, we worked the three to eleven shift. After we got off, we would head down to the French Quarter and stay out until four in the morning, dancing to jazz music and drinking concoctions called Hurricanes at Pat O'Brien's. During the second week we treated ourselves to a cheap motel room so we wouldn't have to sleep in a tent during the day. It was one of the most enjoyable parts of the trip.

When we got our paychecks, we said good-bye and headed toward Texas. "Texas," Barbara said. "A wonderful state of ignorance." Surprisingly, the car made it all the way through to the New Mexico border without a problem. But at Tucumcari, it rebelled again. We blew the right rear wheel bearing and had to stay overnight in a horrendous motel with grungy old linoleum on the floor, ancient yellow sheets on the bed, and a bare bulb on the ceiling. It reminded me of J.J. The room was only two dollars a night and so depressing it made us want to cry. Instead, we laughed and made the best of it.

The next day, Barbara's birthday, we had planned to celebrate by getting a nice motel room in Albuquerque and having a good dinner in a decent restaurant. My car had plans of its own. Outside Santa Rosa, the universal joint broke. It happened near a gas station, which meant that we only had to push it and wouldn't have to pay to have it towed. But we spent all the birthday funds and more to get it fixed. When the mechanic told us he would be unable to get a new universal joint until morning, we asked him if we could camp behind his station. He offered us better accommodations—an old van. This wasn't one of those carpeted, customized vans; it was a rusted hulk that whistled in the sharp, cold October wind. We hung towels on the windows for privacy and wrapped ourselves in sleeping bags, while we ate Hershey bars and drank from a bottle of Jim Beam, my present to Barbara. I had a single candle, which I lit before singing "Happy Birthday." It was one of the all-time great parties.

"Twenty-three," Barbara said. "I guess I'm getting old. When my mother was twenty-three, she had me. Sometimes I wonder if I'll ever be a mother."

"Of course you will."

"If it's a girl," she said. "I'll name her Lynda, in honor of the lady who gave me the best birthday party of my life."

"And I'll name my first one Barbara, after the best friend I ever had."

We spent the next few hours laughing and telling lame jokes, all of which were made hysterically funny by the Jim Beam.

"May all your days be as good as this one," I toasted.

"It's crazy," she said. "This trip—it's been miserable, but I've never had so much fun in my life."

Three seconds later, she was out cold. I covered her and brushed the hair out of her face. She was snoring loudly. I let her snore. After all, it was her birthday. I lay back in my bag and stared up at the roof while the wind shook the old van. I wondered, for a moment, if she was afraid. Although we hadn't talked about it, I knew I was. As each day went by, I became aware that we were one day closer to the Army—and Vietnam. In spite of myself and the reassurances of our recruiting sergeant, I couldn't help but wonder if we would both come home when it was over. Before drifting off to sleep, I chided myself for the doubts. After all, Barbara and I were invincible; weren't we?

5

This Man's Army

"Raise your right hand and repeat after me," Barbara's father said. There was a sheen to his dress green uniform with the silver eagles on his shoulders and the four rows of ribbons over his chest. It only served to underscore Colonel Kaplan's weariness. He was a soldier who would never have the strength to fight another battle, and he knew it. He was planning to retire in a year. "I, state your full name, do solemnly swear . . ."

"I, Barbara Kaplan, do solemnly swear . . ."

"I, Lynda Van Devanter, do solemnly swear . . ."

"That I will support and defend the Constitution of the United States against all enemies, foreign and domestic . . ."

We took our oath of enlistment in the office of the commander of Letterman Army Hospital. The general and Barbara's father were old friends who had served in Korea together. He and his sergeant major stood behind Colonel Kaplan, ready to congratulate us as soon as Barbara's father pinned the gold bars—"butter bars"—of a second lieutenant on the collars of our civilian dresses. I found myself wishing that my own father were here to share this moment with me. He would be proud.

My black Nova had made it all the way from New Mexico to San Francisco with only two more pit stops—one for a new oil pump and the other for a starter. However, the car wasn't finished terrorizing us. When we arrived at Barbara's father's apartment we went in to say hello before unloading our gear. A minute later, we heard commotion outside. We looked out the window and saw black smoke billowing from the front of the car. The paint was already beginning to bubble. When we got there and opened the hood, flames shot out. It was a few minutes before we were able to smother the fire.

The problem was with the carburetor. Barbara's father had a friend fix it—and anything else that needed fixing—before he sent us on our way again, this time to our first duty assignment, Fort Sam Houston, Texas, where we would take our officer's basic training.

Although Fort Sam was only a hundred years old, it was part of a military tradition in San Antonio that stretched back to 1718, when Spanish troops were assigned to a garrison in the Mission San Antonio de Balero, which was later to become the Alamo. Located only a few miles from the Alamo, the fort was, in its relatively short lifetime, the place where Pershing set off after Pancho Villa, where the Army Air Corps got its start, where Teddy Roosevelt and Leonard Wood put together the Rough Riders, and where Eisenhower spent much of his Army time before becoming a general. It was also the location of the Medical Field Service School (MFSS), where Barbara and I would spend the next two months.

We were disappointed when the man in the housing office told us that there were no rooms for us on post. We had been hoping to live in a barracks environment so we could get an initiation into what real Army living was like. When we arrived at the off-post motel where the Army had leased rooms, we were even more disappointed. From the outside, it looked like a seedy flophouse. But when we got to our suite, we realized that we were in Fat City.

There was a living room, a kitchen, two bedrooms, and such amenities as paneling, a television, comfortable chairs, and a refrigerator. We had to share the quarters with two other nurses, but we still had far more living space than we were accustomed to.

Barbara and I took the twin beds in one bedroom. Sandy and Ann shared the double bed in the other room. Although Sandy Shepherd and Ann Best were graduates of the same school in Cleveland, that was about all they had in common. Sandy was my age, but looked much younger. She was pretty, bubbly, and unattached, and liked to party as much as my friend Gina did. She also liked to dance as much as Barbara, and the two of them were playing Motown records before we'd finished unpacking.

Ann was six years older, a bit on the hefty side, and engaged to be married as soon as the course was finished. She looked matronly and wore her dark brown hair in a style that looked like something out of the fifties. She was very pleasant and easy to get along with. Since neither Ann nor Sandy had a car, we decided to use the Nova for transportation. Uncharacteristically, it served us well. Colonel Kaplan's friend had done a good job of fixing it.

We began our training by learning that we were "a ragtag band of wimps and washerwomen." "I've spent a lot of years in this man's Army," our company commander told us. She was a five-foot-three-inch crisply starched Regular Army officer—a lifer—who couldn't have weighed one hundred pounds soaking wet. But she did her best to convince us that she was to be feared. "I've seen thousands of medical professionals through basic training. I've taught thousands of maggots like you to march in cadence and to adapt to the Army way of life. I've made officers and gentlemen out of thousands of civilian scumbags. But this is the most disgraceful, disorderly, disgusting, disheveled, disjointed, despicable group of misbegotten, misguided miscreants that it has ever been my misfortune to lead. However, I assure you twerps that before you leave here you'll become soldiers or die trying."

I turned to Barbara. "She can't call us those names."

"That's lightweight stuff," she said. "You should hear what they call infantry trainees. Once, when my father was stationed at Fort Dix, I overheard a drill sergeant say to one of his men, 'Your best friend, Jody, is already pumping your girlfriend, Mary Jane Rottencrotch, asshole. When you walked out the front door, he slipped in the back.' It's supposed to help turn the guys into killers."

They weren't attempting to turn us into killers, but I began to think before the morning was out that they were trying to change our gender. Although our company was divided about evenly between men and women, with a mix of doctors, nurses, and administrative officers, the sergeants always referred to us as gentlemen. Some, who were not quite familiar with the finer points of the English language, even went so far as to call us "gentlemens."

One of the first things they taught us was the meaning of the old Army expression "Hurry up and wait." There was always a rush to go wherever we were supposed to be, and then a long, boring wait while supply sergeants and administrators took their sweet time. When we got our new Army clothing, we found out that the military has two sizes—big and bigger. The shirt from my long johns hung down to my knees and the arms extended three or four inches beyond my fingers. We got so much field equipment that it was nearly impossible to fit everything into the Nova when it was time to return to our apartment. That night, we unpacked mess kits, helmets, gas masks, sleeping bags, rucksacks, canteens, shovels, and heavy canvas tents, in addition to green woven straps that were somehow supposed to be snapped together over our shoulders and around our waists so we could attach the assorted items a soldier needs in the field. This was our web gear.

We also started a routine that would be repeated every night until the end of the course. We sat on the living room floor around cans of black polish, Brasso, and cotton balls as we learned to shine our brass and polish our boots the Army way. The brass was easy. We'd put Brasso on, let it dry to a white film, then buff it off with a soft cloth. After it sparkled, we would carefully measure the uniform to locate the precise spot for the brass. Our commander carried her own ruler and a small T square. If the brass was on wrong, we could get demerits. Too many, and we'd have to repeat the course. Nobody wanted to do this one again. We soon learned to mark the correct spot lightly on the uniform with ink. It was our first lesson in improvisation and shortcuts.

Our combat boots took some real work. Barbara showed us how to spit-shine. First, we would get a good basic coat of polish on them and quickly buff it. Then, we'd dampen the cotton balls in water and begin the long tedious process of rubbing the boots, our fingers making tiny wet circles until we could see our reflections. Some people cheated by using a coat of floor wax over a regular black shine. We did ours the right way.

When we finished, Barbara played music and marched around wearing her baby doll pajamas, untied boots, web gear, and a helmet. We followed her, each of us putting together our own special uniform from the odds and ends that lay in the middle of the floor. We were all soldiers now. It was a lark.

If the Army was a lark, our initial training was a joke. We started by learning to march. We looked about as bad as Abbott and Costello and most likely encouraged our drill sergeant to consider early retirement. "Not that left, lieutenant. Your other left." Any time we did a turning or flanking movement, our platoon would come apart into at least two sections going off in opposite directions. The funniest maneuver was "to the rear, march," which usually ended up with a collision involving a third of the platoon. It took a long time, but we did finally learn to march with some precision. We also learned to sing while we marched. The songs were raunchy enough to embarrass a truck driver.

In the classrooms, we encountered instructors who were as bad at teaching as we were at marching. They were usually bored sergeants who read their lectures directly from their notes, sometimes not bothering to look up or change the inflection of their voices. If we were lucky, we got overzealous junior officers who generated so much enthusiasm for their subjects it could make a person sick. We learned about the mission of the Army, the chain of command, organization of combat units, and a lot of other things that had almost nothing to do with our own mission of saving lives. During those times, the high point of the day came at five o'clock when the last tiresome class was finished and we could all head for The Pit, an appropriately named casual club downstairs in one of the school buildings where everyone went for cheap drinks.

A few weeks into the course, when we started going to Camp Bullis, a subpost twenty miles northwest of Fort Sam, the quality of our training changed drastically. Here the instructors caught our interest. There was, however, one drawback to training at Bullis—four o'clock formations. That meant we had to be out of bed by two thirty to give us all enough time to use the bathroom, get dressed, drive onto the post, park the car, and make the long walk to the assembly point where the buses would meet our company. I'm not sure what was worse: standing at attention bleary-eyed in the cold at 4 A.M., or rolling out of bed at 2:30 A.M.

Every morning when the alarm would ring, I'd feign sleep, hoping that Barbara would shut it off. She was as good at pretending to sleep as I was. After five minutes of buzzing, I would get annoyed enough to shut it off myself. "Barbara, get up."

"I am up."

"Then get out of bed."

"You get out of bed first."

It was a point of honor to be the last one awake. Inevitably, we'd lay there half dead until far past the time when we should have got up and Sandy or Ann would yell, "If you two don't wake up and get into the bathroom, we're going to be late for formation.'' We would drag ourselves out of bed and end up in the bathroom at the same time, elbowing each other out of the way as we tried to comb our hair and brush our teeth. Putting on makeup was out of the question.

Bullis was where we learned to fire the M-16 and .45 caliber pistol, to set up a field hospital, and to read a map and compass. Barbara and I took our land navigation test as a team. She got our directions from the compass and I read the map. I was certain we were off track, but we usually seemed to hit the right points, although we were definitely behind in time. Barbara wasn't a whole lot of help. I'd be bending over a checkpoint, making some notes, and I'd look up to find her off in the middle of a field, heading in the wrong direction. ''We're supposed to go the other way,'' I'd yell.

She'd laugh. ''Don't you know you have to stop and smell the flowers along the way?''

Once when we came to a field of daisies, we skipped through them singing songs from *The Sound of Music*. We lay in the middle of the field and stretched our arms and legs to make angel marks like the kind that little kids make in the snow. We laughed the whole time. For a while, I closed my eyes and lay quietly. ''Maybe we should be taking this more seriously,'' I said. When I opened my eyes again, Barbara was skipping around me and dropping flower petals on my forehead. ''He loves me,'' she sang. ''He loves me not.''

''You're out of your mind, Kaplan,'' I said. ''You've gone stark raving bonkers. They're gonna put you in the padded room.''

When the instructors taught us low crawling, most people moved around on their hands and knees. They didn't want to get dirty. We visited the mock Vietnamese village, where a soldier dressed in black pajamas and a conical hat showed us how to avoid trip wires, pungi pits, and other booby traps. We tended to take it as a joke.

''What if they're not telling us the truth, Barbara? What if we end up in combat?''

''Come on, Lynda. Don't be ridiculous. They always keep nurses in safe areas.''

They tried to teach us about the different kinds of smoke. We thought it looked pretty in yellow, purple, green, and red, but we never learned what the different colors meant. How could we take it all seriously when they kept reassuring us that we'd never really be under fire?

The one thing we did take seriously was the medical portion of the training. After we set up our field hospital, we practiced handling mass casualty situations—Mas-Cals—with some of us taking the role of wounded, while others performed their medical specialties.

The wounded were on litters and had tags attached to their bodies, explaining the nature and extent of their injuries. It was our job to examine them and to decide whether to send them directly to an operating room, to set them aside for later surgery, or to choose which ones were so severely wounded that they probably wouldn't survive. This was triage. It was the subject that the cadre stressed the most. Essentially, we were deciding who would live and who would die. It was a sobering thought, and a cold, calculated process that was especially hard for someone twenty-one years old and fresh out of nursing school. During the early part of training, many people were repulsed by the idea of "playing God." After a while, the instructors got their point across: If we didn't make the decisions, many more people might needlessly die. When a hospital is in the middle of a push—a period of heavy casualties—if you spend ten hours working on a guy whose chances of living are marginal, you could lose six others who all stood a better chance with less effort. We had to start thinking about the odds.

Back at MFSS, we sat in an amphitheater listening to a lecture on the precise method of doing an emergency tracheotomy. Our practice was done on a goat that had been anesthetized and laid out on a table before us. Feeling slightly giddy, we each took our turns performing the surgery, all the while wondering if we would ever have the nerve to do it on a real person.

We graduated from basic shortly before Christmas, and after a brief vacation with our families, Barbara and I headed for our next training assignment—William Beaumont Army Medical Center, in El Paso, Texas. I saw J.J. only once during Christmas and found myself far less enthusiastic about our relationship.

Barbara and I had to live off post again because of the housing shortage. This time, we didn't have to share an apartment with anyone else. We each had our own bedroom. We were moving up in the world.

Although we arrived in January, the operating room nursing course we were scheduled to take didn't start until the end of February. In the meantime, we were put to work on the hospital's psychiatric ward. It was filled with guys who had come back from Vietnam with severe problems. They were given ninety days to straighten out or the Army would dump them in a VA facility. Many patients were potentially violent and others were meek as lambs. All had one thing in common: They were tortured by their memories of the war. Some would spend their time screaming and crying for dead friends; others would sit in silence twenty-four hours a day, oblivious to all that went on around them. Still others would go through apparently normal times, only to erupt in violent episodes when it was least expected.

Scottie Larson was one of the latter group. A onetime high school football star, Scottie had been drafted when he flunked out of the University of Minnesota. He had spent his entire time in Vietnam living in "the boonies" as an infantryman, and he was one of the survivors when his company was overrun by a North Vietnamese regiment six months earlier. Although he had been shot in the shoulder and leg, both were superficial wounds. He appeared to be fully recovered—except for his periodic suicide attempts.

One day, he managed to sneak out of the ward without anybody finding him. Every available person immediately began searching for him. Barbara found Scottie two hours later. He was on top of a water tower behind the psychiatry building with a brick in his hand. She cautiously approached the tower. Other people had noticed him at the same time. She waved them back. "Come down, Scottie," she said. "You're going to hurt yourself."

"Back off, slope whore!"

"I'm not a V.C., Scottie," she replied. "It's me, Barbara. This isn't Vietnam. You're home. This is America. We're in Texas."

"Fuck you, gook cunt. The captain said to hold this hill. You're not going to trick me."

"Scottie," she said patiently. "I'm Barbara. Don't you remember me?"

He lifted the brick to throw it. "I'll kill you. I'll kill every fucking V.C. in this country."

"Wait, Scottie," she said calmly. "Give me a chance to prove this isn't Vietnam." She pointed to different landmarks around the area, trying to convince him he was in no danger. There was a football game in a distant field. The Viet Cong didn't play football. A new

Chevy Camaro was parked in a nearby lot. V.C. didn't drive Camaros. She pointed to her own red hair. "How many V.C. women have you seen with red hair and green eyes, Scottie?"

She sat in the grass at the base of the tower, and leaned back casually on her elbows while looking up at him. She appeared to be merely another nurse relaxing in the grass and enjoying the view. "Why don't you come down, Scottie? We'll talk about it."

He had lowered his arm, but still held the brick in it. "I don't want to come down. I'm gonna jump."

"If you jump, you might kill me, too," she said. "Why would you want to do that, Scottie? Don't you like me?"

"I guess I like you all right," he said. "But I wish I were dead."

"Come down and let's talk."

"I don't want to talk."

"Then we don't have to talk. But you should come down before you hurt yourself."

She continued the dialogue for at least forty-five tense minutes, sometimes being forceful and direct, other times philosophizing with him about life. She talked about the weather and the Dallas Cowboys and his old high school girlfriend. He said his grandfather used to let him milk the cows on the old farm near the edge of town; that the Cowboys were nowhere near as good as the Vikings; that his company commander had been an incompetent and should have been shot by his own men. Eventually, he dropped the brick on the walkway and climbed down the ladder to where Barbara was waiting. Two big orderlies ran forward and grabbed Scottie's arms. Barbara smacked one. "Leave him alone," she screamed.

The men gave her a strange look, but they backed off and let her lead Scottie back to the ward. He leaned heavily on her shoulder, crying as they walked. Later, I took Barbara to the officers' club for a few well-earned drinks. "Maybe I should have let him jump," she said.

"He didn't know what he was doing."

"We promised him help," she said. "Someone to talk to. Those asshole doctors doped him up as soon as I got him in bed."

"You handled yourself terrifically out there," I said.

"It's part of the job."

"How did you feel?"

She looked directly into my eyes. "Scared shitless," she said.

Barbara had a goldfish that she won at a carnival. She liked animals and would always stop to scratch a dog's ears or rub a cat's stomach. She would have preferred a dog or a cat of her own, but she knew it didn't make sense to get a pet if she was going to Vietnam soon. So she got the fish.

It used to swim happily around its little glass bowl while Barbara sat watching it and talking to it. She named it Trouble. "I had a long talk with Trouble," she would say. "I asked him if it isn't time for him to get married?"

"What did he say?" I'd ask, playing along.

"He said he's not mature enough to get married yet. He wants some time to party before he gets saddled with a family and responsibilities."

"He does seem content."

"Sure, but I'm worried about him," she whispered. "He needs to settle down. Between you and me, I've started noticing that he drinks like a fish."

We spent nights discussing Trouble's future. Would he grow up to be a big fish in a small pond, or a small fish in a big pond? Did he have enough potential to go to Harvard, or would he have to settle for Princeton? Did he get upset when we ate fish for dinner?

Five weeks after she got him, Trouble died. Barbara cried during the funeral ceremony, which we held in the bathroom. I read from the Bible and Barbara gave the eulogy. "He was always such a happy little fish," she said. "It came so unexpectedly. The last time I talked to him he had plans."

When she finished, we sang "What a Friend We Have in Jesus" as we poured him from his bowl into that other bowl that would lead him through the sewers to what Barbara called "the great goldfish bowl in the sky."

At the very moment Barbara flushed, I had an impulse I couldn't stop. "And away goes Trouble down the drain," I sang. Initially, Barbara didn't appreciate my humor. Then an impish smile crossed her face. "Ashes to ashes, dust to dust," she said. "There goes Trouble with the Drano and rust."

We broke out the beer and gave him a good Irish wake.

When our course started, we covered everything a surgical nurse needs to know to function effectively in the OR. The instructors emphasized plenty of practical experience. We got the opportunity to work as the circulating nurse, the one who stays outside the sterile field and directs the OR traffic, and as the scrub nurse, the one who works next to the surgeon, handing the instruments. Procedures were strictly enforced so that bacteria and other microscopic organisms could be kept out of the sterile field. We were taught to sterilize our equipment, how to set up a Mayo stand—the stand that holds the surgical instruments—and how to anticipate the needs of each surgeon. Some had difficulty absorbing the material, but Barbara and I had gone through a grueling rotation in the OR at Mercy and knew the material inside and out. Our course averages were hovering around 98 and we hardly had to crack a book to keep them there.

Since our hours were better than they had been in basic training, we found ourselves with a more active social life. Barbara started dating more than a half dozen guys and sometimes would have as many as three different dates on a Saturday—one for brunch, another for the afternoon, and the last one for dinner and dancing. Although I was still engaged to J.J., I started dating, too. Barbara and I doubled occasionally, and sometimes I'd find my date more interested in her than me. It didn't phase me until Kirk came along.

Kirk was someone Barbara and I had been introduced to at the club one night when he was having dinner with a friend. They were both infantry captains on temporary duty in El Paso. The friend was better looking and Barbara got him. But Kirk was smart and funny. After two dates, I began to wish that he was on permanent duty with me. However, he never called me again. A mutual friend told me why. I found it hard to believe, but inside, it knew it was the truth. I brought it up one night when Barbara returned from a date. "Did you and Kirk have a good time in Nuevo Laredo last night?" I asked.

I expected to find her full of remorse. She didn't miss a beat. "Sure," she said. "We danced to one of those crazy mariachi bands and he had me rolling on the floor with his funny stories about the soldiers in his company."

Something inside snapped. "I thought you were my best friend," I screamed.

"What are you talking about?'

"You knew how I felt about Kirk. You could have at least had the decency to say something to me before you went out with him."

"It wasn't my fault he called me," she said.

"You could have said no."

I thought I saw a trace of guilt on her face, but she wasn't giving an inch. "You don't own him, Lynda. You only went out with him a couple of times."

"You knew how I felt," I shot back. "You've already got half the guys in this town. What do you want: another notch on your belt?"

Apparently, I touched something inside her. "The nerve of you!" she yelled. "Don't try to get sanctimonious with me. I'm not the one who's two-timing a fiancé."

"Leave J.J. out of this. He has nothing to do with it."

"Except to prove what a high and mighty hypocrite you are."

"Me? I don't go sneaking around behind my best friend's back with her boyfriend."

"Who said I was your best friend?" she replied.

I stomped out of the apartment and didn't come back until I was sure she would be asleep. I had decided that I was never going to speak to her again. I would move out and get another apartment as soon as my next paycheck came. If I saw her on the street, I would walk to the other side.

We spent the next week in silence, saying only those things that were absolutely necessary.

"Barbara, kindly turn that record player down. I'm trying to study and don't appreciate your poor taste in music."

"Lynda, please have the decency to wipe off the table after you eat. It can be difficult living with a slob."

"Do you have to leave the top off the toothpaste tube, Lieutenant Kaplan?"

"It's about time you did your share of the vacuuming around here, Lieutenant Van Devanter."

She said she was sorry in the middle of the week. Not for going out with Kirk, but for calling me a sanctimonious hypocrite. The apology wasn't good enough.

I continued to give her rides to school, partly because I couldn't leave her stranded, but mostly because it gave me a chance to make her feel guiltier. *I* was good enough to be concerned about her needs after *she* had broken my heart.

"Can't you ever be on time, Kaplan? We're gonna be late again."

"I would have been early, Van Devanter, if you hadn't hogged the bathroom."

By Saturday afternoon, the argument started to get absurd, with the two of us complaining about the silliest things like folding the dishcloth in the wrong direction and not closing the medicine chest all the way. In the middle of another bout, we both started giggling. The giggles turned to full-blown laughter and then tears.

"I'm sorry for everything, Lynda," she said.

"Me, too. I've been acting like a jerk."

"Look, if that moron is going to come between us, I'll never see him again."

"It doesn't matter," I said. "I don't really care much for him anyway."

When Kirk called later to ask Barbara for a date, he got a two-word answer: "Drop dead."

Near the end of the course, I came down with pneumonia and spent two and a half weeks recovering after my hospitalization while Barbara took care of me. By that time, I had missed too much class work to stay in the program. The officer in charge presented me with three options: I could remain in El Paso and take the course again with the next class; I could get the specialty in a year of on the job training (OJT) in a stateside hospital; or I could go to Vietnam and be officially classified as an OR nurse after six months of OJT in an operating room. She agreed that I had the knowledge necessary to be a good OR nurse without the piece of paper.

I informed her that I wanted to go to Vietnam.

My orders came through within a week. Next, I called J.J. and told him that I wanted to break our engagement since I had orders to go to Vietnam. I was going to send the ring back, but he flew out to El Paso. It made things more difficult, yet he couldn't change my resolve.

Then I sold the car. I was sad to see it go.

Finally, I offered my good-byes to Barbara. "I'll write a lot of letters," I said.

"Don't bother," she said. "I just got my own orders. As soon as the OR course is finished, I'll be right behind you."

6

New Blood

June 8, 1969. First Lieutenant Sharon Lane, a twenty-six-year-old woman from Canton, Ohio, had been with the 312th Evacuation Hospital in Chu Lai, South Vietnam, for little more than a month. She was in her second year of military service, having spent the previous year at Fitzsimons General Hospital, near Denver. A graduate of the Aultman Hospital School of Nursing in Canton, Sharon completed her Army basic training at Fort Sam Houston. Now, she was working on the 312th's Vietnamese ward, located in a quonset hut on the hospital compound. She and another nurse, Lieutenant Patricia Carr of Louisville, Kentucky, were taking a break before waking their patients. "I was sitting behind the desk," Lieutenant Carr said. "Lieutenant Lane was sitting on an empty bed." At 5:55 A.M., a Viet Cong rocket exploded next to the hut, sending shrapnel out in all directions. Within seconds, Sharon Lane became the first Army nurse to be killed in Vietnam as a result of hostile fire.

A few hours later, my plane began its descent to Tan Son Nhut Airport in Saigon.

The jet, a stretch 727 owned by a commercial airline, had been modified to jam in as many warm bodies as possible, regardless of the discomfort. Our seats were so close that even I was cramped. I could imagine how the 350 larger men with me must have felt.

I'm sure we spent at least twenty-four hours in the air, although crossing the international date line caused me to lose all track of time. Whatever the time, it was too much as far as I was concerned. There had only been two short refueling stops—one in Hawaii and the other in the Philippines. By now, my legs were so stiff I doubted if I would ever walk again. The pain in my backside had long since disappeared and turned into a sort of generalized numbness. My lower back ached and my feet were swollen. I felt dirty and tired. I wanted to get out, and if given the option, might have even considered doing so over the Pacific Ocean.

When we had left Travis Air Force Base in California, they told us the trip would be a lengthy one. Somehow all those hours in the air felt a lot worse than they sounded. The stewardesses, who were older than most, fed us dry sandwiches and warm sodas. When the sodas ran out we were left with metallic-tasting water. About the only thing I enjoyed was the movie *Rachel, Rachel,* a film starring Joanne Woodward as a small-town spinsterish schoolteacher who is still a virgin at thirty-five and whose life is dominated by an overbearing, sickly mother. It brought me close to tears, but the other soldiers on the flight would have probably preferred a John Wayne or Clint Eastwood flick.

My seatmates were both from the infantry. One was a college-educated private who had been drafted. He made no secret of his unhappiness. "There's no love lost between me and the Army," he said. "They ought to let jerks like Johnson and Goldwater do the fighting. If they hadn't snagged me, I could have been pulling down good bucks in advertising by now, working at my uncle's agency." The other was a sergeant first class—a lifer—who had already served one tour in Vietnam with the 101st Airborne in '67, and who had requested this second assignment. "There ain't nothin' back in the good old U.S. of A. for me," he said. "You'll see for yourself, if you don't go home in a body bag. Last time I was here, I couldn't wait to get back to the world. Was countin' my days from the moment I stepped off the plane with all the other 'fresh meat.' Gonna buy me a car, find a woman, and all that crap. But when I went home, all I could think about was 'Nam. After a while, the place gets to you, and then all that bullshit back in the world don't mean nothin'."

In the middle of our final descent to Tan Son Nhut, the plane began jerking wildly. The next thing I knew, we were on our side and personal gear was falling from the overhead racks. I glanced out the window at the ground directly below. Then I saw explosions. There was a burning in my stomach and an overpowering fear that paralyzed me as I observed the bombs and red tracer rounds. We went into a steep climb. My hands were shaking. In a single moment, every idealistic thought I had ever had was gone. To hell with "Ask not . . ." and all those other high-sounding phrases. There were people on the ground who were trying to kill us. I'd had enough of this grand adventure. I wanted to go home. Right now!

As the plane climbed, the lifer chuckled at my fear. "Don't pay it no mind," he said. "V.C. love to fuck with us. It don't mean nothin'." A minute later, the pilot's voice came over the intercom. He sounded as if he were on the Houston to Chicago run and was making a routine flyover. "Men, we just came into a little old firefight back there and it looks like them V.C. ain't taking too kindly to us droppin' in on Tan Son Nhut. So we're gonna take a little ride on over to Long Binh and see if we can't get us a more hospitable welcome. Keep your seatbelts buckled and we'll be down faster than you can say Vietnam sucks."

The pilot's reassurances and the smooth landing at Long Binh helped to restore my confidence. But if there had ever been any cockiness in me before this trip began, there sure wasn't any now. In its place was a cold, hard realization: I could die here.

I spent the next three days at the 90th Replacement Detachment at Long Binh, a city that reminded me of Baltimore during the 1968 riots, when the streets had been filled with Army trucks, tanks, and soldiers, and everybody was on edge, expecting trouble to break out any minute. But these streets were quite a bit different from those of Baltimore. As we rode in buses and the backs of trucks to inprocessing stations, we saw water buffalo pulling bamboo mats piled with bundles of sticks. Women dressed in black pajamas and conical woven bamboo hats tended the animals or worked in rice paddies. Other women, small and fragile, walked through the city in *ao dais,* long contoured dresses slit to the waist and worn over white pants. The *ao dais* seemed to waft in the breeze like brightly colored silk curtains.

The Vietnamese men in the area were soldiers or farmers. They were dressed in either olive drab camouflage jungle fatigues and boots, or in black pajamas and sandals. Yet even without the different clothing it would have been easy to distinguish the two groups. The farmers always seemed old and weary. The soldiers looked like young boys. There didn't seem to be much middle age here.

Most striking were the children. They had round serious faces and sad almond eyes. Rarely did they smile. In many ways, they were like little adults in their hand-me-down American clothes and bare feet.

They tended the animals and worked the fields alongside their parents.

It was a place where the war was always present. Coiled barbed wire dominated the countryside, snaking its way up and down the roads, around the villages and through the fields. Guard towers rose high in the air, dwarfing all other structures. In each one, a soldier silently watched for Viet Cong, his M-16 rifle always at the ready.

While I waited at Long Binh for my in-country assignment, I began to learn that the picture of war painted by my recruiter was quite a bit different from the reality. Although Sharon Lane may have been the first nurse the V.C. actually killed, she wasn't the first American woman to die in Vietnam—not by a long shot. No sooner had I met some other nurses than I began hearing the stories. At least six U.S. Army nurses had died in Vietnam before I arrived—two in '66 and four in '67, all in helicopter crashes. And there were plenty of doctors, corpsmen, and other medical personnel who had also been sent home in body bags. Yet that wasn't the whole story. Navy and Air Force medical people were dying, too.

"Safe?" said one older woman, a major who had laughed at my naïveté. "Honey, whoever fed you that line should be horsewhipped. There might not be many nurses dying, but there are enough being wounded to discourage anyone with half a brain from being here."

She told me about the rocket and sapper attacks on hospitals. Sappers were specially trained enemy soldiers who were able to silently infiltrate even the best defended installations. They kept everyone in a continual state of fear. "The V.C. don't care whether you're a nurse, a clerk, or an infantryman," she said. "All they know is that you're an American." What made it worse, she told me, was that you couldn't distinguish between the V.C. and friendly Vietnamese. "Your hooch maid could be the one who's bringing the V.C. maps of your compound so they can try to kill you at night," she said. "And if they don't succeed, she'll be back there the next morning, singing as she washes your clothes and shines your extra pair of boots. It's a crazy war."

One thing everybody agreed on was that assignments to certain medical facilities should be avoided at all costs, because of their unreasonable workloads and constant danger. One unit that was near the head of this list was the 71st Evacuation Hospital, a MASH-type facility in Pleiku Province close to the Cambodian border. Pleiku was an area of heavy combat and the casualties were supposedly unending.

Unfortunately, on my third day at the "Repo Depot," I found out that the 71st would be my new home. "It may be a shitty job," the bloated assignments officer told me as he sat behind the desk in his plush air-conditioned office. "But look at it this way: Pleiku is in the mountains and is probably the only place in this whole damned country where the temperature ever gets below eighty degrees."

I thought then about my cousin Steve, who was a helicopter door gunner with the First Infantry Division, "The Big Red One." I knew he was stationed somewhere in the south part of Vietnam, in the Mekong Delta I thought, and I'd been hoping that I might be assigned somewhere near him. His family was worried about him and I'd promised I would try to look him up and keep an eye on him. Since I was going north to Pleiku, that would be pretty much out of the question. But at least we were now in the same country and maybe I could get down to see him.

Steve Kramer was the oldest of thirteen children born to my Aunt Ginnie and Uncle George. He was about a year younger than I, and had gone to Vietnam about eight months before me. He and I were the only ones out of our thirty-some-odd cousins who were the right age for Vietnam, and now we were both in the war.

I went up-country with two other second lieutenants, Michelle Neuman and Coretta Jones, flying in a six-passenger single-engine plane to Nha Trang and hopping a supply helicopter from there to Pleiku. Michelle was a petite blonde, with blue eyes, a pageboy haircut, and the face of an elf. From the time she was an infant, everyone had called her Mickie, a name that seemed to fit perfectly her bubbly personality. She had been raised near Boston, but had gone to a nursing school in San Jose, California, to get away from home. When she laughed, it sounded more like a giggle. She was a whirlwind of undirected energy, and she was one of the most fun people I'd ever known. She was forever trying to tell jokes and usually forgetting the punch lines. Even when she remembered them, she would giggle so hard that she wouldn't be able to get the words out. Of course Mickie's punch lines never mattered. Her giggle was so infectious that it would be impossible not to laugh with her. If I didn't know better, I would have sworn that she had invented the word "cute." Everybody liked her immediately.

Coretta was far more subdued than her outgoing friend. She had gone to the same nursing school as Mickie, but since Coretta was two years ahead, they hadn't got to know each other until recently, as the result of a one in a million coincidence. Ten days earlier, they had found themselves the only women on the same plane out of Travis, headed for Vietnam. Coretta was three years older than Mickie and two years older than I. She had worked in the emergency room of a hospital in Oakland, California, her hometown, before deciding to join the Army to "find something better." She was tall and black, with a body that was slightly overweight but very attractive. Although at that point, I thought of myself as a girl, there was no question in my mind that Coretta was a woman. She carried herself with a quiet confidence and seemed to be one of the few people who really listened when others talked. However, the thing that stood out the most was her compassion. There wasn't anything about her that you could point to and say made her compassionate, but her concern for others always came through. Maybe it was an expression given off by those big brown eyes or from her warm smile. Whatever it was, I knew instinctively that she was a person who could be counted on in a crunch.

When we arrived at the 71st Evac Hospital, we were met with an enthusiasm that was hard to believe. I don't think I've ever felt so welcome anywhere. But everyone had a strange habit of referring to us as "turtles" or "FNGs."

"Why turtles?" I asked.

"Because it took so long for you to get here," one of the nurses said. "The people you're replacing have waited a whole year."

"And what's an FNG?"

"What else?" she said. "A Fucking New Guy. Welcome to the war. We could use some new blood around here."

There was a list in the emergency room that had the name of every person assigned to the hospital. Next to each name was the person's blood type. When the hospital ran out of blood, someone would go immediately to that list. As a result, replacements were more than just people who could take over some of the workload; they were, literally, new blood.

We all experienced a degree of shock when we saw the hospital compound for the first time. Coretta made her evaluation less than five minutes after we had left the helicopter. "This is the damnedest hospital I've ever seen,'' she said. That was probably an understatement.

After signing in at headquarters, we got an abbreviated tour. The 71st consisted of a group of ramshackle wooden buildings and metal quonset huts, all covered with a layer of red dust and protected by a fence, barbed wire, bored guards, and Vietnamese soldiers in tanks. The ER was about fifty yards from the helipad and was connected to the post-op/intensive care unit and the operating room—actually six operating cubicles, three on each side of an open hallway and divided from each other by five-and-a-half-foot-tall cabinets. The building housing them was called the surgical-T, because of its shape. Next door to the surgical-T was the morgue. As we walked past it, a nurse wheeled a gurney through its double doors. I felt like I wasn't supposed to look.

Our guide was a six-foot-four-inch hulk of a man who must have weighed 250 pounds and who looked like he could lift a tank with one arm. He wore dirty, wrinkled fatigues and his jungle boots were coated with a layer of red dust. His clothes hung on him. I had the feeling that he was the kind of man who would have looked sloppy even in a tux. He appeared to enjoy the role of tour guide, and he seemed to like the three of us instantly, although he didn't bother to tell us his name.

When we were finished with the business part of the tour, our guide offered to show us the ''important sights,'' which were the park, the banana trees, and the pool. The park was a narrow strip of ground behind the headquarters building and between a couple of other buildings he referred to as hooches. It was called the Bernard J. Piccolo Memorial Peace Park, in honor of the popular commander who had just left. The banana trees were a couple of scrawny things near the commanding officer's trailer. The signs in front of them identified them as the Bernard J. Piccolo Memorial Banana Tree and the Elizabeth L. Piccolo Memorial Banana Tree. He said both names fully, as if to combine them into the Bernard J. and Elizabeth L. Piccolo Trees would have been highly irreverent. And God pity anyone who had the nerve to call them Bernie and Liz. Such sacrilege would never be permitted. It was important to always respect Bernard J. because he had been ''a truly wonderful man,'' and Elizabeth L., because she had waited faithfully back in the world while her husband ''did his duty for God, apple pie, and country. Amen.''

Our last stop was the pool. "Only evac hospital in-country with our very own pool," he said proudly.

"Don't tell us," I said. "You call it the Bernard J. Piccolo Memorial Swimming Pool."

He laughed. "No, actually the people around here were thinking of calling it the Captain Bubba L. Kominski Memorial Swimming Pool, in honor of just possibly the second best neurosurgeon on the entire continent of Asia, with perhaps the exception of Upper Mongolia. But Bubba Kominski is far too modest to allow anything like that."

"Why Bubba L. Kominski?" I asked.

"Because the good captain just happened to save the life of an infantry lieutenant who just happened to be the son of an engineer colonel who just happened to be grateful enough to the 71st to donate some men and machinery to our noble effort to make life on this planet more meaningful. In short, Captain Bubba L. Kominski, gentleman, scholar, neurosurgeon of distinction, and father of the six-month-old Glenda Lee Kominski, just happened to be the man responsible for getting this pool built."

"Sounds impressive," I said teasingly. "And when do we just happen to get to meet this wonderful Captain Bubba L. Kominski?"

Our guide smiled broadly, put his enormous, meaty hands around my waist, and lifted me more than a foot off the ground until I was at eye level with him. "You're looking at the man," he said. "Captain Bubba L. Kominski at your service."

Bubba got us temporarily set up with cots in the living room of Colonel Bernard J. Piccolo's trailer, which was vacant until a new commander arrived. "They're gonna have to kick a couple of doctors out of a hooch so you girls can have more permanent quarters," he said.

The next day, Mickie, Coretta, and I started to work. Coretta was assigned to the emergency room. Mickie and I joined the operating room staff. None of us was quite ready for duty at the 71st.

That first shift was a shock. There were *only* fifteen wounded soldiers who needed surgery. I saw young boys with their arms and legs blown off, some with their guts hanging out, and others with "ordinary" gunshot wounds. In addition, at least another twenty-five DPCs—delayed primary closures—were scheduled for the OR. These were guys who had been brought in with wounds a few days earlier. Since wounds coming into the 71st were usually dirty, and the possibilities of infection high, doctors would stop the bleeding, remove the metal fragments or bullets, and clean the wound during the initial surgery. Then, rather than close the outer skin immediately, they would leave the wound covered with sterile fine mesh gauze and antibiotics for a few days to make sure infections didn't get a chance to start. Later, when the risk of infection was lessened, the guy would be brought back into the OR for a DPC.

My first case was a D & I, debridement and irrigation, with Bubba Kominski. "I bet you thought us world-renowned neurosurgeons were above mere donkey work like this," he said. "Well, Van, lesson number one is that everybody around this death factory is a jack of all trades." The D & I was probably the most common operation in Vietnam. When a soldier got a frag wound, he would usually have little holes all over his body, where the fragments had broken the skin. Our job, after we stopped the bleeding, was to remove the metal fragments and cut away any dead skin—debridement—and then to clean the wound with sterile saline solution to reduce the risk of infection—irrigation. Bubba called it, "making big holes out of little holes." He said our kid had stepped on a Bouncing Betty.

"A Bouncing Betty?" I asked.

"It's a land mine," he answered. "An explosive charge bounces up to about waist level before going bang. The V.C. like it because it tends to deprive our upstanding young men of a part of their anatomy that usually spends a lot of time at attention when it's in the presence of unclothed beautiful women. Fortunately, this young trooper had his back to the charge. Family jewels all in place, but it sure took a bite out of his ass."

The next lesson that Bubba taught me was to forget most of the things I had learned in nursing school and at the OR school, starting with the arrangement of my instrument tray. "You can always tell the FNGs by the way they set up their Mayo stands," he said. In almost every OR, there are specific ways to organize the instruments. Every item has a place, and the best scrub nurses can find things blindfolded. The system is based on the idea that the only person using the tray will be the scrub. She normally hands the surgeon what he needs. If he forgets this rule, he is usually reminded with a quick rap across his knuckles.

However, as Bubba quickly pointed out, we had neither the time nor personnel for us to follow these standards. Stateside operations are usually performed by a surgeon with at least one assistant plus a scrub. In Vietnam, I would be expected to be both scrub nurse and assistant, and sometimes would find myself without a free hand with which to give instruments. He proved his point immediately. ''Get on the other side of the table,'' he said. ''You're going to start cutting with me.''

''I don't know how to cut,'' I said.

''That's why I'm going to teach you, Van. Welcome to med school.''

Bubba was an excellent teacher and I learned quickly. From that case, we went to a neuro case, one in which a nineteen-year-old boy had gotten a bullet lodged in his back, pressing against his spinal cord. As Bubba cut down to the vertebrae and started working his way to the spinal cord, I saw another facet of his personality. He became very intense, and concentrated every ounce of his being on the delicate work that had to be done. It would have been obvious to even an untrained observer that Captain Bubba L. Kominski was a virtuoso with a knife. He may very well have been accurate in calling himself ''the second best neurosurgeon in Asia.''

The wounded soldier had been brought in paralyzed, but Bubba hadn't been quite sure if it was because the spinal cord had been cut or only bruised. Although a bruise could also be serious enough to cause permanent paralysis, it would leave some hope.

It turned out that our kid's spinal cord was moderately bruised, with the bullet lodged against it. ''No question about it,'' Bubba said. ''We got us some damage here.'' He used his tiny instruments to slowly and meticulously cut away pieces of vertebrae and remove the bullet, taking special care not to do any further damage to the spinal cord. ''Hey, Van, we got a bleeder that let loose. Could you give me some suction while I tie it off?'' I was extremely nervous. One mistake could end whatever small chances this guy might have to walk again. Finally, Bubba dropped a bullet into the specimen bowl.

As he finished the surgery, I asked, ''Do you think he'll walk again?''

''Hard to tell,'' he said. ''But if he does or doesn't we'll never know. We just patch them up and send them away. We never hear what happens after they're gone.''

''Isn't it frustrating?''

"You'll get used to it, Van. This is an assembly line, not a medical center."

One thing I knew I'd never get used to was something I encountered later in the day when I had to work with another doctor on my first serious burn case. The soldier, whose entire body had been charred beyond recognition, had been at the 71st for the past three days. His patrol had been accidentally attacked by one of our own helicopters. Of the ten men, he was the only survivor. In spite of the work that was being done to keep him alive, he was undoubtedly going to die. Almost his entire body, except for his feet, had been seared by napalm, a jellied petroleum substance that oozes down the skin and into the pores, carrying flames with it. By now, he was covered with a sickly blue-green slime, called pseudomonas, a common bacterial infection among severely burned patients. I could barely look at the kid while we scraped away the infected dead tissue, trying to get down to a viable area so he might have some chance of healing. Long after we were finished with him, I was unable to get the smell of pseudomonas and napalm out of my nose. It seemed to be in my clothes, my hair, and even the pores of my skin. I would live with that smell for the next year. It was disgusting.

When I went to the mess hall that night, all the food smelled like the burned soldier. I had managed to control my stomach during the surgery, but twice that evening, when I thought about it, I retched.

Those first days in the OR were a blur of wounded soldiers, introductions to new colleagues and almost constant surgery during our twelve-hour shifts. The pace was tiring, but everyone said we were in a slow period. "If you think this is something," said one nurse, "wait until you find yourself in the middle of a push." I gradually began learning my way around the OR and started to become familiar with the different surgeons, their personalities, their strengths, and their weaknesses. In almost every way, they were similar to their counterparts in civilian life, with one major exception—there were no prima donnas here.

I also found myself working as an assistant surgeon whenever I was assigned to scrub on a case. Some doctors were frustrated with my performance and angry that I didn't already know everything that they had been taught in their residencies. Others were more patient.

One of the most understanding teachers was a thoracic surgeon named Carl Adams. "If you want good help," he said, "you've got to be willing to train them." He taught me to tie off blood vessels and even talked me through my first spleenectomy, when I had to remove what remained of one soldier's spleen while Carl worked lower in the belly on more pressing problems.

"I want you to feel around the spleen until you get the vascular system between your fingers," he said.

"Got it."

"Good, Van. Now slip your fingers behind it and hold it right about where you can feel the clamp."

"Okay. Done."

"Perfect. Now put another clamp in there." Carl always did a double clamp in case the first one didn't hold.

"It's clamped."

"All right now, Van. All you need to do is cut off the spleen and tie the blood vessels. Got it?"

"Yeah."

Although he had only been at the 71st for about a month, Carl was an old hand at combat surgery. He had spent more than eight months at another evac hospital in Vietnam. I liked working with him. Not only was he a natural surgeon with an instinct for problems that others might not be able to find, but he was also an interesting man who could talk about everything from the French Renaissance to the Chicago White Sox. I always learned something new from him.

Carl wasn't very tall—about five foot eight—but with his black hair and mustache, he bore a resemblance to the young Clark Gable. He also had some of Gable's rogueish look about him, but that was deceptive. Carl Adams was one of the gentlest and most sensitive men I had ever known. He gave everything he had to his patients and would frequently spend all night sitting by the bed of a wounded soldier who stood only a marginal chance of surviving. In his short time at the 71st, he had already been credited with pulling out some guys who, according to the oddsmakers, should have died. Shirley McKnight, a nurse who had also spent some time at Carl's other unit, said that they called him "Miracle Man" while he was there.

Born and raised in Minnesota, Carl had been drafted away from a wife, two kids, a thriving practice, and a house in the country. When he spoke in that special way that showed how much he missed them, it was easy to see that he was a good husband and father. Although only thirty-five, he had been married for sixteen years to the woman who had been his high school sweetheart. He was also one of the few married men who had had the strength to remain faithful to her for that entire time. Most of them became what we called "geographical bachelors."

When we worked together, Carl loved to play the part of the old hand, and he would rib me about being an FNG. But he was always gentle with his jokes. Mostly, as we stood over exposed hearts and lungs, blown-out bellies and rivers of blood, he tried to be philosophical about what was going on around us, quoting men like Napoleon, Lincoln, and Shakespeare. Yet when he would get tired, not even his philosophical nature would keep him from showing how deeply it hurt him to spend time sewing kids back together when he thought the reasons for them being blown apart were so foolish. I, of course, tried to prove to him that the war was a noble cause to preserve democracy.

"You really believe that?" he would ask quietly.

"Of course I do."

"Is that why you always wear that rhinestone flag on the lapel of your fatigue shirt?"

"I think we should be proud of our country, Carl," I said, "and proud of our flag."

"So do I," he answered with a sigh. "But I'm afraid this time, we may find that our country is wrong."

Once, when he finished with a patient he knew was going to die, he looked across the table at me and said, "I am tired and sick of war. It's glory is all moonshine. It is only those who have neither fired a shot nor heard the shrieks and groans of the wounded, who cry aloud for blood, more vengeance, more desolation. War is hell." He shook his head and then asked, "Do you know who said that, Van?"

"Who?"

"William Tecumseh Sherman," he answered. "He was supposedly a national hero. Why didn't we learn from him?"

Dear Mom and Dad,

I'm trying to get some sleep, but the damned mosquitoes and the smell of this bed aren't going to let me.

I'm stationed at Pleiku in the Central Highlands. You can mark that on your map along with Long Binh, Bien Hoa, Nha

Trang, and Tuy Hua, which are the places I've seen so far. My new address is:

2LT Lynda M. Van Devanter N5272354
71st Evac Hospital
APO San Francisco, California 96318

Use it frequently, please.

The hospital is in a rather heavy area of fighting so we get a large number of casualties. Some of these guys are really messed up. It's pathetic.

We're in the middle of a monsoon season now, so it rains all the time. But you get used to it. The guys say the real monsoons haven't arrived yet. Wait until the fall.

One thing Pleiku has over the rest of this godforsaken country is the temperature. Long Binh was probably the worst heat I've ever endured. It was even difficult to breathe there. In Pleiku, it's so damp that everything is mildewed, which is why my bed smells so bad. One thing you could do which would make living much easier is send me an electric blanket. When left on most of the day, I'm told it dries out the bed. That way, the sheets aren't soaked when you climb in at night. It also takes away the mildew and smell. A mechanic's light to hang in my wall locker would be handy, too. This dries out clothes. Mine are already mildewed so badly that they have watermarks. Neither of these items are available over here, but they would definitely improve things. It's hard enough to be a girl without having clothes that look like hell and smell like mildew all the time. That must be the worst thing about this tour. That and the bugs.

My hooch (a building housing people for sleeping purposes) is a real hole. It's filthy and buggy. And there's no hot water. I don't think I'll ever get used to it, but I'll endure. After all, as everyone keeps reminding us, "This is a hardship tour."

I'm working in the operating room twelve hours a day, six days a week, but that varies with the patient load—sometimes we work eighteen or twenty hours.

I'd better close. I've got to get some sleep. Please write. My mailbox is the only empty one in the OR.

Love,
Lynda

By the end of the first week, Coretta, Mickie, and I moved out of the trailer and into the hooch, which we would eventually share with four other nurses. It was a fifteen-by-forty-foot shack in a row of identical buildings. Over the front door was a sign that said FUB-1. One of the former occupants told me that the sign stood for "Fucking Unbelievable Boys." "We knew how to party with the best of them," he said. "You women might want to change the Boys to Broads, but remember, you're still expected to live up to the traditions of this hooch."

Our cubicles were six-by-ten-foot boxes that felt more like closets. The Pleiku red dust was everywhere: on the pale green walls, the floors, and even the ceilings. We spent hours trying to scrub it out, but were unsuccessful. "This place isn't much," Coretta said. "But I guess it's better than nothing."

"What are you talking about?" Mickie asked. "This *is* nothing!"

The night we moved into FUB-1, Bubba invited us to a Welcome Turtles celebration that he and Captain Slim Moffitt, his roommate, were throwing at the Bastille. "Just go to the Bernard J. Piccolo Memorial Peace Park and make a right," he said. "You can't miss it." Coretta and Mickie were too tired. I went alone.

The Bastille was not only where Bubba and Slim lived, it was also the social center of the 71st. The place actually consisted of two parts. The main section was simply a double-wide room on the end of a hooch that was almost identical to FUB-1. Since Slim was a music buff, he had a powerful stereo system and close to a hundred tapes on his side. Bubba had a small refrigerator and bar on the other side. It was the perfect place for a party. However, the thing that made the Bastille most interesting was not the main room but the bunker. Outside the door of the main room, Bubba and Slim had constructed a six-by-eight-foot structure entirely out of sandbags. It was high enough to stand in and large enough to fit fifteen or twenty people. They had built it so not even a rocket attack could stop their parties. "If there's one thing we're serious about," Slim said, "it's partying."

Slim, who in spite of his nickname, was at least as big and hefty as Bubba, was a nurse anesthetist who planned to make the Army a career. However, he didn't fit the image of the hard-charging, rock-solid lifer who walks around with a broomstick up his back. Although he always wore fatigues, he never buttoned the shirt and rarely wore an undershirt. As a result, anybody who wasn't at least six foot two inches tall usually found themselves talking to Slim's hairy stomach. He and Bubba were ideal roommates. From the pictures they had on display, it was painfully apparent that they both missed their families. One entire wall was filled with shots of Glenda Lee Kominski, Bubba's first child, whom he hadn't yet seen in the flesh, and another with photos and letters from Terri Kominski, his wife. Pictures of Slim's wife, Alice, and their three boys filled a third wall. Alice had a knack for writing hilarious letters that described the antics of their boys. Since anesthetists usually had some free time during an operation, Slim would bless us with readings from Alice to keep our spirits up while we worked.

"You can always tell the FNG," he said as I entered the Bastille wearing a flak jacket and helmet over a yellow culotte dress. "Nobody wears flak jackets and helmets around here."

"According to regulations, we're supposed to," I said. "Besides, what happens if we have a rocket attack?"

He laughed. "We haven't had a rocket attack for weeks."

"But what if?"

"Relax, FNG," he said. "The V.C. wouldn't dare interrupt our party."

It didn't even take an hour for the Viet Cong to prove Slim wrong. When the first rocket exploded on our compound, I immediately panicked, and everything seemed to go black. By the time I realized we were under attack, I was already sitting in a corner of the Bastille's bunker, shaking with fear. Apparently, somebody had led me there. Slim was kneeling next to me, calmly telling me that everything would be all right. The others simply continued the party. I didn't believe Slim. "Come on, Van," he said. "This is nothing. It happens all the time. Want me to get you another beer?"

As the rockets continued to explode, other sounds began to creep into my consciousness. Foremost was the ear-piercing siren, and the voice over the loudspeaker: "Attention all personnel. Take cover. Pleiku air base is under rocket attack. Take cover. Security alert condition red. Option one." I heard some other people casually talking about the New York Yankees and their chance for winning the '69 pennant race. On Slim's stereo, Jimi Hendrix was blaring the "Star-Spangled Banner." In the corner next to me, three nurses talked about a patient they had helped to pull through a crisis. Everyone else was standing, except me. *Don't these people know they're supposed to stay low during a rocket attack?* Between the sea of legs, I could see occasional flashes of light outside the doorway. There was a series of explosions that sounded especially close. I screamed. "That's only outgoing," somebody said. "Artillery Hill's giving it back to the V.C." Jimi Hendrix went into a new song and a couple of legs moved as if they were dancing. Everything took on a surreal quality. Then someone sat next to me and grabbed my hand. "You don't need to be afraid, Lynda," he said. "You're safe here." It was Carl Adams. His voice was reassuring.

"I want to go home," I said.

"Everybody does," he replied. "We've all gone through periods like this. You'll be all right."

I grabbed his hand tightly. When Slim returned with the beer he told Carl that they were calling for a chest cutter in the OR. Carl eased himself out of my grip and disappeared into the flashing night. Slim encouraged me to drink the beer. By the time that can was finished, I was feeling more confident. Within minutes, we were telling stories and laughing. Someone passed a marijuana cigarette to Slim. He took a hit and handed it to me.

"No thanks," I said. "I've got my own brand."

He laughed. "Van, do you know what this stuff is? It's top grade Montagnard grass." It had a thick sweet smell. I examined it closely. "It'll help relax you," he said.

I took the first hit of my life. "Inhale and hold it," Slim said. I held it until I thought I would choke and then exhaled. I felt no effect. I certainly wasn't more relaxed.

About an hour after the rocket attack had started, it abruptly ended. The siren stopped and people began walking out of the bunker. Slim and I were the last ones in there. I was determined not to leave my nice, safe little corner. "Come on, you guys," Bubba said. "Let's go inspect the damage."

"How do you know it's over?" I replied. "We could walk out there and end up in the middle of another attack."

He and Slim both chuckled. "Don't worry," Bubba said, taking the tone of a patient schoolmaster with his slow student. "Once it stops, that's it for the night. It never starts again. That's the way the V.C. work. It's all just harassment. They need target practice and we've got a nice red cross they can aim at. They set the rockets by Seiko watches out in the field and then leave. By the time our guys try to do anything about it, the V.C. are gone. They've had their fun for the night.''

Reluctantly, I went with the two men. As we walked across the compound, we saw a group of people clustered near the commander's trailer, my previous home. Hundreds of holes were in the side of it where shrapnel had pierced. Three feet away was an enormous crater. I walked into the trailer to see what other damage had been done. The cot where Mickie had slept was on its side. A big fluorescent light fixture was lying on the cot that had been mine. If I had been there, it would have landed on me. *I could have died.* I stood with my mouth open, transfixed by that piece of metal on the bed where I had slept. After awhile, I heard footsteps behind me. Mickie and Coretta shared my shock when they too saw the damage. ''It looks like somebody's playing for keeps,'' Coretta said.

When I went back outside, Bubba and Slim were examining one of the two scrawny banana trees. ''I'm a little concerned,'' Bubba said. ''The Elizabeth L. Piccolo Memorial Banana Tree has taken some shrapnel. I hope it isn't too traumatized.''

I stared at him as if he were crazy. ''This trailer and that hooch over there are half destroyed; we could have been killed, and all you can worry about is an ugly little tree?''

''Yup,'' he said. ''There's one thing you have to remember, Van. You can always get a new trailer, a new hooch, or another doctor. But there's only one Elizabeth L. Piccolo Memorial Banana Tree. The Army doesn't issue replacements.''

''I'm talking to a couple of lunatics,'' I said.

Bubba smiled and turned to Slim. ''Looks like she catches on real quick, partner.''

With all the beer I had been drinking, I began to encounter a bit of urgent pleading from my bladder. I was afraid to walk back to the Bastille alone, so I dragged Slim and Bubba away from their precious banana trees to escort me. Having one of these big hulks on each side made me feel safer as we headed for the ''lady's lounge.''

''The lady's lounge?'' Slim said. ''What's she talking about?''

''I think she means she has to go pee-pee.''

Before we got halfway to the Bastille, I heard a high-pitched whistling overhead. In a split second, I was in a muddy ditch. Bubba and Slim were there a millisecond later, landing on top of me and completely covering me with their massive bulk as the first rocket exploded. The ground shook. Another rocket came. Then another. Then a whole barrage. The sirens started again. There were sharp flashes of light. My ears were ringing. I felt crushed and had trouble breathing. But I didn't want them to remove their five hundred pounds. They were using their own bodies to provide me with extra protection because I was the FNG. New people were to be kept alive until they learned enough to keep themselves alive. That was fine with me. However, there was one minor problem that was quickly becoming a major one. My bladder was at the point of bursting.

"There's only one way to deal with that," Bubba said as another rocket exploded a few hundreds yards away. "You'll have to go wee-wee in your pants."

I was mortified. "No way!" I said. Viet Cong or not, I wasn't going to wet my pants.

"I think we've got one that's potty trained," Slim said.

"Then she'll have to hold it."

Unfortunately, I knew that if I continued to fight against my bladder's natural tendencies, I would eventually lose, especially with all this extra weight on top of me. Finally, I made what the Army would have called a command decision. "I'm going to run to the latrine," I said.

"Like hell you are," Bubba answered.

I gritted my teeth and tried to put up with the pressure for a few more minutes, while rockets exploded all around us. Maybe it was fortunate that I had to go to the latrine so badly. It helped to take my mind off the continuous explosions. But I knew I couldn't hold out indefinitely. "Look, you guys," I said. "I've got a better idea. If you get off me, I can crawl down to the other end of the ditch and pee. I will tell you here and now, do not look. I expect you to follow my wishes."

Both of them laughed, but they lifted themselves enough so I could crawl out. I moved about fifteen feet through the mud and then turned onto my back, taking care to keep myself as low as possible. With great difficulty, I managed to lower my culottes and underwear. Holding my body parallel to the ground with the back of my head practically in the mud, I hoisted myself so that I was supported by my arms and legs. Bubba and Slim were roaring with laughter. "I told you not to look," I screamed.

"We're not looking," they answered in harmony.

"Promise?"

"Are you nuts?" Bubba said. "You think we're going to risk having our heads blown off so we can see your ass? We may be crazy but we're not fools."

As I began relieving my bladder, I found out something I should have learned years earlier: the human body is not built to neatly accommodate that particular biological function in the position I had chosen. By the time I put my culottes back on again, my legs and clothes were so wet and dirty that I might have been better off following Bubba's original suggestion.

A few minutes later, the helicopters started. "Incoming wounded," Bubba said. "I have a feeling we're in for a long night."

7

Mas-Cal

"This kid's in shock. Get a couple of IVs into him."

"Somebody want to check that tourniquet? His limb's discolored."

"We need more plasma. Where the hell is it?"

"If we don't get his ass into the OR in the next five minutes, he's had it."

"This one's got no reflexes. Shove him over with the expectants."

"Goddamnit, I knew it was going to fucking happen. Those fucking fucked-up fuckers in the fucking mess hall ought to be fucked. I told them not to serve any more fucking fruit cocktail. I don't care how fucking stupid it sounds, every fucking time they serve fruit fucking cocktail, we end up with more fucking wounded than we can handle. I warned those fuckers."

"Snow him with morphine. He's going to die within the hour."

"Got a big belly wound here."

"Call Bubba to look at that head and order five pints of AB negative blood from the lab."

It was my first Mas-Cal, short for mass casualty situation, and although the instructors back in basic had warned us what to expect, no amount of warning could have ever prepared me for the sheer numbers of mutilated young bodies that the helicopters kept bringing to the 71st. "Now you'll see how we really earn our money," Slim said. The emergency room floor was practically covered with blood. Dozens of gurneys were tightly packed into the ER, with barely enough space for medical people to move between them. And the helicopters were still bringing more. Dead bodies in Glad bags were lined up outside the ER doors, to be moved to the morgue as there was time. The moans and screams of so many wounded were mixed up with the shouted orders of doctors and nurses. One soldier vomited on my fatigues while I was inserting an IV needle into his arm. Another grabbed my hand and refused to let go. A blond infantry lieutenant begged me to give him enough morphine to kill him so he wouldn't feel any more pain. A black sergeant went into a seizure and died while Carl and I were examining his small frag wound. "Duty, honor, country," Carl said sarcastically. "I'd like to have Richard Nixon here for one week."

I started to prepare another soldier for surgery. He grabbed my arm. "I can't feel my foot," he kept saying. He was cold. Somebody had covered him with a blanket to keep him from slipping into shock. I put a couple of IVs into his arms. "Nurse, I can't feel my foot!" I glanced down at the lower part of his blanket. "Your foot's still there," I said. "We'll have you fixed up in no time." I pulled the blanket back from his chest and cut his fatigue shirt off. When I removed the blanket from his legs so I could cut away his pants, I was shocked to see the lower part of his left leg lying on its side, separated from his knee by a bloody jagged wound. The medic in the field had applied a tourniquet to keep it from bleeding out.

I had to get that foot out of the way so I could cut the boot off his other leg. But I kept thinking that if I picked up the lower leg and carried it off, he would scream. I knew I would then lose my grip and scream, too. I didn't want to break down. I let it lay for the moment.

Coretta came to give me a hand. "You okay?" she asked. "You look like you're going to get sick."

"I'm fine," I answered.

We removed the old field tourniquet and put a pneumatic tourniquet around his leg so we could relieve the pressure once in a while to keep the stump from becoming gangrenous. He kept asking about his leg and we tried to distract him while we doped him up with pain medication. Later, when we brought him back to the OR, we lifted him from the litter to the operating table. I stood next to the empty litter, looking down at the lower leg. "What am I supposed to do with this?" I asked nobody in particular.

"Throw it in the trash," somebody said. "It's no good to him now."

I wrapped the leg in a pillow case and sent it to the pathology lab.

After I put on my surgical suit and scrubbed, I found myself working again with Carl Adams on the first of many cases that we would handle together during the next seventy-two hours. Our initial soldier had a gunshot wound. The bullet had entered the left chest wall at the nipple line. Someone in ER had put in chest tubes to drain the wound and get the lung expanded again.

"Let's get him on his side," Carl said.

We turned him onto his right side and lifted his left arm over his head. Carl made the incision and together we tied off the bleeders. With a pair of large retractors I held the ribs apart while he went in and removed the bullet. He repaired the rest of the damage in the chest cavity, irrigated with sterile saline, and closed. "That was an easy one," he said. "Don't start getting cocky on me."

The next case was far more complicated. The soldier had been wounded through the stomach, but at an angle where the metal fragments went up from the stomach into the chest. Apparently, the guy had just finished eating a big meal before he was hit. Partially digested lima beans and ham were splattered throughout his chest cavity. "Sometimes it's easier," Carl said, "if you tell yourself they're not people you're working on, but merely bodies. We're not in a hospital, Van. This is a factory. If you look at it any other way while you're working, you might make yourself crazy." When we got into the chest and started cleaning the wound, we found more than food. There were dozens of worms crawling around. We tried to get all of them out before Carl began searching for the frags. It was a slow, tedious process. "Wait until we get one of the Vietnamese with their undigested fishheads and rice," Carl said. "They'll make this job look pleasant."

After he had taken care of the chest wound, he moved into the belly. It was also a mess. There probably wasn't a single organ that hadn't been damaged. Carl moved the intestines out of the belly and onto the sterile drapes to give himself more room to work. We covered them with lap pads that had been moistened in warm sterile saline. As his hands moved through the belly, reparing damage, he began to make some order out of what was formerly a jumbled mess. When he was finished with the other organs, he started on the intestines, visually inspecting them and running his fingers along the underside to carefully check for any hidden frags that might later cause an infection. He ran the bowel four times and had already gotten a dozen frags when he started to put it back in the belly. Then he stopped for a moment. "Call it instinct," he said, "but I'd better run that bowel one more time." Slowly, he felt his way along the bowel again, until he found a final frag near the retro-peritoneum, the inner back lining of the abdominal wall. It was the first time I had seen him rely on his instincts, but it wouldn't be the last. Carl had a knack for sensing problems in areas that other competent surgeons might overlook. I thought he was wonderful.

"The cooks brought some food into the outer office, Van. We ought to eat after this case."

"What time is it, Carl?"

"Breakfast time."

"I'll wait and eat when we're through with our last case."

"Are you kidding? That could be three or four days from now. If you don't eat, you'll collapse."

"I can't eat in the middle of of all this."

"Then you'll have to learn."

"I have a stomachache, Carl."

"Try some antacids. It's pretty common."

Even in the worst of cases, Carl never panicked. He could be looking down at a soldier with blood spurting out of a dozen holes and half the insides blown away, and he would assess the situation in a cool, calm manner, starting to make order out of a mess almost immediately. In the middle of the first afternoon, we came up against one case that would have thrown terror into the most proficient of surgeons. The soldier had multiple frag wounds of the chest. The left lung was collapsed, and the right was partially collapsed. A metal fragment had lodged itself in the heart muscle. In a stateside hospital, an operation to remove the frag would have been conducted by a top heart specialist, with the aid of an artificial heart, so the real one could be kept still while surgery was being performed. Unfortunately, we had neither a heart specialist nor a heart machine at the 71st and if the frag wasn't removed, the soldier would die. Carl would have to work on the heart while it was still beating, and move quickly enough so that he would not cause any more damage. It would be like trying to change a tire while a car is moving.

He began by making stitches around the edge of the frag so he could immediately tighten them as soon as the metal was removed, and, hopefully, hold that section of the heart together at least a little bit until he could get the other stitches in. If he made a single mistake, his work would all be in vain. He held a forcep in one hand, ready to grab the frag. In the other was the end of a suture. His movements were swift and sure. Carl told Slim to start pumping blood into all four IVs. We held our breath and I said a quick silent prayer.

In a split second, Carl removed the metal fragment and pulled the suture tight. Immediately, blood came spurting out at least eighteen inches high. Without losing an instant, he dropped the frag into a bucket and tied off the suture. Blood was still escaping at a rapid rate, but Carl continued to stitch the heart as calmly as if he were working in a bloodless field on a less essential organ. Every few seconds, he'd have me sponge away some of the blood so he could see well enough to tie a knot. He had to be extremely careful to avoid puncturing the other side of the heart with his needle. He timed himself so he sutured in rhythm with the heartbeat.

Finally, that blood stopped flowing. When I looked up at his face, I could see that the tension and lack of sleep had taken its toll. Sweat was rolling down his forehead and along the side of his cheeks. I wiped it away with a sterile 4×4 sponge. His eyes met mine across the table. "You were great," I said.

"No compliments now," he answered. "The job only counts if this kid lives. Let's take a look at his left lung."

"Quick, Van, what's your favorite food?"

"My mother's homemade lasagna. How about yours, Carl?"

"Give me another suture. Mine's lasagna, too. Would you cut right here above the knot? There's this little restaurant in Saint Paul. My wife and I go there at least once a month. The cook makes the best lasagna I've ever tasted. Another clamp, please."

"Mosquito?"

"Yeah."

"You obviously haven't tasted my mother's lasagna if you think the best is in Minnesota."

"Suture, Van. Ah, but does your mother have the red checkered tablecloth, candlelight, and violin music? Cut it right here."

"Done. Carl! I think I've met a true romantic."

"Bah, humbug. Give me another suture."

During the second night, we did three belly cases, a chest case, and a couple of multiple frag wounds. At one of the other operating tables, a surgical tech had fallen asleep and fell into an open belly while the doctor was repairing a kidney. The tech was carried out of the OR and left to sleep on the floor of the office, but only for an hour. The belly had to be washed out and the whole operating field sterilized again. After a few others fell asleep at the tables near morning, and it looked like the casualties would never end, we all began grabbing some sleep between cases whenever we had the chance. Some people pulled chairs together and slept stretched across them, while others were satisfied with the floor. The OR supervisor's office was comfortable, but the linen closet was quieter. Around midmorning, I found myself a spot in an out-of-the-way corner of the emergency room.

"Van, wake up. The next case is ready."

"Shit! What time is it, Coretta?"

"Eleven. You've had about twenty minutes sleep."

"Any time to grab a bite?"

"Better not right now. You and Carl are assigned to a burn case next. A squad was napalmed by friendly fire. When you smell that OR, you're liable to lose your lunch."

Carl and I went through three burn cases that afternoon, cutting away entire chunks of charred flesh that was so crisp it could be broken in half. The crew in the ER had been unable to remove all the clothes because the soldiers were in such pain. They had to be anesthetized before we could even start prepping them. In some spots, the heat had been so great that the clothes and skin were melted together. Just when we thought we were finished with burns, we got another case, the only survivor of a helicopter crash. In addition to a body that was almost covered with third-degree burns, the soldier had traumatic amputations of both legs. When we removed the pneumatic tourniquets after we had stopped the bleeding at the stumps, we pulled off layers of crispy skin that had stuck to the material. In the middle of the darkest humor, the doctors and nurses would call these patients crispy critters.

"Let's close the peritoneum with O Chromic, Van. You like baseball?"

"I was once the best catcher in the league, Carl. Here—O on a taper."

"Yeah, that should do it. I used to pitch. Cut, please? Had a curve that was good enough—another suture—to get me a tryout with the Yankees in the days when they practically owned the pennant. Scissors, please. Are you a Yankee fan?"

"Nope. Washington Senators."

"Senators? Why bother rooting for a bunch of losers?"

"Loyalty. Harmon Killebrew was my hero."

On the second night, we came under another rocket attack. When the shrapnel hit the surgical-T's metal walls, it sounded as if somebody had taken a handful of gravel and thrown it against the quonset hut. Since there were no windows, I couldn't see the explosions, but I still felt their concussion and jumped each time another rocket hit. "You'll have to steady yourself," Carl said, "or you're going to give this guy an accidental tonsillectomy from the stomach up."

We lowered the table closer to the floor and Carl and I performed the surgery while kneeling. The anesthetist lay on his back, monitoring his gauges from there. In the beginning, my hands shook so badly I could barely hold the instruments. Carl talked quietly and joked with me until I calmed down. After an hour of kneeling, our legs were falling asleep and the pain in the knees was unbearable. We tried raising the table some and operating from a position that was half standing and half squat. That was also painful, this time for the thighs and lower back. Finally, we decided to put the table back to the original position regardless of the V.C. rockets. Besides, by that point, we were so tired we might have even welcomed death. At least then we would be able to get some rest.

"Don't go to sleep on me now, Van."

"Huh? What? Oh, Carl. I wasn't going to sleep."

"I asked for a sponge."

"Right here."

"Clamp that bleeder?"

"Sure thing."

"Why don't you get started on the spleen while I'm down here in the belly?"

"You mean take it out myself?"

"That's right. I've talked you through enough of them. It's time you did one on your own."

"Got a question for you, Van."

"Huh?"

"What day is it, Van?"

"Wednesday. No, Carl, wait. Maybe Thursday."

"Day or night?"

"I think day. Last time I was out in the ER, I thought I saw light through the doors."

"How's the situation out there?"

"Maybe a dozen left, Carl. Mickie says the choppers have stopped bringing new wounded. The rest are all dead."

"Are you sure it's daytime?"

"Not exactly."

"It's probably night, Van. It feels more like night."

"Maybe it does."

Our final case was a pale soldier whose entire belly was blown open. His guts were hanging out and had been held in place by blood-soaked bandages. He was a kid, a boy who didn't look old enough to shave. His face was as smooth as a baby's bottom, and he had a collection of bright red freckles that stood in defiant contrast to his gray white complexion. He had fallen on a V.C. mine. I noticed that his chart said he had been in an area that was classified. I asked Carl about it.

"The kid's unit was over the fence," Carl answered.

"Over the fence?"

"Sure, Cambodia."

"We don't have any soldiers in Cambodia."

"We don't? Who told you that?"

"The government. The newspapers back home."

"Don't believe everything you read and don't believe anything the government tells you."

While I got the soldier prepped and the anesthetist put him under, Carl grabbed a cup of coffee to help him stay awake. When he returned, he looked totally drained. He could barely walk a straight line. I wondered if he would be able to handle another case without sleep. I helped him into a new pair of gloves and he stared blankly at the belly that had been destroyed beyond recognition. "What am I supposed to do with this?" he said dejectedly. After a half minute of hesitation, he started to work in his quick, methodical way, clamping off every bleeder he could locate while I suctioned the blood from the wounded soldier. The boy was losing it as fast as I could suction him out. We had four IVs pumping blood into him. Slowly, the belly started looking better as Carl removed frags and pieced organs back together again. The work that Carl was doing would have been difficult for any surgeon; it was especially tough for one who hadn't slept for at least three days.

It seemed like we were in that belly for hours. As we worked, we could hear the other surgical teams finishing their final cases and leaving the OR one by one, to return to their hooches and a long-awaited sleep. Everyone was so exhausted that the good-byes were barely audible mumbles. Eventually, we were the last ones. We were almost finished when suddenly the soldier went into cardiac arrest. Carl and the anesthetist worked feverishly to resuscitate him. The kid came back for a minute and then arrested again. They pulled him out of it once more. He arrested a third time. Carl frantically tried to put life into this dying boy.

"I've got no readings," the anesthetist said. "Give it up, Carl."

"Fuck off," Carl said. He cut into the chest to do open heart massage. It was a last-ditch effort that rarely was successful.

"Still nothing, Carl. He's had it."

"Shut up and keep working!"

"Carl, he's dead!"

"Then I'll bring the fucker back!"

"Carl!"

He finally stopped trying to resuscitate the soldier, put his hands on the table, leaned forward and shook his head. "I'm tired," Carl said.

He walked out of the OR and back to the office to do the report. After the anesthetist left and a corpsman removed the body, I started to clean the room so it would be ready if another case should come. It was the first time that I had really noticed the mess. Three days' worth of debris was on the floor. Half-empty instrument trays were scattered around the OR. Almost every inch of concrete was covered with blood. Stained sheets lay in one corner. As I was cleaning the operating table, Marcia Coleman, a first lieutenant and the head nurse on nights, came into the room. ''You look wiped out, Van,'' she said. ''Go to bed. We have other people who can clean up.''

''It's my responsibility. I'll take care of it.''

I started wiping blood off the crash cart, but after a few minutes, I told myself it was hopeless. So I went to work cleaning the other equipment. The job seemed overwhelming. Everything was covered with blood. It would take me at least eight hours to do it right. I tried to wash the walls, but I got discouraged there, too. Finally, I just gave up. I walked back to the office. ''You were right, Marcia,'' I said. ''I can't do it anymore.''

I went into the women's changing room and stripped off my bloody scrubs. My fatigue pants and T-shirt underneath were also covered with blood. There was blood all over my body, but I was too tired to wash it off. I lifted my fatigue shirt from a nail on the wall and put it on, leaving it unbuttoned over my bloody T-shirt. As I walked out of the room, my boots left a trail of blood. Carl was walking out of the men's changing room when I passed it and he was also covered with blood. We walked outside together. It was night.

''You're good help, Lynda,'' he said. It was one of the highest compliments a surgeon could pay a nurse. As we walked through the darkness toward the hooches I could hear the sound of small arms fire and helicopters in the distance. How much longer would it be before they sent us more broken bodies? An hour? Two? I shuddered at the thought.

Carl put his arm on my shoulder in a gesture of comradeship. ''I've thought of little but sleep during the past seventy-two hours,'' he said. ''And now I'm too tired to sleep.''

''I know how you feel,'' I replied.

''You do,'' he said, looking at me thoughtfully. ''Can I buy you a drink?''

''Yeah. I need it.''

We went back to his room and he played quiet music on his stereo while we both drank Scotch. We sat cross-legged on the floor, using a packing box as a coffee table. Carl spoke slowly about our war, too tired to reach back in history for his usual colorful quotes. I talked about how I had felt watching the last boy die and how hard it was to put aside the parts of me that wanted to cry for all the dead soldiers.

"You'll learn how," he said. "Or you won't survive this year."

Sometimes we didn't talk with each other as much as we talked at each other, neither of us listening to what the other was saying, each lost in a world of our own. We were both trying to sound philosophical about the death surrounding us, and, for a while, we succeeded. But after too much talking and too much Scotch, I began to shake. In spite of my attempts to hold back the tears, they came. He touched my hand and then moved next to me, wrapping his arms around me and running his fingers through my hair while I sobbed. Finally, his body began to shake and he cried with me.

"Why do they have to die, Carl?"

"Who knows?"

"I don't understand."

"Nobody does," he said.

"But there's got to be a reason."

He grabbed my shoulders and looked into my eyes. "I've had my fill of this war, Van," he said. "I need someone to hold me. It's the only thing that makes any sense."

"I need it, too."

Carl and I didn't make love that night. We slept together in his bed, two bodies covered with the blood of hundreds of young boys, holding tightly to whatever island of sanity we could find. But we also knew we would soon be lovers. And when that time came, it would have nothing to do with his wife and two kids and the house in the country. We were just tired and lonely and sick to death of trying to fix the mutilated bodies of young boys.

I was always bothered by the attitudes of some people who believed that women in the military were either whores or lesbians. But I think I know how the whole thing may have started: In a war, in a situation where there is nothing remotely resembling sanity around you, you tend to try to find some sense of normalcy, some feeling of comfort, some communication with another person on a level removed from that environment of destruction. You want to share moments of happiness. When you work under the intense conditions of a combat zone, you find yourself forming stronger bonds than you might have imagined in a peacetime world. You spend hours, days, and weeks working with a person, sharing the agony and joy, the laughter and tears, the hopes and disappointments. Inevitably, the time will come when you've finally experienced all the pain, emptiness, and ugliness you can stand. And in that final, quiet moment, all you want to do is lean against somebody and cry so they can hold you and love you and remind you that, after it's finished, you're still human.

Unfortunately, many people who haven't experienced that need don't understand.

> *Hi Mom and Dad,*
> What's happening? I still haven't gotten any mail and the spiders in my mailbox are getting bad. We're working harder now because of the heavy fighting at Dak To and Ben Het. If you notice a week or two go by without any word from me, it's probably because we're having a push and can't leave the OR. Don't start worrying.
>
> It seems funny to sit here on the steps in front of my hooch and see nothing but fatigues on everyone—jungle fatigues, camouflage fatigues, tiger stripes, everything. Circling the skies are C-130s, "Spooky" helicopters watching out for us, and Sopwith Camels headed for aerial recon at Ben Het, which is about twenty miles from here. Our guys are completely blocked in at Ben Het. Charlie has cut off the road to Dak To and the ARVNs are screwing up badly. The casualties are bad and the sky is filled with dust-off (medevac) choppers. I'm tired, but I'll probably be called back to work soon.
>
> The sounds here are the strangest. We have everything from complete silence to the rumble of engines, the clatter of choppers and the whine of jets. Then there's the dull thud of outgoing artillery and the screaming whistle and earth-shattering crash of incoming rockets. A couple weeks ago we had our first rocket attack since I've been here. It was the most frightening thing I've ever experienced. Now, I'm almost used to the sound of outgoing artillery at night, and seeing flares reassures me instead of frightening me.
>
> The most beautiful sight here is the sunset. You've never seen such clouds, and the colors are fantastic.
>
> I found my recruiting sergeant the other day. He is in supply on Artillery Hill and, although I chewed him out for getting me into this mess, he has been a boon in bad times. He acquires many little luxury items otherwise unobtainable. I've started learning how and where to swipe necessities. We put a tabletop on the shower floor

over some two by fours so we don't have to stand on the moldy cement, and we stole some paint to cover the crud in the latrine. We also picked up a few little things to decorate our rooms. I even got a coffee can with a hole in the bottom to use as a cover for the ceiling light in my room. Could you please see if you can find some nice decals and posters that I could use? I would especially like a lampshade. It would make the room a lot more feminine.

I love you all. Please write soon.

Love,
Lynda

8

One Giant Leap For Mankind

Captain Bubba L. Kominski—"gentleman, scholar, and just possibly the second-best drinker in all of the continent of Asia, with the possible exception of Inner Mongolia"—regarded his unofficial position of hospital social director as a sacred trust. So the drinking and merrymaking didn't get out of hand, he ordered us to follow one hard and fast rule: No parties at the Bastille unless there was something worthwhile to celebrate. He informed us that this rule would be strictly enforced. Failure to follow it would bring immediate unmentionable consequences.

"What might be a worthwhile cause for celebration?" I asked.

"That's simple, little lady," he said. "In this armpit of a country, surviving another day is reason enough for anyone."

Those initial months in Pleiku became a blur of long hours in the operating room followed by equally long hours at the Bastille. We partied as hard as we worked and when we slept, it was frequently because we had passed out from too much alcohol or too much exhaustion. We were loud, boisterous, and unruly, almost relentless in our pursuit of anything that would block out the faces and moans of dying boys. When people laughed, they did it with a roar; when they cried, it was usually in private. We learned to live for today, because tomorrow might not come. When it did come, we learned to blot out the bad memories with the right amount of booze or grass. The booze came through regular Army supply channels. We bought it at the PX, along with our stereos, tape decks, and snacks. The pot came through irregular channels that were as strongly established. For a dollar, it was possible to get pure Montagnard gold, packaged like regular cigarettes. The smell was the only way anyone could tell the difference. My brand was Kool. They even came filter-tipped. There was also all the opium, hashish, and heroin anyone could want and it was available at bargain basement prices. Fortunately, few of us felt we needed them.

What we did need was love, understanding, friendship, and companionship; the things that would keep us human in spite of all the inhumanity being practiced around us. Carl and I filled many of those needs for each other. He was patient and gentle, giving freely of himself and making our limited time together more natural than I would have ever imagined. We talked easily and laughed a lot. When he would hold me and kiss me softly, I felt protected. We spent precious hours together comforting one another and leaving the war outside the hooch. He told me stories about his childhood in Michigan and how he would do crazy things like rolling down "Suicide Hill" in an old garbage can, or tying his sled to the backs of cars and letting them pull him through the snow-covered streets. Once, he mistakenly hitched a ride to a Chevy that headed for the interstate. After losing his nerve and rolling off at somewhere around fifty miles an hour, he watched his sled take off forever, sending sparks up as it bounced along the plowed road. While he lay on the side of the road, dizzy, bruised, and with a broken arm, he vowed to take up a safer winter sport—ice hockey. Later, with his skates and hockey stick, he earned an athletic scholarship to the University of Minnesota, but his real talent wasn't on the ice; it was in the water. From the time he was eight, Carl had been collecting trophies for his freestyle and butterfly strokes. He was strong enough to go to the Olympic tryouts in '56, but his freestyle was only good enough to place him seventh in the hundred meters and his butterfly was totally outclassed.

I told him my own swimming stories, about how I always seemed to come in second and how much I had envied my sister, Jean, for all her first-place trophies. A few times, when Carl and I went to the pool, he was kind enough to let me win our spontaneous races, yet when I watched his style, there was no way I could tell myself that those victories over him were anything but charity.

Once, when my sister Mary sent me a papier-mâché apple, Carl and I spent an entire afternoon hanging it, being very careful to get it in exactly the right spot. When we finished, we held each other and talked for hours. Although I was very inexperienced with men, he made me feel confident and I wanted to please him. With him, I was happy; away from him, I ached for his touch. We told each other that it was love. I tried to make myself forget that he would be returned to the world at the end of August, to a woman who loved him as much as I did and who could give him far more than I ever could.

But for now, we had each other, and in spite of the rocket attacks, the casualties, and the Army, we had romance. We took long walks around the compound, looking up toward the sky or down toward the ground, never to the sides where we might see the guards and tanks and barbed wire. When we worked nights, we spent our days lying by the pool or making love in the afternoon. When we worked days, we would spend our nights partying at the Bastille or lying together in the darkness. And when we were in the middle of pushes, we still found the time for that one word, or look, or touch that made it all bearable, that reminded us that we had our own little world away from the war, a world filled with peace, a world where flowers grew and children played and men recited poetry. Carl sometimes called me Annabel Lee and his favorite lines were those by Edgar Allen Poe: "And neither the angels in heaven above/ Nor the demons down under the sea/ Can ever dissever my soul from the soul/ Of the beautiful Annabel Lee." He told me that regardless of whatever happened in our separate lives, ours was a love that we would always know was a good love, one we could look back on with fondness and without guilt.

I knew he was right.

"Lights on. Down two and a half. Forward." The voices of the astronauts were muffled by static, but still audible as they played over AFVN, the Armed Forces Radio Network in Vietnam. It had been a slow day and night in the OR, with no more than a couple of casualties whose wounds were minor, so we all gathered around the small radio in the ER to listen. It was almost as if everyone, including the V.C., was so interested in the moon landing that they had forgotten all about the war. AFVN had devoted almost all its airtime to the Apollo 11 mission that night and we all knew while we listened that we were witnessing one of the great turning points in history. "Forty feet, down two and a half. Picking up some dust. Thirty feet, two and a half down. Faint shadow. Four forward. Drifting to the right a little."

From Houston: "Thirty seconds."

"Drifting right. Contact light. Okay, engine stop."

"We copy you down, Eagle."

"Houston, Tranquility Base here. The Eagle has landed."

It was 4:16 A.M. Saigon time. At that very moment, a loud cheer went up throughout the Pleiku area and the sky filled with rockets, flares, and fireworks. We were all proud to be Americans.

When the day shift came on, we traded places with them at the Bastille, so we could continue celebrating the event. It was a party that had been in the planning for weeks. "This here moon thing," Bubba had said, "is just possibly the second-best reason in the universe to have one hell of a party." Slim had made a tape of the Apollo transmissions during the night, and he replayed them for us while we began to get seriously blitzed. Although it had been raining for the past few days, this morning was only hazy with the sun occasionally poking through the clouds. On another tape deck, someone was playing songs about flying and the moon. Mickie and Coretta showed up in flight suits they had scrounged from the Air Force. They wore oversized fishbowls as helmets. Although neither of them bore the slightest resemblance to Buzz Aldrin or Neil Armstrong, Mickie and Coretta gave us a drunken Vietnam-style recreation of the moon landing when they fell off the roof of the Bastille and landed on their backsides. Instead of making their own historic walk, the two of them crawled into the Bastille to find a place where they could sleep it off.

"Never could see why people want to fly to the moon when we have a perfectly good earth," Coretta said.

"Ohhhhh," Mickie moaned. "I'm starting to feel the effects of zero gravity."

Carl and I were lying next to each other on the roof. My head rested on his shoulder and his arm was around me. I could hear the rhythmic beating of his heart and his slow, steady breathing. It was reassuring. "I don't care what those scientists say," I told him. "I still think the moon is made of green cheese."

"Limburger," Carl said. "The minute those guys get out they'll be overcome by the smell."

Shortly before noon our time, when Armstrong and Aldrin opened the hatch on their lunar module, Bubba and Slim gave us plastic cups filled with champagne. Someone turned up the radio volume when Armstrong told Houston he was "on the porch."

"Neil, this is Houston. You're loud and clear. Break break. Buzz, this is Houston. Radio check and verify TV circuit breaker in."

"Roger, TV circuit breaker's in," Aldrin said. "LMP reads loud and clear."

"And we're getting a good picture on the TV. Okay, Neil, we can see you coming down the ladder now."

"Okay," Armstrong said. "I'm at the foot of the ladder. The LM footpads are only depressed in the surface about one or two inches. Although the surface appears to be very, very fine-grained as you get close to it. It's almost like a powder. Now and then, it's very fine . . . I'm going to step off the LM now."

It was 11:56 A.M., July 21, 1969, Saigon time, when Neil Armstrong reached the surface of the moon. "That's one small step for a man," he said, "one giant leap for mankind."

We toasted and I swallowed the champagne in one gulp. For a few minutes, we were all silent, contemplating the significance of the moment. Then someone put "Sky Pilot" on the stereo and the party resumed.

Later, when Carl and I walked back to the hooch, he sadly looked up at the sky and shook his head. "I've seen hundreds of kids die in this past year," he said. "If they can put a man on the moon, then why can't they get us out of Vietnam?"

There was a graffiti wall in the women's changing room of the OR. The next day these words appeared: "U.S. lands on moon. . . . Who cares?" and: "Today the moon . . . tomorrow, Vietnam."

Dear Lynda,

I don't have much time right now, but I wanted to let you know that I've arrived in Vietnam. My orders were delayed because my father died last month. The cancer finally got him. He told me he was proud of me. I've been assigned to the hospital at Cam Ranh Bay. Looking forward to seeing you again.

Love,
Barbara

Dear Mom and Dad,

Things go fairly well here. Monsoon is very heavy right now—have barely seen the sun in a couple of weeks. But this makes the sky that much prettier at night when flares go off. There's a continual mist in the air which makes the flares hazy. At times they look like falling stars; then sometimes they seem to shine like crosses.

At 4:16 A.M. our time the other day, two of our fellow Americans landed on the moon. At that precise moment, Pleiku Air Force Base, in the sheer joy and wonder of it, sent up a whole skyful of flares—white, red, and green. It was as if they were daring the surrounding North Vietnamese Army to try and tackle such a great nation. As we watched it, we couldn't speak at all. The pride in our country filled us to the point that many had tears in their eyes.

It hurts so much sometimes to see the paper full of demonstrators, especially people burning the flag. Fight fire with fire, we ask here. Display the flag, Mom and Dad, please, everyday. And tell your friends to do the same. It means so much to us to know we're supported, to know not everyone feels we're making a mistake being here.

Every day we see more and more why we're here. When a whole Montagnard village comes in after being bombed and terrorized by Charlie, you know. There are helpless people dying everyday. The worst of it is the children. Little baby-sans being brutally maimed and killed. They've never hurt anyone. Papa-san comes in with his three babies—one dead and two covered with frag wounds. You try to tell him the boy is dead but he keeps talking to the baby as if that will make him live again. It's enough to break your heart. And through it all, you feel something's missing. There! You put your finger on it. There's not a sound from them. The children don't cry from pain; the parents don't cry from sorrow; they're stoic.

You have to grin sometimes at the primitiveness of these Montagnards. Here in the emergency room, doctors and nurses hustle about fixing up a little girl. There stands her shy little (and I mean little—like four feet tall) Papa-san, face looking down at the floor, in his loin cloth, smoking his long marijuana pipe. He has probably never seen an electric light before, and the ride here in that great noisy bird (helicopter) was too much for him to comprehend. They're such characters. One comes to the hospital and the whole family camps out in the hall or on the ramp and watches over the patient. No, nobody can tell me we don't belong here.

Love,
Lynda

Hi, Lynda, this is your father. Right now, I'm home by myself. After you suggested it, we scooted out to Gem and found ourselves a nice little old cassette recorder and player so we could start sending you tapes. I hope everybody here doesn't suffer from mike fright.

One of the things the moon landing made me realize is how commonplace everything seems once it's happened. We've all picked up a feeling of ennui. Gee, these guys were up on the moon, they were wandering around on its surface, they shot the thing up there and shot it back down, and an awful lot of people are terribly unimpressed. It sort of reminds me of an old joke: This young boy takes his uncle to a circus where a guy climbs a 150-foot pole and stands on his head. On his right foot he hangs two or three circular horseshoes and twirls them. He does the same thing on his left foot. With his left hand, he juggles three balls, and with the right hand, he plays a clarinet solo. The young boy says to his uncle, "Ain't he the greatest?" The old guy looks at him and says, "A Bennie Goodman he ain't."

So many of us look at everything that happens with that attitude. We forget that there are so many wonderful things that people are doing. Regardless of whether these guys had been the first or the twenty-first guys on the moon, we should be proud of them and never take them for granted. It's a great, great achievement for these good old United States.

I guess there were a lot of things that I never did tell you before you left home. One is that I'm proud that you're doing what you're doing. Even before the Japanese bombed Pearl Harbor, I was trying to get into the service. At the time, I thought I had it made in the Marine Corps. They were taking young college graduates as possible officer candidates, so I went down and saw old Colonel Miller at the Marine Corps Reserve in Washington.

When he saw my glasses, he suggested that I take them off when I came back for the eye exam. I had already memorized the chart so I'd have no problem.

When I went for my physical, the doctor started asking me a lot of usual questions. Pretty soon in the game, I suggested taking the eye examination because I was afraid of forgetting the chart. But this guy was a pretty sharp operator. He said, "I know damned well you wear glasses." So I had to show him my glasses. He looked through them and said, "That refraction's too big for the Marines, buddy boy. You go home."

Later, I took the physical for the Army a couple of times but my blood pressure was too high for them. That was about the time that Nancy came along. I went back and appealed my case with the surgeon general. He ordered the Army to give me another physical, but they weren't buying. They wouldn't take me. It wasn't that I was anxious to be there, but I felt like I owed a little something to my country. I guess this is why I'm so pleased that you're in the Army. I'm living vicariously now. You are me and I'm in. As I said before, I'm very proud.

The three men arrived in an ambulance on a quiet afternoon when I was hanging out in the ER, waiting for something to happen. It was a very slow day and those kinds of days could be painfully boring. The ER nurses had just finished cleaning and bandaging some cuts on a little Montagnard boy who had fallen on the barbed wire outside the compound. Fortunately, the only thing that had really been hurt was his pride.

When the men came through the doors—two walking, one being carried on a litter by corpsmen—they all looked half dead. Their faces were drawn and their eyes bloodshot. Their eye sockets were hollow and dark. Their hair was over their ears. Each was so pathetically thin that it looked like a good wind would blow all of them away. They reminded me of a pack of wolves who hadn't eaten in a month and who had been beaten every time they had gotten near food. It was surprising that the two on foot even had the energy to walk.

The man on the litter, Sergeant Gary Flores, had a bullet wound through the thigh. It had become infected by weeks of dirt and neglect. His buddies—PFC John Peterson and Corporal Brian Barth

—had carried him more than fifty miles through jungles and over mountain trails. All had cuts and bruises covering their bodies. There were dozens of freshly healed scars and dozens more that oozed pus. They had gone without boots for six weeks and their feet were a mess. X rays would later turn up broken ribs on all. One of the walking wounded had a fractured arm. Yet when they arrived, they couldn't help but smile. And we smiled back. Then they laughed. It was the joyful laugh of free men. Soon, the laughter was accompanied by tears. "The medic in the field told me I could lose this leg," Sergeant Flores said. "It's still the happiest day of my life."

The three were members of a unit that had been operating over the fence for at least six months. They had been ambushed two months ago and were taken prisoner by the V.C. After a few weeks, they escaped, but were forced to find their way through hostile territory without maps, compasses, weapons, or food. It was luck that brought them into contact with an American unit.

As with most ex-POWs, the first thing they asked for was steak and ice cream, probably the worst food they could have had because of their dysentery. With some difficulty, we convinced them that it would be in their best interest to wait while we treated them with mega-doses of vitamins, antibiotics, and electrolyte replacements. We fed them gelatin and broth in spite of their pleas for more substantial food. Fortunately, Sergent Flores's leg was not as bad as the medic had told him. We had him out of the OR two hours later.

When the men finally got their steak and ice cream two days later, they disregarded the nurses' warnings to eat moderately. Each barfed up his food. That was expected. But they still said they had enjoyed every bite.

I wondered a lot about their high spirits. Would they be as happy when, in a few weeks, they were back at their unit tromping through the boonies with packs on their backs and rifles in their hands? Maybe next time they walked into an ambush they wouldn't be so fortunate.

Hi, Mom and Dad,

There's been some action lately and we were told we should write our families to tell them we're alive and safe. They figure you'll hear about it on the news. Well, I'm here to tell you it's never as bad as the papers make it out to be. We did go on red alert and there were some rockets and mortars and small arms fire, but no one on our compound was hurt.

Ben Het seems to be about over. The damned lily-livered ARVNs finally got there *after* the North Vietnamese pulled back into Laos and Cambodia. President Ky went up there yesterday and gave the ARVNs medals. If the GIs, Australians, Montagnards, and CIDGs had anything to say about it, the ARVNs would all be strung up by their fingernails.

I'm glad to hear that you all are flying the colors. Keep it up. It means a lot to us.

Love,
Lynda

"Have you no pride?" Bubba asked rhetorically. "We're all flabby, I tell you." He was, to put it mildly, a little high on Jack Daniels when he went into his sermon in the middle of a party at the Bastille. "We've been enjoying too much of the good life and forgetting that we have a divine obligation to take care of these here bodies which are temples of the Lord."

"Amen," somebody shouted.

"Now I ask you, brothers and sisters, do you think the Lord likes living inside all this flab?" He was turning into a bona fide evangelist right before our eyes.

"No," we all answered.

"Do you think the Lord appreciates all these alcoholic beverages we consume?"

"No!"

"Does he like to see His children smoking the demon weed?"

"No!"

"Say hallelujah, brothers and sisters."

"Hallelujah, Brother Bubba. Hallelujah!"

"Well, brothers and sisters, I've seen the light. It's time we changed our ways and started taking care of His temples."

"Amen."

"And because He loves you, He has chosen Brother Bubba, just possibly the second best preacher in Asia, to show you the way."

"Hallelujah, Brother Bubba. Hallelujah."

"So, I'm telling you now, the first thing we are going to do is give up our evil habits."

"Hallelujah, Brother Bubba."

"We're gonna stop drinking."

"What!?!" The word was sounded in a collective voice. "You're crazy!"

"Say hallelujah, my children."

"Fuck off, Brother Bubba," we answered.

"And we're gonna stop smoking that wacky tobacky them Montagnards grow."

"No way man," said a voice from the corner.

"Say hallelujah, brothers and sisters."

"Brother Bubba eats shit," someone else said.

"Then, brothers and sisters, we are going to exercise our temples."

"Exercise?" Slim shouted. "Are you nuts?"

"And when we're ready, I, Brother Bubba, am going to lead you all into our very own First Annual Seventy-Worst Ejaculation Hospital Olympic games. Say Amen."

"Boo." We carried Brother Bubba kicking and screaming to the pool, where we dunked him a few times to sober him up. However, when the alcohol wore off, he still hadn't come to his senses. He was determined to lead us in athletic competition. We were little match for Bubba's will—or for his biceps.

For starters, he organized a daily exercise class, which was officially optional. However, Bubba proved himself a skilled arm twister, guilt inspirer, and general pain in the neck. Besides, he threatened to ban all nonparticipants from any future parties at the Bastille. When that wasn't good enough, he threatened to wring their necks.

Everyone attended the sessions.

We started out groaning and complaining, but before long, we found ourselves enthusiastic about the exercise. It was a great way to get rid of our frustrations. When he finally got around to deciding which events would be part of the Seventy-Worst Ejac Games, we were all ready for a little competition. As soon as we signed up for the games, the classes were disbanded and we began conducting our own training sessions. Everyone had his or her own secret formula for success and we were all determined to be winners. Carl and I registered for most of the swimming events, some track events and the three-legged race. We were also part of the Bastille volleyball team that would challenge the administrative-type lifers who worked in headquarters.

During our training period, we almost completely stopped drinking. We spent more time doing laps in the pool and less time lying in the sun outside it. When I worked nights, I ran in the morning and swam in the late afternoon. When I worked days, I swam in the morning before my shift and ran in the evening after I got off. Although Bubba had originally wanted to cancel all parties at the Bastille until after our Olympic Games, he realized that such drastic action would result in mutiny. He was also afraid of being assassinated by some crazed party addicts who just had to have a regular fix of music, laughter, and fun. So instead, he continued the Bastille's fine tradition, but limited the consumption of alcohol. It made the parties less raucous, but we still enjoyed ourselves.

As Olympic day approached I became more aware of another day that was coming closer—the day Carl would say good-bye and return to the world. Sometimes, when I sat on the side of the pool while he swam, I would get scared and feel a pang of emptiness in my heart. I'd only known him for two months, but already he had become the most important person in my life. He was the one who helped me deal with all the death and destruction, the one who taught me how to be a decent assistant surgeon, the one who held me during rocket attacks, the one who told me funny stories, and the one who showed me how to love a man. When we were together, I wondered how I would survive without him. When we were apart, I thought about him constantly. What would I do?

"You'll have to get tougher," he said.

"I don't want to get tougher."

"It's the only way you'll survive Vietnam."

We won the three-legged race, beating out another doctor and nurse team by less than a second. Coretta and a dust-off pilot came in third. Carl swept all the men's swimming events, even after Bubba made him swim with a ten-pound weight tied to his waist. I came in second in every women's swimming event, losing to Mickie each time, and I was last in every footrace I ran. In the volleyball game, the lifers creamed us 12–5, but the game was played under protest, since Bubba claimed two of their players were ringers, transferred in for the game.

Carl and I decided not to attend that night's party at the Bastille.

Instead, we went to my room with a candle, a bottle of wine, and a desire to be with each other. We were far more protective of our time together as his time to leave approached.

Before we could even light the candle, we heard that familiar sound—incoming choppers, dozens of them. We didn't bother to wait for the call before heading to the emergency room.

It would be another long night. My stomach began to hurt again.

Hi, Mom and Dad,
How's the world? Have you seen the sun lately? If so, let me know what it looks like. I've forgotten. The last time I wrote, the sun had just peeked out for five minutes. It disappeared and hasn't been seen since. We've put out a search and rescue mission to find it, but they haven't been heard from either. I think they cut the border and headed for Bangkok to wait it out. Today, Bugs Schweichert, one of my OR techs who has been here for a year and a half, finally admitted that a true monsoon has arrived. The rain has been coming down literally in sheets so hard you can't see. And the wind is forty to fifty knots with gusts to seventy-five. This has been constant for eight days so far. Bugs said we should wait until we haven't seen the light of day for a month before calling it a real monsoon, but today changed his mind. Even so, he said this weather is nothing compared to what we can expect in the fall.

The weird thing is the bitter cold. I'm freezing because I didn't bring anything warm. I didn't even bring my field jacket. I can't believe I'm spending summer in the tropics. That's hysterical. Actually, though, it's better this way. Everybody else in the country has monsoons with hot weather. The steam can be unbearable. This weather is such a dramatic change from the heat when I got here. But we find a lot to laugh about. When you say you swam to work and the wind picked you up and tossed you all the way back to your hooch, it's close to the truth.

Aunt Ginnie sent me one of Steve's pen-and-ink drawings. It's the scene of "Skating on the Creek." I've hung it on the wall of my room, and it really adds a touch of home to this godforsaken place. The snow and the skaters, the trees and the bridge add a note of needed tranquility. Please pass along to Aunt Ginnie my gratitude. I really appreciate her thinking of me.

I haven't been able to get in touch with Steve yet, but I keep trying.

I better go now. There's work to be done. I miss you all.

Love,
Lynda

"The conduct of the ladies around here is not very commendable," the short fat major said. She closely resembled the Nazi, the nun from my nursing school days. But Major Mary Ellen Swanson was neither a nurse nor a nun. She was a medical services officer who worked as one of the hospital's administrators. Her specialty was supposed to be supply and transportation, but she spent more time watching over the camp's morals than doing her real job. Unfortunately, she was influential enough with the commander and executive officer to make herself someone to contend with. She designed a new slot for herself —Morals and Ethics Officer—and convinced the C.O. to make the job officially one of her extra duties. We were forced to attend all her lectures. All were bad, but this was one of the worst.

"There's been too much hanky-panky going on," she continued. "Too many women have been entertaining men in their billets after hours and too many ladies have been involved in illicit entertainment elsewhere. I remind you that we have a curfew of twenty-four hundred hours and I expect it to be followed. I also expect that men will be entertained in a ladylike manner and you will have them out of your billets before twenty-four hundred hours. For any of you ladies who still think like civilians, I remind you that twenty-four hundred is midnight. Now you won't have any excuse for not following the rules. The senior occupant of each billet will be responsible for enforcement and don't be surprised if I make rounds once in a while. I hope I make myself clear."

"Does that mean she has to kick out *her* lover by midnight, also?" Mickie whispered.

"No way," Corletta answered. "The prohibition only applies to men."

Having to sit through morals lectures was bad enough, but hearing that kind of talk from Major Swanson was an outrage. It was common belief that she had a long-standing relationship with one of the other nurses, a petite blond captain who worked on one of the wards.

Although the two of them denied it, and the word had never got into official channels, it was rumored that the "ladies" had been discovered in *flagrante delicto* once by a new nurse who had burst into the major's room to offer help when she had heard what sounded like screams of pain. The sounds had resulted from a bit of pleasure. It seems that the good major was unable to keep quiet, and she and the captain were oblivious to anyone else when they were involved. The major's other hoochmates, especially those with neighboring rooms, described the noise as something that was more akin to a battle cry than a love sound. Those who had heard it nicknamed her the Orgasmic Banshee. It wasn't that anyone objected to the major's sexual preferences or even to being awakened by her—she sounded no worse than a rocket attack. The general attitude was "whatever gets you through the night." There were far more important things than that to offend our sensibilities. Who could really care about two women finding comfort with each other when there were hundreds of boys dying every week?

But we were highly offended by the major's arrogance in trying to stop us from having as normal a life as we could under the circumstances. Yet her attitude was typical of the Army's double standard. If the guys wanted to go carousing to all hours of the night and screw ninety-seven prostitutes in a day, it was to be expected. "Boys will be boys." Every PX stocked plenty of GI-issue condoms and according to the grapevine, some commanders even went so far as to bus in Vietnamese girls for hire to keep morale high. However, if we wanted to have a relationship, or to occasionally be with a man we cared deeply about, we were not conducting ourselves as "ladies" should. And if we might be unladylike enough to want birth control pills, which were kept in a safe and rarely dispensed, we could expect the wrath of God, or our commander, to descend upon us. We wouldn't have been surprised to find a request of that nature noted in our efficiency reports.

Major Swanson continued, "It's also been brought to my attention today that the ladies are using the gentlemen's latrines when they visit the gentlemen's billets. Please stop. It embarrasses the men and I don't like it. I want you ladies to act like ladies. You're all officers and members of the United States Army. I happen to be quite proud of my corps and I'd sure hate to see its reputation go down over here."

"Did somebody say something about going down?" Mickie whispered.

"Yeah," Coretta answered. "I think the major said she wants to go down on the whole United States Army."

"Does that include men?" I asked.

"Don't be ridiculous," Coretta said. "That broad wouldn't know what to do with a man if she got one gift-wrapped."

The lecture was brought to a halt by the overwhelming sound of tanks outside the building, making it impossible for anyone to hear the good major. Before it was finished, Coretta had already come up with a plan to keep our major from enforcing her curfew. It involved a microphone, a tape recorder, and a little ingenuity. "We'll blackmail the bitch," she said.

"Isn't that a little unethical?" I asked.

"So's war," she answered. "But nobody's stopped the fighting yet."

Coretta's plan was to place a microphone outside Major Swanson's window and get one of the lovemaking sessions on tape. Since the Orgasmic Banshee was so loud, we wouldn't have to worry about getting inside her room with a microphone. All we needed to incriminate her was her name and that of the captain and some explicit expressions of love. Anything else would have been gravy. Once we got the tape, we would make a duplicate and send it to her with a pointed note suggesting that she cease and desist from persecuting those who chose to make love during war.

We discussed the situation with the others at the Bastille and decided to use Carl's room as our operations center, since it was the one closest to Major Swanson's hooch. The day our plan was to be put into action, we stocked the room with a couple hundred feet of wire, two extra tape recorders, and three cases of beer. Coretta, who had already started to earn a reputation as a top-notch scrounger, came up with a super-sensitive microphone borrowed from a friend of hers on Signal Hill. She also sweet-talked one of the communications specialists into rigging the wiring so there would be no last-minute problems. We were all in our hooches by curfew.

As soon as our lookout saw Major Swanson and the captain return to the major's room for the night, word was passed from hooch to hooch. We silently moved toward Carl's hooch. It was like night-stalking. Coretta zigzagged across an open area and placed the microphone outside the major's window, while Mickie fed out the wire from a spool. I kept lookout. When we returned, the beers were opened and the waiting began. Our communications expert turned the system to top volume and the microphone picked up even the softest whisper. Everything was working perfectly.

We spent the next hour drinking the beer while we listened to the major and her captain discuss a lot of things that were great for the rumor mill, but not for our purposes. Shortly after one in the morning, we could tell by the turn of the conversation that the women were getting ready for some fun in the sack. There was some rustling, a few spoken endearments, and the squeak of bedsprings as they entered the field of battle, and then something we had not planned for: A rocket attack.

We had forgotten that the air raid siren was outside Major Swanson's window. When it went off, the equipment in Carl's room magnified its sound by at least ten times. There was a high-pitched screeching that was enough to burst every eardrum in the place, and it was at least three or four minutes before anyone had the sense to turn the sound system off. When it was over, Blake McCarthy, our urologist, got up from the floor and shook his head. "Swanson must be one hell of a lover," he said. "I've heard a lot of women scream from pleasure in my life, but I've never heard *anyone* scream like that."

Before we could make another try, we heard that familiar sound—incoming choppers. "Chinooks," Bubba said. Those were the Army's largest helicopters. They could carry as many as fifty casualties in one trip. More than one chopper meant real trouble.

"There's no sense in waiting for them to call us," Coretta said.

Carl smacked his right fist against his chair. "Don't those fuckers ever stop?" he grumbled. "When I'm back in the world, I don't ever want to remember one single thing about this fucking hole. It's all been nothing but a bunch of crap."

I felt his words as if they were a knife wound. After he realized the implications of what he had said, he tried to make it easier by touching my cheek and telling me he would never forget me, or what we shared. Maybe he was right. But I knew that once he was back with his wife, two kids, and the house in the country, he would try to forget me, along with all his memories of the war.

A week later, after we had said our good-byes, I remembered a line of Leonardo da Vinci's that Carl was fond of quoting: "In rivers, the water that you touch is the last of what has passed and the first of that which comes; so with time present."

I would never forget Carl Adams. And in my heart, I knew I would always love him. However, his advice was correct: I'd have to be tough to survive alone.

Dear Mom and Dad,

Guess what came in the mail yesterday? A big box containing an electric blanket, a mechanic's light, Hostess Ho-Hos, soap, Tampax, and popcorn. Would you believe it had to be repacked in San Francisco? Packages get tossed around a great deal on their way here, so you'd better pack a bit tighter. It was on a convoy from Qui Nhon to An Khe that was hit. It took a week for them to find everything. The poor package really went the rounds. Thanks a million.

The light is working really well—together with the de-mildew bag you sent, they have dried my clothes out. We have a little Montagnard, fourteen years old, who does our laundry. I made her popcorn this morning and she went crazy for it. She'd never had it before and keeps calling it pop instead of popcorn. She's so cute. I'll send you a picture.

I also got the perfume you sent the other day. The plastic on the bottle was broken, but it's what's inside that counts, and I have what's inside. Perfume is such a morale booster. Ask any guy over here. The patients get a kick out of it. Most of them are grunts—infantry—and spend all their time smelling each other. Perfume is a lot more pleasant.

The 71st is being transferred to An Khe, about thirty miles east of here. Reason is classified, but suffice it to say we're needed. Half of us are supposed to be there by the fifteenth of September, the rest by December. I won't be going until December. I'm supposed to be running the OR when our supervisor moves to An Khe in September. Nothing is definite yet. I'll let you know final plans when I can.

I better close. I'm awfully tired. Take care and write. I love you.

Love,
Lynda

9

God's Will Be Done

"So the North Vietnamese general said to me, 'I cannot understand why you do not like me, Father Bergeron. You call yourself a servant of the Lord. I thought it was one of the teachings of your religion that the Lord loves everyone, rich or poor.' " The priest's pale blue eyes twinkled and his whole face seemed to light up as he related the incident to those of us who had been taking a break in the emergency room.

He continued, "I smiled and swallowed another sip of his wine. It was a wonderful, full-bodied Burgundy, perhaps a little sweeter than I prefer, but not at all disagreeable. 'General,' I said, 'you are correct in believing that the Lord loves you, but fortunately, I choose my friends more carefully than does the Lord.' "

We all laughed at the thought of this gentle, soft-spoken man, Father Jacques Bergeron, not only defying the dictates of generals—ours and theirs—but also returning their arrogance and pomposity with ego-deflating humor. We loved his stories and eagerly anticipated the visits of the tall, gray-haired man who somehow managed to move easily among all the different groups in both secured and unsecured areas. He told tales about everyone: the ARVNs, the NVA, the Vietnamese, the Montagnards, the Americans, and the Viet Cong.

He held his hands up to silence our laughter. "But my story is not finished," he said. "The general was not done with me." He lowered his voice, as if now we were all conspirators. "This man was not just any general. Although he is brutal and ruthless, he is also very educated and is at ease with the ways of our culture. Unfortunately for me, he wanted to discuss the Bible. He questioned me on Creation, the flight of the Jews, and the birth of Jesus. However, he was most interested in the story of Noah and the Ark. I think I might have overstepped my bounds when I told him I was skeptical about that part of the Bible. 'But father, how can a man serve a master and doubt that master's doctrine?' he asked."

Father B flashed us an impish grin. "I told him my skepticism only concerned one minor point. 'You see,' I said, 'because I meet so many men like you on both sides of this war, I find it very difficult to believe that there were only two jackasses in the Ark.' "

We shrieked over that one.

"Laugh, my children," Father B said. "But can you imagine how I felt when the most brutal of all Ho Chi Minh's generals pointed his pistol at me? It was obvious that he did not share our sense of humor. I tried to leave his table. There really was no good reason to stay. The wine bottle was already empty and this fellow is far too selfish to open a second one for company. But he ordered two very hostile guards to convince me it would be in my best interest to converse with him for a bit longer."

Father B took a deep breath and leaned forward. "Naturally, I stayed," he said. "I deplore violence, especially when it is against me."

A few of us chuckled.

"The general sneered at me. 'You probably believe me to be that entity you Catholics call the devil,' he yelled. I told him I hardly considered him that important. The sentiment left him slightly offended. 'Then do you believe I have sold myself into the service of the devil?' he asked. I told him that not everyone like him has sold his soul to the devil; some are smart enough to rent it by the day."

Although Father Bergeron's stories had the ring of hyperbole, we believed every word he told us. He was usually a very modest person and he related as many stories about himself as he did about other people. He was also the one who told us that God created man after He made the other creatures because he didn't want any advice while the work was going on. And although he took his missionary service seriously, he was fond of quoting Oscar Wilde, who called missionaries "the divinely provided food for destitute and underfed cannibals."

"I am not here to convert anyone," Father B had said in one of his more pensive moments. "Merely to try to ease the suffering of some. I believe that is God's will."

He was very playful with everyone and loved to weave humor into any discussion of religion, especially the dialogues that were in danger of becoming too stuffy. "Like G. K. Chesterton, I believe the test of a good religion is whether you can joke about it," he said.

The first time I met Father B, in June, he and Carl had been engaged in a theoretical discussion about the existence of God, especially in light of the power of science. Father B was as good as Carl at quoting from history. "Major Adams," he had said, "I can think of no better source to answer your doubts about God than the former German Catholic Cardinal von Faulhaber of Munich. Albert Einstein once told him that he respected religion but believed in mathematics. The cardinal informed Einstein that both were merely different expressions of God's precision. Einstein asked what the cardinal might say if mathematical science ever came to conclusions directly contradictory to religious beliefs. 'I have the highest respect for the competence of mathematicians,' said the Cardinal. 'I am sure they would never rest until they discovered their mistake.' "

Father Bergeron was a regular visitor at the 71st, arriving at least once every two or three weeks to tell his stories, offer his help, or borrow medical supplies. We all called it borrowing, but we knew we'd never see any of it back. Although giving away medical supplies was highly prohibited, we'd sneak him whatever we could—antibiotics, dressings, vitamins, and hardware. Once, when he arrived in a battered, broken-down jeep, he even talked the motor pool sergeant out of another jeep while his was getting fixed.

We worried about Father B because he spent so much of his time working with people who lived in dangerous areas. He never carried a gun or sought protection. He took the danger philosophically. When we would try to discourage him from making a particular trip, he would quote from the Twenty-fourth Psalm: "The Lord is my light and my salvation; whom shall I fear?"

Besides talking us out of medical supplies, he also had a knack for talking us into certain missions of mercy that were prohibited by Army regulations. According to the rules, the only civilians we were to treat on compound were those who had war-related wounds. But Father Bergeron knew how to locate our soft spots and we found ourselves bending the regs to handle cases that he brought. One was an old woman who had a fifteen-pound goiter that was larger than her head. It was so enmeshed with blood vessels and interwoven muscle tissue that it took us almost twelve hours to remove it. The woman had been living with the goiter for twenty years and had compensated for its weight by leaning back when she stood. After it was gone, she was unable to keep her balance and had to be taught how to walk again.

Another case which came during a slow period was a little Vietnamese girl who had shortness of breath and such chronic congestive heart failure that she could hardly sit up anymore. The problem was a congenital heart defect that resulted in not enough oxygen in the blood. If she didn't have help, she was sure to die within a year. When Father B first arrived with the girl, Bob Gordon, a lieutenant colonel who was our chief surgeon, refused to do the operation or to allow anyone else in the hospital to perform it. The surgery was extremely delicate and we had neither the expertise nor the proper equipment. However, Father B was not a man who knew how to accept no as an answer. If she would die in a year, he argued, there was little risk when balanced against a potentially full and happy life. And wouldn't it be possible to get from Saigon many of the tools needed to do the surgery successfully? And since we had so many skilled surgeons, surely we had one who could perform the operation.

The little girl was so adorable with her long black hair, sad almond eyes, and a gentle smile that could melt a glacier. Father B had properly prepared her to play on Bob's sympathies.

It took a week of convincing by Father Bergeron and half the medical staff, but Bob relented and ordered surgery for the girl. The equipment was scrounged from Saigon, the surgeons reviewed procedures on the heart, and the girl's parents were warned not to expect miracles. Bob put her chances of survival at only fifty percent. He did the surgery himself, with another surgeon as his assistant.

When they were successful, everyone felt the joy as if it had been a personal triumph. During the next few weeks, the little girl was the darling of the 71st as she slowly began her recovery. Within a month, she was playing like any other normal child. Father Bergeron predicted a very long and happy life—if the war didn't get her first.

Dear Mom and Dad,

It is now nearly three weeks since I have heard from anyone. How about it, you guys? Does anybody know I'm here? If you all only knew how bad it is to look day after day at an empty mailbox and wait while they holler every name but yours at mail call. Just a few words, please. I'm at a very low point.

The move to An Khe was canceled and now it's supposedly back on. The latest rumor is that everything is so up in the air because we're waiting on the V.C. The last four nights, they've been walking mortars into Pleiku Air Base, our sister compound. This morning, they hit what they were aiming for—the flight line. It was just practice. We're waiting for the real thing—expected in a few nights—so we can't mobilize too well. They've also been doing a job on An Khe in the last week. The newest word is we're moving on 15 September again.

I heard the radio say that Ho Chi Minh died. God only knows what that will mean. Will they increase activity or will the new leader pull out? I've gotten to the point where I don't try to anticipate moves—if something happens, it'll happen. I'm not going to get an ulcer over it.

My mood is getting the better of me. I'd better close. Please write.

Love,
Lynda

Although Father Bergeron rarely talked of his past, the rumor mill was filled with so many stories about him that it was impossible to separate fact from fiction. Depending on who was talking, Father B had come from either a very wealthy background or a very poor but educated background. His parents had been either missionaries, or farmers, or landlords. He had experienced a happy childhood or a sad childhood. It was hard to get any of this information from him because his stories were always about Vietnam.

"I rarely think of my life in France before I came here," he said. "It's been so long, it almost seems that I've been in Vietnam forever."

Some believed he had been an artist before joining the priesthood, but most of his comments seemed to indicate that he had once been a businessman. Of some things we were reasonably sure. He was sixty-four years old and had participated in the French Resistance during World War II. He had originally come to Vietnam in the forties when it was still a French colony and he told us that once, during the fifties, when the Viet Minh had fought the French, he had met Ho Chi Minh.

"Ho seemed a fragile man," Father B had said. "He was very much an intellectual and did not appear to be someone who was likely to be a national leader. But appearances are often deceptive."

Father B talked little about politics. When he did address the topic, it was apparent that his only allegiance lay with the people who were war's victims. "It is not my place to take sides in a political issue," he said. "However, if Ho ran today for an election in the south, he would win by a landslide. What does that say about democracy in Vietnam or about the idea that the people of the south are being protected from the evils of communism? I know the communists as well as I know you. You are both the same. The only real villain is the war. I can only hope that God forgives us all for allowing it to continue."

He spoke frequently about the immorality of war. When he talked, it was with a sadness that seemed unusual in him. He saw all war as an abomination and told us that the only people who should be allowed to be soldiers were those who had gotten the countries into conflict. "Let the old glory mongers and politicians fight their own wars," he said. "And let the young men and women get on with their lives. If the older men were the ones dying, there would be fewer wars." He also felt that it was not necessarily a good idea for anyone to try to westernize Vietnam. Unlike other missionaries, he never attempted to "civilize" the people by shoving his own views down their throats. In fact, he was fond of quoting lines from Buddha and Oriental philosophers and pointing out their relevance to modern life in the Western world.

Dear Mom and Dad,

I hang my head. Mail call just brought six letters from you in addition to the nicest care package I've ever seen. Postmarks go back as far as a month. I don't know what the holdup was, but mail call was bright for the first time in a *very* long time. I'm sorry I misjudged you. It's hard to keep my spirits up when there's no mail to cheer me.

The move to An Khe was canceled again. The rumor mill is still buzzing, but this is supposed to be the final word.

Love,
Lynda

Everyone at the 71st loved Father Bergeron. We never doubted that most people who knew him, on both sides of the war, loved him as much as we did. That was why we were so shocked and angered when we received the terrible news.

We were in the middle of another push when Bubba told us that word had come that Father Bergeron had been tortured by the V.C. the night before. When they were finished, they cut off his head and placed it on a stake in the middle of a village in the north of the province as a warning to others who were American sympathizers.

Father Jacques Bergeron wasn't an American sympathizer any more than he was a Viet Cong sympathizer. He was merely a good man who wanted to see the war end, so the Vietnamese people could live normal, happy lives.

Later that day I was assigned with Don Higham, a general surgeon, to work on a North Vietnamese colonel who had been captured the previous night. "I should cut this sucker's head off to even the score," Don said. "We can hang it on the post at the front gate and laugh at all those bastards. After all, what goes around, comes around. Payback is a motherfucker."

Don was just venting his rage and would never have done anything so barbaric, but the thing that surprised me the most was that I wanted him to follow through on his threat. In fact, I might have been glad to assist.

10

Same Same Stateside

"Got another burn case, Van. Docs want him in OR immediately."

"Not again, Coretta. Don't those V.C. know when to stop?"

"The V.C. didn't do this one. Friendly fire did."

"Shit! I'll never get used to that smell."

"Of course not. Nobody does."

"Chopper's down at the Air Force base, Van. Dust-off says they've got two more crispy critters. Better get the OR ready."

"I can't handle another burn case, Bubba."

"Me neither, little lady. But we will."

"Let's hustle to the pad, Van. Chopper with six crispy critters."

"Six. But Mickie, how?"

"Napalm. A jet jockey overshot his target."

"Oh, God, that smell."

Dear Mom and Dad,

This letter is going to be short and sweet since I'm dead tired. The last couple of weeks have been unbelievably busy. I've been working at least sixteen to eighteen hours a day without a day off in almost three weeks. I know we will get some time when this is over, but for now, I'm beat. There's no one particular thing going on, just a lot of little things coincidentally happening at the same time. One day it's a chopper crash, next day a Lambretta (small Vietnamese bus) accident. Then a mine explodes in a convoy or something else happens. Plus, there are always the guys who are wounded in battle. It's now 10:30 P.M. and I've been scrubbed since 7 A.M. My fingers are wrinkled. But I'm finished for the night. There are still two operating rooms running. The night crew can handle the rest. I just hope we don't have to get up again. I think I'll get good and drunk. Let them call somebody else.

Love,
Lynda

Once Carl was gone, I tried to bury my loneliness in work. I missed him, probably more than I've ever missed anyone in my life. A few times, I thought of breaking my promise and writing him a letter. But I didn't want to interfere in his other life. He was back in the real world with his wife and kids, where all of us wanted to be. What could I possibly offer him now?

I checked the mail each day for a card, a letter, some sort of reminder that I was not forgotten. Carl never sent a word. Maybe it was best that way.

However, I could still hear his voice telling me I had to be tough to survive. And as each day passed, I found myself developing a harder shell to protect my emotions. For the first few weeks after he went home, I drank heavily and used more grass. But after a while, I started avoiding them because they lowered my defenses. Before, they had effectively deadened all pain and kept me from feeling the suffering of others. Now, they only made me feel it more. I was getting tired. This war was beginning to look different that the one I had believed in only a few weeks earlier. I started listening to the local discontents who railed against Nixon, Congress, the joint chiefs of staff, and the whole U.S. government. Every time another person died on my table, I came one step closer to agreeing with them. I still tried to remind myself that we were in Vietnam to save people who were threatened by tyranny, but that became more and more difficult to believe as I heard stories of corrupt South Vietnamese officials, U.S. Army atrocities, and a population who wanted nothing more than to be left alone so they could return to farming their land. I saw kids—American eighteen- and nineteen-year-olds and little Vietnamese and Montagnard kids—who were dying of diseases that I thought had been eliminated from the face of the earth. There were cases of malaria, polio, typhoid, cholera, and tetanus. One day, I saw some dead American soldiers lying outside the morgue. They had been ambushed by an NVA unit. The butchers had cut off our soldiers' penises and stuffed them into the GIs' mouths. I was outraged by the scene, but not as outraged as I became when I later saw a similar scene, only this time with dead Viet Cong. It was the first time I realized that our clean-cut, wholesome American boys could be as brutal as the "godless communists."

Neither group was as bad as the ROKs. The ROKs were soldiers from the Republic of Korea. They were part of a token international force that had been assembled in South Vietnam so the U.S. need not claim this as a solely American war. The ROKs handled most of the interrogations in our area and were some of the hardest soldiers there. They practiced every conceivable kind of torture, and often the interrogations ended in death regardless of whether the person was a V.C. or just an innocent Vietnamese who happened into the wrong place at the wrong time. One of the favorite forms of torture was referred to as the "Bell Telephone Hour." They would connect electrical wires from a field telephone set to the victim's testicles or vagina. If presented with an answer they didn't like, they would crank the phone to produce a shock. The pain must have been excruciating. Yet that wasn't the worst type of interrogation.

The preferred technique was far more gruesome. I saw the results of that method on a night when we received an unconscious V.C. suspect for surgery. He had been scalped. It wasn't a quick scalping. It had taken place over a number of hours, a little at a time, to bring about the maximum amount of suffering. They had made the man stand on his toes while they attached his flesh to a hook. Each time he moved an inch, he was in agony.

By the time we got that case, I was already insensitive enough to the suffering to laugh when one of our own surgeons lifted the flap of scalp and said, "No sense wasting this. Know any bald guys?"

During those months after Carl left, I lost my direction and found myself becoming a person I would never have been before Vietnam. Maybe he would have said I was merely getting tough. Like thousands of Americans, I began calling the Vietnamese—both friendly and enemy—"gooks." I would have thought I was above that sort of racism; after all, hadn't I marched in the United States for civil rights like a good Catholic girl who believed all oppression was wrong? I began to understand how many of my friends had felt during my early months there. I had looked down on them for displaying just the kind of attitude I was beginning to develop. Now, I saw the Vietnamese as nothing more than a group of thieves and murderers. It was especially difficult because V.C. looked the same as anyone else. Rather than try to distinguish between the friends and enemies, I learned to hate all of them. They were the ones who kept killing American soldiers. Why should we bother saving them?

Once, in the middle of a push, I was directed to scrub on a belly case. When I looked at the chart, I realized I would be working on a prisoner of war, an NVA lieutenant colonel. I was furious. I stormed up to the nurse in charge. "We still have GIs out there," I said. "What the fuck are we doing this guy for?"

"We're following triage protocol," she said. "This soldier is next."

"But twenty minutes ago, this jerk was out there trying to blow us away."

"And now he's wounded and needs our help, Van. Get to work."

"If you're such a gook lover, why don't you scrub on the case?"

"Because I've ordered you to do it."

In addition to being upset, I was extremely confused by the whole episode. I could understand that as a human being, he had a right to proper care, but every bone in my body told me that he wasn't worth the effort. In fact, he could have been the officer who had ordered Father Bergeron's execution, or the battalion commander who was responsible for every single case we got that day. I wanted to spit in his face. Instead, I spit in my hands. That was how I scrubbed for the case before donning sterile gloves. If he died of an infection, fuck him.

A part of me knew that after it was over, I would be ashamed. I had taken a vow as a nurse to help all human beings no matter what race, creed, color, or sex. According to that vow, they were all entitled to quality care. But my bitterness far outweighed any vows I had spoken in a graduation ceremony. I did what I had to do for that POW and not one bit more. All the time we worked on him, I wished that he would die.

But he didn't.

When we were finished and it was apparent that the NVA colonel would live, the surgeon suggested we literally charge an arm and a leg for the operation. I offered to get the saw and we all laughed hysterically. Some day, I would hate myself for having laughed. But not now.

> Hi, Lynda, this is your old dad speaking. Right now, I'm here by myself with the tape recorder. I feel like an airline pilot when I speak into the microphone. "This is your captain speaking."
>
> The man who runs the painters left a few minutes ago. I think I wrote you yesterday or the day before that we had some painting done upstairs in your old room. It came out pretty well. Now we're thinking very seriously about getting the back porch enclosed. It would make the whole house warmer in the winter and it would give us an extra room in the summer. We were even thinking if we got it enclosed, we might put a little electric heat out there for the winter and maybe make it into a family room.
>
> We've also been talking about getting a color television in the living room and Mom's getting rugs for the front of the house. The rugs we have there now are shot. I don't know what other plans she has. I think she's got a few more she hasn't told me yet.

The pregnant Montagnard woman was wheeled into the OR right after we finished with a guy from the 4th Division who was certain to spend the rest of his life as a quadraplegic—if he survived. Bernie Weinbaum, a general surgeon, scrubbed on the woman's case, along with Gail Carlton and me. An extra table was rolled into the room and Steve Michelson, who had some experience in pediatric surgery, stood by in case the frag had penetrated the woman's uterus and was inside the baby. Although the X rays weren't clear, we fully expected to find a wounded baby.

We tried to give the woman oxygen by mask and she fought us. I spoke some Jarai, her native language, and told her that we were not trying to smother her, but were going to help her and the baby breathe better. It took a few minutes of convincing, but the woman finally relented. She was still talking when the anesthetist, Slim, put her under.

While Slim threaded his endotracheal tube in through her mouth to connect her to the anesthesia machine, Gail scrubbed the woman's belly and I set up the instrument tray for a Caesarian section. I laid out the towels in a rectangular pattern around the wound and placed sheets on top of them. We attached them to the skin with towel clips. Then Bernie made the incision. It was routine at that point. We cauterized the small vessels to stop the bleeding and tied off two of the bigger ones. Next, he opened the peritoneum, being very careful because of the huge uterus pressing against it. Bernie made a tiny nick in the peritoneum, slipped his finger into it and made the hole bigger. Then he began cutting with the Metzenbaum scissors.

Following that, he made another incision in the uterus and again split the tissue with his fingers before cutting, this time with curved Mayo scissors. The amniotic fluid immediately started pouring out. Bernie reached in and pulled out a tiny wet baby boy and dropped him onto the sheets of the woman's belly. We clamped the cord and wrapped the baby in a towel. His heartbeat was barely audible and his breathing shallow. There was a frag wound in his chest. I carried him to Steve's table. When the baby was anesthetized, Steve made his initial incision and went in after the frag. He was too late. The baby died on the table.

We followed that case with a soldier who had his belly blown apart, and another soldier who had lost his manhood to a Bouncing Betty, and one who had been severely burned in a helicopter explosion, and one who had lost both legs at the knee, and another, and another, and another.

"Just once, Coretta, I wish I could get that smell of burned flesh out of my nose."

"You and me both, Van. But I think it's going to be there until we get back to the world."

"Not quite," said Kenny Jones, a male nurse who was working on his third tour. "That smell follows you. We're all gonna be smelling that shit until the day we die."

I popped another antacid tablet. It was getting to be a habit.

> Hi, Mom and Dad. I'm too tired to write now, so I figured I'd send you a tape instead. The last couple of weeks have been really bad. Some of our guys have been getting hit pretty hard. We've been working up to eighteen, twenty-four and thirty-six hours at a time for weeks. When we get time off, I just sleep.
>
> I don't know what the newspapers at home are saying right

now, but we keep hearing that the war is over because of the negotiations. That's a bunch of garbage. In the last two and a half or three weeks, I've seen more GIs come in here seriously hurt than I have seen since I've been here. Most of the fire bases around here are getting hit like hell. You know, it's getting kind of hard to explain my feelings about this whole thing. In the past couple of weeks I've seen a few of my friends come in pretty blown up, guys who've been at our parties or who've been in the hospital before. It's harder when you see it happen to somebody you've known. And over here, you get to know people really fast.

We worked on a couple of guys yesterday who were really banged up. We spent twelve to fourteen hours on each one, and they would have died if it wasn't for the doctors. One of the guys had four holes in his heart. Sometimes, these guys will come into the ER bleeding and they'll look up at you and say, "I must have died. I'm dead, aren't I?"

It's depressing and yet it's almost reassuring at the same time. They know that somebody cares enough to be over here when they don't have to be. I think the thing that's most depressing about the whole situation is the fact that nobody's admitting that something is going wrong over here.

It would be a lot easier if our government would just make up its mind. I wish that somebody would decide whether or not we're going to have a war. We should either pull out of Vietnam or hit the hell out of the NVA. This business of pussyfooting around is doing nothing but harm. It's hurting our GIs, the people back home, and our image abroad.

But out of it all, I guess there's some satisfaction for me in knowing that I'm doing a job that's needed. I don't think there are many other places where you can feel as needed in nursing. Here, you're always doing something that's necessary. For the first time in my life, I feel like I have to keep going or people might not survive. It's time for me to return to the operating room, so I'd better say good-bye.

Amos Giovanni was a male nurse who looked like he had it all. Everyone who had worked with him said he did an outstanding job on his ward. He was tall, dark, very attractive, and according to some, far more intelligent than the rest of us. Amos was also quiet and reserved. He rarely showed up at any of our Bastille parties. He said he preferred to stay alone in his room and when there was time off, he spent it reading. Raucous parties were not his style. But he never spoke in a haughty or condescending tone. He was always extremely pleasant to the rest of us.

However, Amos Giovanni was also as cold as ice. He didn't show the least bit of emotion. Everyone thought it was because he was better able to control his feelings than the rest of us. Our opinions changed drastically after Slim found him barely alive one night, following an apparent suicide attempt. There was a simple note next to his bed: "I can't take it anymore. There's too much death and suffering. Please don't try to stop me." If Slim hadn't come into the room when he did, Amos might have been successful.

We immediately carried Amos to the ER, where we tried to pump his stomach. We put a tube down his throat and got some IVs going. Although Slim had found, in Amos's room, a store of drugs that included codeine, Librium, Valium, and a half dozen others, indications pointed to Darvon as the one he had ingested. It had been prescribed for back pain. Within the hour, the guys in the lab told us our hunch was correct.

I spent the next five hours on the ER telephone, trying to get patched through to the Eli Lilly company in the United States. The call had to go through the Military Air Radio System (MARS), a complicated network of long-range radio connections that required the operator in Saigon to call the operator in Japan, who would get somebody in Guam, who would reach someone in Hawaii, who would connect with someone on the mainland, who would make a long-distance call to Eli Lilly. The number of links in the chain made it very easy to lose contact in the middle of a conversation. It was extremely frustrating.

I went through six attempts before getting the man at Eli Lilly, and after we began talking, we were cut off four more times. The experience was more difficult because of the terrible connections and communication rules that made it tough to hold a normal conversation. I was forced to shout at the top of my lungs to be heard, and after every sentence I had to end with the word "over," so the person on the other side would know when to talk. The man at Eli Lilly was even less accustomed to the military's communication methods than we were.

I relayed dozens of questions from the doctors, but the man had few answers. The most important query was in reference to an antidote. There was none.

He said that all we could do was to support Amos on a volume-controlled respirator—one that forces a predetermined amount of air into the lungs—give him some IV stimulants, and hope that his system could eventually get rid of the Darvon. However, he wasn't very hopeful.

Since we didn't have a volume-controlled respirator, we supported Amos through the night on a pressure respirator—one that is regulated by the resistance in a person's lungs.

Amos arrested three times, but the doctors kept him alive. They were concerned that even if he did live, he might have extensive brain damage. All we could do was hope.

We sent him to Saigon on a helicopter the next morning. Coretta and Mickie packed up his belongings and sent them on another flight. From Saigon, Amos was shipped to Japan. We never learned whether he survived or not.

> Hi, Mom and Dad. Sorry I haven't written but in the last couple of weeks, we've been in the OR so long that when I'm done I can't even see well enough to thread a suture. That's why I'm taping this letter. I don't remember if I told you, but several weeks ago, when I had my last day off, three other nurses and I were flown by helicopter to Camp Enari, which is the headquarters of the 4th Division. They wanted to make us honorary members of the division.
>
> You wouldn't believe how well they treated us. They couldn't have done more for us if they had crowned us Queens for a Day. They came down here at five o'clock in the afternoon and took us to a reception with the assistant division commander and several people who work for him. Then we were put up in a VIP trailer with air-conditioning, hot water, and all the comforts of home. It was unbelievable.
>
> We ate at the general's mess and had a cocktail hour with real hors d'oeuvres, before sitting down to shrimp cocktail. I hadn't seen shrimp since I left the world. I went so totally wild over it that the colonels at my table laughed at me and gave me their own shrimps. After that, a real honest-to-goodness waiter, with a

uniform, asked me how I wanted my filet mignon done. *Filet mignon!* I took it medium rare. And we had a choice of butter or sour cream for our potatoes. I said hang the calories and poured a soup bowl full of sour cream over mine. And for dessert, they offered me a choice of chocolate, strawberry, or pineapple sundae. I sat there stunned and couldn't believe what I was hearing, so one of the colonels ordered all three for me.

The next morning, we went back to the general's mess for eggs Benedict. I was completely flabbergasted. Then we were presented with certificates and unit crests from the 4th Division. It was a salute to the nurses of the 71st Evac Hospital. The general kept telling us that we were the backbone of the entire medical system and that it was about time someone saluted us. It really made us feel good to know that they knew we were doing all we could for them.

After the ceremony, they took us to a landing zone called LZ Oasis, about twenty miles south of the 71st, where we saw an underground hospital that was completely covered by five feet of sandbags. Everything that wasn't covered with mud was covered with dust. The guys slept in unbelievable conditions. Next, we went to Fire Base Golden Dragon, about five miles south of Oasis. It made me really appreciate the few conveniences we have up here. At least the water we have at the 71st is potable. The guys at the fire bases are lucky if they can get enough drinking water. Also, we have showers. Maybe they're cold, but at least it's running water inside a building. The guys at Golden Dragon have a tank of water on top of a little wooden support. They pull a little handle to let water out of the tank. And if it starts to rain, everybody runs out with a bar of soap to get clean.

I'm really impressed by the bravery and courage of some of these guys. If you could imagine the fear, the things that they face. They're not only facing the enemy, they're facing the actual physical terrain of the country and the diseases. Then on top of that, they've got to fight the other inhabitants—the wildlife.

I came on duty one morning just in time to see a chopper crew removing three GIs who had been pulled from their guard posts and out of their beds by a tiger. They were literally ripped to shreds. I never even thought that tigers were over here. I guess I should have. If you see an elephant walking down the road, it's nothing unusual. Water buffalo graze in the backyard.

I'm getting settled in here now. I scrounged some paint and covered my walls in a bright pink. I also got a little refrigerator from one of the guys who went back to the world. I have it at the head of my bed. And there's a mattress for under my bed. Now, during rocket attacks, I don't have to lie on a hard floor. I can spend the time listening to music and drinking beer from my refrigerator. It makes things more bearable.

I talked to Barbara on the phone the other night. She's at Cam Ranh Bay, working at the 6th Convalescent Center. She seems to be all right, but she says she's tired and is getting too much harassment. She sounds different these days. It might be the phone connections.

For some reason, I think I've missed you all more in the last few weeks than I've ever missed you. Since I've been over here, I've finally come to realize some of the things that are so precious back in the world. I wish I was with you. If I've never told you before, I love each and every one of you very much. I'm going to have to sign off now. I just got off duty, but I'll have to go back on in a couple of hours. I need some sleep. Take care. I'll talk to you later.

Hi, Lynda. This is your father. In your last letter, you asked me to price the Sony 230 recorder so you could compare prices in your PX. I can find all kinds of Sonys, but I can't find the 230. Sooner or later I'll run across it.

I had some fairly good news today. Dr. Farmer told me my blood pressure is the best he's ever seen it. It was only 160/85.

We're beginning to think that maybe we're going to bring the little old white trailer home from the mountain and sell it. I don't know that Mom and I ever need a trailer that big anymore. Whatever trips we take, I guess there won't be too many people going along since you're all older now. I'm thinking very seriously about getting a truck camper. Some of our friends have them and are having a ball.

If you notice some background music, it's from Mary's room. Mary was so intent on getting herself a big fat stereo with an amplifier that she bought a two-hundred-fifty dollar job. But by golly, whatever happens with Mary always seems to go wrong. Her stereo broke down a couple of hours after we got it. I took it back and got it fixed, but it broke again within two hours. We got her a brand-new one. I hope this one lasts.

There isn't much else happening, so I'll say good-bye for now. I love you and miss you very much.

There's a standard one-liner used by hundreds of comedians that goes something like this: "I spent a month in that town one night." They could have been describing the 71st Evac. It wasn't that the time dragged, just that each day was filled with a month's worth of experience. As the casualties kept coming in a seemingly endless torrent of human flesh, I began feeling as if I were turning into an old woman. We were living by a different clock in Pleiku, and learning that chronological age has little correlation with how old some people feel. Holding the hand of one dying boy could age a person ten years. Holding dozens of hands could thrust a person past senility in a matter of weeks.

Sometimes I found myself thinking about Amos Giovanni and wondering if his suicide attempt had been successful. Maybe he knew more than the rest of us. After all, whether he was now dead or a vegetable made little difference: He would no longer have to face the suffering. For him, it was over. In many ways, I envied him his peace. I also found myself envying Carl for being back in the world. I constantly wished that he was here so I could feel some of the love and remember that I was a person. But as the pressures and exhaustion built, I discovered another curious fact: I was no longer able to cry. Even if I wanted to. Somehow, when I reached that point, it became easier. If you can't feel, you can't be hurt. If you can't be hurt, you'll survive.

However, Carl had awakened something in me. He had shown me that I needed someone, if not for love, then at least for comfort. I thought that if I was careful, and didn't get too attached, I would not be hurt. Others had entered into relationships with that attitude. I would try it myself.

The man was Pete D'Angelo, an infantry sergeant. He had come to the hospital to visit one of his soldiers who had been wounded in a firefight ten miles north of Pleiku City. Pete was one of those few men who looked right at home in jungle fatigues. When he appeared in the emergency room to thank us for saving his buddy's life, I felt an immediate attraction. He was lean, handsome, and aggressive. He was also tired, short-tempered, and as introspective as a piece of wood. He dealt only in the here and now, and if it wasn't concrete, it wasn't worth talking about. He led a scout platoon, a supposedly elite group of men he jokingly referred to as "the losers, convicts, and crazies." He would go into Cambodia with his small unit to gather intelligence. That was all he told me about his missions. The rest, he said, was classified. We had supper together in the mess hall that night and he returned to our compound a few nights later for a Bastille party. I found myself enjoying his company, and felt grateful to have a few moments of fun come back into my life.

Unfortunately, I had never figured I would develop any feelings for Pete or that he would fall in love with me. I was wrong on both counts. He began making more frequent visits when he wasn't in the field and I found myself looking forward to even a few moments with him. Once, when he had returned from an eight-day mission, he came immediately to the 71st Evac, before he had been debriefed. He was wearing a beard and needed a haircut. The gate guard refused to let him on the compound, so Pete did what he called "the right thing to do under the circumstances"—he decked the guy.

I hid him in my room all that night. The next morning, before he left, we shaved him and cut his hair.

As the weeks went by, I found myself becoming closer to Pete. He began opening up and he talked frequently about his men and how proud he was of them. He told me stories that sounded so crazy that no one outside of Vietnam would have believed them. There had been one time when his platoon had liberated a whorehouse and carried the prostitutes through the streets as heroes. Whenever the unit wasn't on an operation, Pete spent a lot of time either at the MP station bailing one of his men out of a jam, or in his captain's office, explaining why it was impossible to civilize them. They were all incorrigible and Pete was the perfect person to lead them.

But not everyone thought that Pete was the perfect person for me. Ann Sieger, the head of the ER staff and a good friend, probably gave the best reason. Ann was a captain who had served a previous tour in Vietnam in '67. "Van," she said, "the last time I was here, I fell in love with a guy who flew Cobra gunships. When we were together it was like heaven. When we were apart, I worried myself sick over him, especially after the first time he was shot down. We had planned to get married as soon as we got back to the world. Unfortunately, the second time the V.C. knocked him out of the sky was his last.'' She smiled sadly. ''It's hard enough to survive a year in this place, Lynda. It's almost impossible after you've lost someone you love to the war. Please take my advice and stop seeing Pete before it gets too serious.''

I ignored her warning until the middle of October when, one night, a helicopter brought Pete to the 71st Evac—this time as a casualty. His wounds were minor: He'd been shot once in the leg and had taken a few pieces of shrapnel in his shoulder. But the moment he was wheeled through those double doors, I knew I would have to stop seeing him. Ann was right. I wasn't going to risk the pain. If I spent all of my time worrying about him, studying the face of every incoming casualty to make sure it wasn't him, my sanity would never survive. Dealing with wounded strangers was hard enough. I realized that it was also better that I was a long distance from my cousin Steve. If I'd been stationed near him, I'd have been constantly watching for him to come in wounded.

It was as if a wall had come down in front of me. I would never let Pete penetrate it again. Although I didn't have the courage to tell him in person that I wanted to break off our relationship, I avoided him so many times that he finally figured it out on his own. I never got a chance to say good-bye.

Dear Lynda,

This letter will come as somewhat of a surprise to you. Me too. For one reason, I write about as regularly as the moon has an eclipse. For another, this is a love letter. Much to my chagrin, even I am capable of love letters.

At this moment, I am in your room listening to tapes and smoking. You are at your Bastille with your friends. If that sounds jealous, it is not really. More a matter of an awakening of sorts.

The urge that has fallen on me to write this is hard to put into words, like so many feelings and emotions are. Let's say it is because I owe you.

Not long ago, when I met you, I was an ill-tempered, introverted, skinny, nervous wreck. I was, if you will allow, a frustrated killer. Though that all may sound a bit dramatic, it is nonetheless true. I was old enough to know what I wanted yet too immature to cope with my lot.

And you were the one who brought me around to believing in life. I laugh now as I think about it. You were so pretty and unassuming. And I was moody, withdrawn, surly, and very, very childish. But you won.

Actually, I'm in a little trouble tonight. I am supposed to be on duty at the fire base. I'm needed there now about as much as a tuna fish sandwich at a feast. But tomorrow, I'll have the batallion executive officer standing on my chest. Of course, I'll lie. I'm the world's foremost liar, as you must know. Naturally, I'll tell him that I had to come here and see this woman I so adore. And that I'm hopelessly in love. It isn't altogether untrue. In my own left-handed way, I do love you.

So, in the end, there isn't really a way to tell you all the things you have been to me. Words are so shallow. But then I rather doubt I could look you in the eye now and say it all. I don't think I would anyhow. You are far too much of a woman for my faltering words and a desperate embrace. I won't try to see you again and I do believe this is the best way. I won't bother you anymore.

There are many things I would like to say in closing. But I guess it doesn't matter. I wish you, Lynda, the very best of everything. Most of all love. And remember that once there was a man, if even of questionable character, who was nuts about you.

Keep your chin up, kid,
Pete

That was the last time I ever heard from him.

The next time I got a day off, I hitched a chopper ride, along with some wounded soldiers who were on their way to the 6th Convalescent Center at Cam Ranh Bay, an idyllic blue-green body of water along the South China Sea. When I arrived, I found white sandy beaches, lush greenery, and a hospital facility that was far more modern and cheerful than the 71st Evac would ever be. It was also clean and relatively safe. Everything at the 6th Convalescent wasn't covered in red mud. Instead of grungy fatigues, the nurses wore white uniforms, and no one had to worry about rocket attacks. It was the kind of hospital we called "same same stateside." From my vantage point, it looked like a perfect assignment. I was jealous of Barbara as soon as I found her, I let her know. "Some people have all the luck, Kaplan," I said as she walked through the double doors of her OR. "Why couldn't I be assigned to a vacation spot like this?"

She hugged me, but didn't smile. She looked exhausted. "If I had any luck," she said quietly, "I wouldn't be in Vietnam at all. Even a grave is better than this hole."

In spite of the surroundings, it didn't take long to see that Cam Ranh Bay had one crucial element in common with Pleiku Province—casualties, and plenty of them. Although most of the guys who reached the 6th Convalescent eventually recovered, many still died. And those who didn't die were usually sent back into combat to again face a possible death. "Yesterday we worked twelve hours on a kid who had seemed hopeless," Barbara said. "I don't think I ever wanted anybody to live as much. And we almost had him out of danger when he arrested. Life's a bitch. Isn't it?"

I had almost four hours before my return flight and I had hoped to spend the time talking over old times, happier times. But Barbara talked very little. She mostly sat and stared at me in a way that made me feel uncomfortable. This wasn't the Barbara I had known back in the world. She was withdrawn and very morose.

"Remember that night in the van in New Mexico?" I asked. "That was some birthday party."

"There was a kid who came through here a week ago, Lynda, and begged me to kill him," she said. "And the thing was, he hadn't been wounded very badly. He just didn't want to go back out to the boonies."

"How about those times we had in New Orleans?"

"One of my father's old friends came through here last month on his way back to the world. He used to take me swimming at Fort Benning when I was a little girl. Now, the doctors have told him he'll never walk again."

"I wonder what ever happened to the Nazi. Think she's still at Mercy?"

"I can't take much more of this, Lynda. I'm tired of seeing all this death and suffering."

"You'll survive," I said. "You have to be tough."

"Yeah, tough," she replied absentmindedly. "I'll have to be tough."

By the time I left, she had managed to smile once. I told myself that Barbara was fine. Perhaps she was overworked and slightly depressed, but who in Vietnam wasn't?

I put Barbara out of my mind that night as soon as I returned to Pleiku. When my chopper descended to the hospital's landing pad, I could see dozens of wounded being wheeled to the ER. I reported to surgery and scrubbed immediately.

That evening's rocket attack came at midnight. We lost the guy who was on the table when the first rocket hit. His heart gave out before we could even cut into him.

11

Baby Come

It was a quiet Saturday afternoon, with a skeleton crew working in the hospital. Bubba had organized another Olympic day for today. It was called the First Annual Seventy-Worst Ejaculation Hospital Gatorade Day. As he explained it, the participants would be divided into two groups: One would drink Gatorade, the other Kool-Aid. The winning team, he said, would prove once and for all whether a balanced electrolyte solution was better than regular drinks. Although everyone pointed out that the experiment would be anything but scientifically rigorous, they agreed to participate because the Olympic Day that summer had been so much fun. Also, they didn't want to disappoint "just possibly the second-best Gatorade drinker in all of Southeast Asia" who was soon going to return to the world where, he assured us, he would resume his position as "just possibly the second-best neurosurgeon in all of North America." Bubba was going home. I was disappointed that I would miss his Gatorade competition and part of his farewell party at the Bastille, but I had been unfortunate enough to pull duty that day. But that's the way it was—one day a friend was there, the next day he was gone.

We had only two cases going in the OR and they were moving without a hitch. I was circulating outside the surgical field and getting supplies, blood, and medication. This day, two enlisted men were working as scrub techs, performing the same job that I had done so many times.

Both cases were easy ones. In room number one, Charlie Hawkins, a general surgeon, was removing a few frags from a soldier's back. In the second room, Glen Proctor, the ophthalmologist, was repairing some damage to a guy's eye. Eye cases always involved very intricate movements and small instruments. They take great attention. As a result, the OR was always quiet when Glen was working.

Although an RN was required during surgery, there was very little for me to do on those cases, especially since they were moving along without a hitch. I told the techs to call me if I was needed, and I started restocking the linen cabinets, which had been badly depleted during the previous week. I first took inventory and then rolled a cart out to the closet to get the linen packs. They wouldn't all fit. So after I unloaded the cart, I went back to the closet and grabbed four more packs, which I carried in my arms. As I walked toward the double doors of the OR, a corpsman rushed into the outer area, pushing a bed that contained a pregnant Vietnamese woman. "Looks like you're going to have a baby," he said.

I turned around. "What?"

"A baby," he said. "You're going to deliver a baby."

"Like hell I am."

Just then, the woman let out a scream, arched her back, and lifted her pelvis in the air. She dropped back to the bed. Sweat was beading on her forehead. Two words could describe how I felt toward that woman, her baby, and the corpsman who was standing around smiling stupidly: pissed off. The nerve of him to bring her to me. The nerve of the ward nurses not to have warned me. The nerve of this woman's doctor for not being here. And the nerve of her: How dare she have a baby in the middle of the war!

"Look, buddy," I said. "You tell your lady that she's at the wrong hospital. I have two surgical cases going and don't have any time for babies."

He shrugged. "I was ordered to bring her down here," he said. "I brought her." He turned to leave.

The woman screamed again. "Wait a minute, private," I said, using my best command voice. "You're not sticking me with this case."

I was too late. The woman started breathing harder, then looked at me and said, "Baby come, baby come." It was time to panic. She started bearing down and pushing. I tried to change her mind. "No, you don't understand," I said to her. "You see, there isn't a doctor here. You'll have to wait for a doctor."

"Baby come."

The corpsman looked more scared than me. "Maybe you better call a doctor," he said.

I snapped at him. "You brought her down; you get your ass to a phone and call a doctor." He ran to the OR office. "And tell him to hustle!" I yelled.

"Baby come," the woman said urgently.

"No, baby isn't coming yet," I said. "He won't come until the doctor arrives. Now if you'll just be patient."

It was obvious that the woman didn't understand a single word I was saying. She was determined to have that baby, regardless of what I told her. I lifted her sheet. "No," I said weakly. Then, "Oh, shit," as a little black bulge became visible between her legs. The child was crowning. I had never delivered a baby by myself. The only obstetrics I knew was enough to pass the course in nursing school. Out of twelve weeks, we had spent a third in the delivery room, where they taught us to put the doctor's gloves on him, hand him the right instruments, and put his forceps together so he could beat the kid's brains out with metal. Nobody ever taught me how to deliver a baby. "Please don't do this," I asked.

I finally realized that the baby was going to be born regardless of what I said or did; I merely had to be there to catch it. With that realization, a sudden calm came over me. I quietly told the woman, in Vietnamese, to "breathe like me." When the next contraction came, I told her to bear down and push. I unwrapped one of the linen packs and grabbed a sterile towel which I held under the crown. On the next push, the little head popped out with the face pointing down. I supported it with my hands. The left shoulder came next. As the baby turned himself to the side, his shoulder popped up. I lifted him up slightly and his right shoulder followed. Then he slipped out.

I stuck my little finger inside the mouth to make sure it was free of mucus. He immediately started to squall at the top of his lungs. He was all wet and squirmy, and I grabbed another towel and wrapped him. "You have a baby boy," I said to the woman in Vietnamese. She started laughing and crying. I felt so proud that I was sure my chest would burst. I laughed and cried with her as I put the little bundle on her stomach. The weight would place direct pressure on the uterus to help it contract properly.

In a few minutes, after the placenta had been expelled, the doctor arrived. "I'm sorry, Van," he said. "We didn't expect—"

"That's all right," I answered.

"Did you want to cut the cord?"

"Thanks."

Somewhere along the line, I had allowed myself to forget about the little wonders of life. In post-op and on the wards, we had rooms full of people with massive wounds, men who would be forever reminded of the bitterness of war. But for those few moments, there was no war, only this miracle of life.

The minutes when I held that beautiful child in my arms were precious. I didn't know where that woman had come from or where she was going, but I was grateful that she had spent the most special time of her life with me. I carried the baby into post-op and held the woman's hand while I dictated the report to the head nurse. As I looked down at his tiny face, so peaceful in sleep, I was certain that nothing would ever happen to him, that all of this craziness would be finished long before he could be touched by war. But something inside me told me I was wrong.

Then I heard that familiar sound—incoming choppers.

And later that night, when I was in the middle of my seventh case, I rememberd the birth with ambivalence. I loved that woman and her baby because they had broken me out of my protective shell and made me feel again. But I also hated them for that same reason.

Dear Mom and Dad,

We still haven't slacked off much, but I got to sleep all night last night after working only thirteen and a half hours. Today I only worked twelve. I don't know when I'll again have this much free time to write. The bad thing is, when we're not doing cases, we've got to give the place a GI cleaning for an inspection by the inspector general. We've been on our hands and knees scrubbing the walls, baseboards, cabinets, furniture, OR tables, everything. And they just get dirty again when we're finished. I am very tired of all this.

The depression gets harder to rise above every day. Harassment is running rampant. Since I arrived, there has been a big changeover in personnel. Our new chief nurse and assistant are nitpicking lifers. They even tried to remove us from our hooch. This hooch was left to us in pathetically dirty shape by the men who moved out. We had to work our tails off to shape it up. I wouldn't even have put my things inside until I had scrubbed it down. I could feel the filth and germs crawling on my body. Then we acquired furnishings to make it look livable. Now they want to move the seven of us out of here. They're going to move dust-off pilots onto our compound and give all our hard work to those rotten men so they can ruin it all over. The worst thing is that there's another hooch that has only three people in seven rooms right next to the parking lot where the dust-off pilots have to keep their jeeps. The chief nurse wouldn't even listen to us when we told her. When we asked to see the commanding officer, she refused us permission, which turned out to be illegal.

So we went over her head and presented our case to the C.O. At least he said he'd consider it. We passed the chief nurse as we left his office and if looks could kill, you'd have one daughter on her way home in a pine box.

I've had it with this place. There's more harassment every day.

I've got to close now. I've got scheduled cases in the morning and don't know how many casualties will come in. I'm beat physically and emotionally and looking forward to R&R very much. I can't wait to take a bath in a real bathtub. It will be fantastic.

I love you all and miss you very much. Please excuse the sloppy handwriting, but I'm pooped.

Love,
Lynda

12

Singing in the Rain

One of the clearest, most oppressive memories of that year in Vietnam was the fall monsoon season. The unrelenting rains and violent winds began in early October and lasted until January with hardly a break. Together, those four months felt longer than any other full year I've lived before or since. The people who had warned me about the season were right: These were the "real monsoons." The red mud was everywhere—on the buildings, in our rooms, on our clothes, and on every casualty the choppers brought. The surgical-T, which was located at the base of a hill, filled with mud and water that came through the swinging double doors. We spent hour after hour sweeping and shoveling mud and water back outside. However, that problem was not half as serious as the ones we faced in the OR.

The fall monsoons brought our greatest number of casualties. It was a good time for the V.C. because they knew the country and were at home with its seasons. To our soldiers, the elements were merely another enemy which, in combination with the V.C., proved unbeatable. If we at the 71st Evac had previously thought we were pushing ourselves to the limit, we were wrong. Before the monsoons, it would have seemed impossible for us to work any harder, but when the casualties increased, we kept going until we dropped. Then, after a couple hours of sleep, we'd start back again. Overworked doctors, nurses, and technicians were falling into almost deathlike sleep at the operating tables. The anesthetists were always the first to go since they were usually sitting and were breathing the leaking gases from their own anesthesia machines. We tried to sleep during every spare moment, taking our rest on floors, chairs, and even on empty gurneys. At one point, I was so exhausted, I took a nap in the expectant area, on a gurney that had previously been occupied by a soldier who had died only minutes earlier. It was still stained by his blood. I was so tired that I could have slept there even if the dead body had been lying with me. As the weeks passed I began to feel like I needed a break or I would crack under the strain. But that break wouldn't come for a long time. Instead, we got more casualties and more rain.

We had cracks in the walls and floors of the OR. The mud that poured down the hill would ooze through the cracks and mix with the blood in ways that were reminiscent of a fifties horror film. Most of the time we shoveled it over to the side and continued with surgery. Often, we found ourselves operating in an inch or more of mud. It was worse during the rocket attacks, when we had to lower the table and kneel in the muck. We tried to keep the rooms as clean as possible, but there was no way to stem the tide. When we had a lot of patients and constant rocket attacks, we knew that we could only handle the most important things. Mud on the floor was a low priority everywhere but in the neuro room, which we struggled to keep spotless. Our rationale was that germs in the brain were far more dangerous than germs in the belly, although in truth, germs in the belly aren't exactly terrific either. After the severe exhaustion set in, it was difficult not to say "fuck it" and live with the mud everywhere, including the neuro room. However, we kept up the fight.

On Halloween, I traded in my "butter bar" for the silver bar of a first lieutenant. The promotion ceremony took place in the communications bunker while the rain poured outside. In the middle of the reading of the orders, another rocket attack started. "I guess we should hurry the ceremony," the colonel joked. "At least if you're going to die, you should die a first lieutenant. The pension's bigger for your family."

> Hi, Mom and Dad. I've got a few minutes to sit with the tape recorder. It's now the fourth of November and the choppers keep pouring in. Sometimes I think if I hear another chopper I'll scream. I hear them all day long, all night long. I hear them in my

sleep. GIs are getting beaten up at Plei Mrong, over at Plei Jarang, and down at Duc Lap and they keep coming here. It's really depressing to walk into post-op these days. At this moment, there are twenty-four or twenty-five patients in there. They're all just as sick as they can be. I've never seen so many really sick GIs pass through post-op.

There was one bright spot today. We had cases all day in the OR as usual, but about six o'clock we only had one going, a kid who had cut off his finger. While we were working, I heard some ruckus out front. We were doing this kid under a local anesthetic, so I looked out to see what the noise was. Martha Raye was out there. When I told the guys in the OR that Martha Raye was out front, the kid said "Shit! Martha Raye! I fuckin' love that lady." I walked out front and said, "Miss Raye, there's a patient in the back who would really like to see you."

She put on a gown, a mask and a cap, and when she saw that the kid was a Mexican American, she started speaking to him in Spanish. It was great. She's an amazing person. I think she's one of the people more GIs would like to see than anybody else, including Raquel Welch. She has something they seem to like. I'm impressed by her.

A lot of people have asked me to tell them things they can send that I don't have over here. If anybody ever asks you, tell them they can send anything at all. I guarantee I won't have it. I can use simple everyday things like cream rinse or hair stuff. I sent to Revlon for a case of Blondsilk around the first part of August. I had brought two bottles with me and had done my hair the first two months. I didn't get the case from Revlon until the twenty-ninth of October. By that time, my roots were about an inch and a half long.

There's nothing over here, no perfume, no Tampax, no toiletries. I don't even have contact lens solution anymore. If anybody finds Soac-lens contact wetting solution, please send me some. My eyes are bothering me. We are without the simplest things here. If you walked blindfolded down the aisle of a drugstore and picked out things, you couldn't possibly miss. And food? What I wouldn't give right now for a loaf of nice, soft, good old plastic-bagged American bread. It's been so long since I've had good bread. The bread over here is mostly homemade, but it's not the same as real homemade bread. It's hard and it falls apart. It would be so nice to have a piece of soft bread.

And a hot shower. I would give anything for a hot shower. Also lasagna. Mom, when I get home, the first thing I want is your lasagna. I haven't had anything lately that even resembles lasagna and I'm so sick and tired of roast water buffalo, buffalo stew, and buffalo burgers.

There are so many little things that people don't appreciate until they get someplace where they don't have them anymore. I miss those little conveniences like being able to go to the refrigerator and pick out a plastic bag of frozen corn, stick it in some water, and boil it up. Fresh vegetables. Fresh lettuce. Lettuce and tomato salad with Italian dressing. Sour cream. Also, now that you all have some access to a cassette tape recorder, how about getting some cassettes, since they're impossible to acquire over here. I'd love to hear everyone's voice, but calling over MARS is a very unpleasant way of talking to anybody.

I'm going to stop now for the night. I'm hoping that there won't be too many cases coming so I can sleep. Good night.

Along with the rains came more cold. We never had snow and the temperatures never got below forty degrees, but with the dampness, it felt cold enough for snow. It was a cold that went all the way to the bone. I was quickly growing tired of it. I wanted some of that dreaded tropical heat that the assignments officer in Long Binh told me I was so "lucky" to be escaping from in June. In the worst of times, I found myself having fantasies of him suffering in Pleiku. I would have loved to throw his fat ass out in the middle of all that mud and let him grovel for a while. Maybe we could all stone him, or better yet, put him in front of a firing squad. We had hated the "Saigon warriors" who pounded typewriters and sent us to nowhere even more than we hated the Viet Cong and Richard Nixon. They were all REMFs—Rear Echelon Mother Fuckers—in our book.

As the months passed, my slowly evolving dislike for our own government surprised me even more than the realities of war. I found myself cursing those people who were responsible for bringing American troops to Vietnam. I began wondering why we didn't leave this war to the Vietnamese and let them settle it themselves. If they wanted to blow each other to hell and back, that was their business. I was still careful to distinguish between my country and its leaders—I remained proud to be an American and continued to wear the rhinestone flag on my fatigue shirt—but as each new soldier came in covered with mud, blood, and his own guts, I moved a bit further from my original position. It all seemed senseless.

Why?

Earlier in my tour, when I had heard about the war protesters, I had felt angry at them for not supporting us. Now, I wished I could march with them to make the politicians understand the terrible price Vietnam was extracting from our young. Most others in Pleiku felt the same way. We even held our own Thanksgiving Day fast—the John Turkey movement—as a show of support for those who were trying to end the war through protests and moratoriums. We heard that the fast had spread to units all over Vietnam.

We operated that day on a boy who had become very special to Denise Murray, a short, blond post-op nurse who had the room across from mine in FUB-1. Denise was a captain, a lifer who had come from a military family. Two of her brothers were Marine majors, her uncle was a colonel in the Air Force, and her father was a well-known admiral in the Pentagon. He was proud of Denise for her choice of career. However, by the time Thanksgiving was through, there would no longer be any future in the military for Denise, and Admiral Murray, Majors Murray, and Colonel Murray would all be sorely disappointed.

It all began with an eighteen-year-old GI from Iowa who had come in a few days earlier with enough metal in his belly to open his own junkyard. We handled him pretty routinely, repairing his left iliac artery, removing his spleen, doing a resection of his stomach and kidney, and running the bowel carefully before putting him back together again. Shortly after we sent him out to post-op with Denise, he began having problems. He was going sour.

At his worst, the boy required almost constant attention. His fever spiked to 104 and he couldn't hold anything down. His case was perplexing. Denise would talk with him when he was coherent, and try to help him when he was not. Unfortunately, during her few days with him, she made a cardinal mistake—she became attached to the kid. That could only mean trouble.

During Thanksgiving, a network camera crew and some reporters visited Pleiku to do a story. When they arrived, instead of finding soldiers happily eating turkey, they chanced upon an ER filled with casualties and they got interviews with the leaders of the John Turkey Movement. Since Denise was the daughter of such a well-known military figure, the reporters asked her if she would give them an interview about the fast. Though she was fasting along with the rest of us, she declined the interview because of the embarrassment it would cause her family.

Our commander was infuriated about the press attention to the fast. Since we were too busy to get away from the surgical-T, he had the mess sergeant send over stainless steel carts filled with trays of turkey, stuffing, mashed potatoes, and gravy, to be consumed between cases. We were all hungry, and the smell permeated the air. Yet nobody touched the food.

Around seven o'clock, after finishing a chest case, I was assigned to work with George Calsavage, the surgeon who had done the original work on Denise's young soldier. Although he wasn't sure, George believed that the soldier's problem was an abscess under the diaphragm caused by a frag that had been left behind, maybe in the colon. The X rays weren't clear in that area, but with so much metal in a belly, it was easy for even the most proficient surgeon to overlook one tiny piece. As I wheeled the boy into the OR, Denise approached me. "I'd like to see the operation, Van."

"It's a septic case," I said. "It's going to be ugly."

"I don't care. I want to be there."

We dressed her in a surgical gown and then wheeled the boy into the septic room, which was an entirely separate area that had floor to ceiling plywood dividing it from the other rooms. We lifted the kid onto the table and I scrubbed his belly as Denise watched from a corner near the doorway. The belly was tight and rigid. After the boy was under anesthesia, George made an incision. He got to the peritoneum and had barely nicked it with the scalpel when immediately the pressure exploded and pus and shit shot out of the small hole, rising so high that some of it hit the overhead fluorescent light. It splattered all over us and our equipment and was accompanied by a putrid odor that caused me to gag. Denise threw up on her way out. It was a turning point for her.

Later, we learned that Denise had found the network camera crew and offered to make a statement about the stupidity of this war. Because her father was Admiral Murray, they promised that her segment would be part of the lead story on the evening news back in the world.

In time, Denise's young patient got better and was sent on to Japan. She got a reprimand in addition to a visit from her father. But she seemed more at peace with herself when it was over.

> Hi, Lynda. This is your old dad again, sending his love from ten thousand miles away. We're expecting quite a crowd for Thanksgiving dinner. If it pans out, I'm going to try and get some of them on tape for you.
>
> I had resolved that I would not discuss with you or even mention anything about some of the wild antiwar things that are going on in the United States today, especially this moratorium bit that was happening in Washington over the fifteenth of November. But since you've asked questions in your letters, I guess it's all right.
>
> This antiwar business is just the kind of thing that turns my stomach. The outfit that ran the whole show here, the commissars of the show—and I use the term advisedly—were in the building practically catty-corner from our own. Some of their characters eat at the same little old sandwich shop where we eat. I was really tickled to see a bunch of elevator mechanics eating there. If you know anything about the blue collar trades, you'll know that the elevator mechanics are the highest paid workers in the country. These are a pretty sharp bunch of boys. When these mechanics came in to eat the first day of this moratorium, they were all wearing badges that said, "Tell it to Hanoi." I loved them for the way they talked about protesting against Hanoi. Nixon's not the only guy in the world who has anything to do with the war.
>
> Somehow or another our government always seems to be to blame as far as the protestors are concerned. I don't know what's the right thing to do in any of this, but I've got to have trust in somebody. I've got trust in God and in my president. Maybe Nixon's wrong in a lot of things, but nonetheless, he's my president and I'm going to support him.

Besides the mud and casualties, the rainy season brought Captain Jack Olsen to Pleiku. He had blond hair, blue eyes, and the kind of handsome rugged features which reminded me of Troy Donahue. Jack and I spent a lot of long stretches together at the operating table, and when you work so closely with someone, the bonds you form are always intense. Ours was a relationship as stormy as the monsoons.

He had been raised in Oregon, as the only child of Swedish immigrants. His father was a doctor with a small practice in Eugene, and his mother had always encouraged him to reach his highest potential. Jack's medical degree was summa cum laude from UCLA and he had completed his surgical residency at one of the best hospitals in San Diego. Unfortunately, the Army drafted him before he could take his surgical board exams. One of Jack's major concerns was that a year of "meatball surgery" would dull his skills before he could obtain certification in his specialty. He was angry with the Army for depriving him of his chance for certification, but his anger never affected his work. Jack Olsen was an outstanding surgeon. He gave his patients everything he had. Although he was less experienced than men like Carl Adams and Bubba Kominski, Jack could hold his own. And with a few more years of seasoning, he would easily equal their skills.

Initially, Jack and I didn't have much of a life outside the OR. By the time we were finished working, we were usually too exhausted to do much of anything but sleep. When we weren't sleeping, we often argued. It was probably because both of us were bone-tired and constantly on edge. Our disagreements were always over the most trivial things. Sometimes it seemed like we battled each other for no reason at all. If he said something was red, I would say it was black. If I said it was green, he would call it pink.

But we also had some good times when the personal storms died down. Jack gave me moments that I will never forget. We would talk often, although I was no longer as open as I had been with Carl. And when we held each other, I felt again that I had found an island of sanity for a few moments. Sometimes in my dreams, I imagined that we could make that island into a peninsula when we returned to the United States. Unlike Carl, Jack was single. There was no wife, two kids, or house in the country. We spoke a lot about the times we would have together back in the world.

When we cut down to a regular twelve-hour schedule for a few weeks in November, Jack initiated an off-duty project designed to solve a liver wound problem that had been plaguing doctors since long before I had arrived in-country. He and I had lost three liver cases in one week alone. He found that totally unacceptable and set out to find a solution. Success would mean that hundreds of lives could eventually be saved.

We had lost the guys because the liver bleeds profusely. Any surgeon trying to repair a liver would find himself in a losing battle with the clock, especially if the wound was a large one. There was only one way to control the bleeding—to clamp off the aorta above the liver. That would create a bloodless field, but in about ten minutes, it would also create dead kidneys and lower limbs. Jack decided to put a tube into the aorta and bypass the liver. That would theoretically give the surgeon his bloodless field in which to work and yet maintain circulation in the lower body. It was a simple, but brilliant solution.

Another surgeon, Brady Coleman, joined Jack in the experiments and I served as their assistant. Whenever we got a free moment, we worked on Jack's project. It involved three phases: First we would test the theory on eight dogs. If that proved successful, then we would try it on cadavers from the morgue. Finally, when we were proficient enough as a team, we would use the new technique on wounded soliders, hopefully saving their lives.

We lost our first dog because of a stupid mistake. We had forgotten to get some dog blood for a transfusion, thinking that we could give him human plasma. I was furious, but I doubt that my anger matched Jack's and Brady's. They were both verbally abusive. However, after the initial setback, we were successful with the other seven dogs. It was time to move on to human corpses.

The first time we walked into the morgue was after a big push. Bodies were strewn all over the place, some still on litters and others in Glad bags. We found hideously contorted faces, formless bags of disconnected torsos and limbs, and an overwhelming stench of death. We worked on the autopsy tables, which had been previously unused. The job was so gruesome, it was almost unbearable. Once, while walking to the table, I tripped over an arm and fell in between two cadavers that were already starting to decompose. I wanted to run out of there and never return. It was bad enough to be surrounded all the time by people dying, but to spend my free hours with the dead was overwhelming. I didn't know how much more I could stand.

Then one day, when Jack and Brady got into a loud argument in the morgue, I knew I had had enough. I screamed at them, "If you people don't have any more goddamned respect for the fucking dead than this, you can count me out." I stormed out of the room and swore I would never set foot inside another morgue as long as I lived.

> Guess who, Lynda. It's the dilapidated old father of yours sitting in your old room upstairs with the tape recorder. The moon's all dark, the radio's playing. I can see the planes coming out of Washington Airport and all the lights out there. I can look up Old Dominion Drive and down Williamsburg Boulevard. I guess this is about one of the prettiest spots I've ever known. The room is a whole lot more comfortable now. We had painting done up here, we fixed up the beds, put new headboards on them, and then brought up a new daybed. Now we have three beds and a nice big rug on the floor and nobody here to enjoy it except me. Every time I sit up here and look out this window, I think back to so many years when you and the others were kids, before we had this room. When I think about moving from this house, I think about giving up this room and I turn against it. There are so many memories here.
>
> I'm real pleased that you got the shine off that butter bar on your shoulder and replaced it with a silver one. It should make a little bit of difference in your pocket and with the people with whom you work. I'm proud that you've made first lieutenant. I'm very proud of you, Lynda, and I love you.

Jack convinced me to stay with the liver experiment, but it took a major concession on his part. He agreed to not perform any more procedures in the morgue. Instead, we made arrangements to do the rest of the work in the OR on soldiers who had just died. That plan cost us sleep on a number of nights, but it was far more agreeable than the morgue. We went through a half dozen bodies before we were ready for the real thing.

Near the end of November, we got a live soldier with a massive liver wound. When he arrived, it looked like he would surely die, but after a tense operation using the new technique, the soldier pulled through. It was a victory; we were entitled to a celebration.

But there was no time for one now. And if there had been time, we probably wouldn't have had the heart to celebrate anyway, because the war, the helicopters, the casualties, the rockets, and the monsoons made everything seem pointless.

I could feel myself sliding quickly downhill and didn't know if I could stop. I was starting to dream about soldiers who had died on my table. Everytime I saw another casualty, I ached. For the first time in my life, I was so tired and disillusioned that I wanted to quit.

13

Hump Day

It was a few days before my hump day, the exact middle of my tour when I would be "over the hump." I was lost in a heavy sleep under my bed when the phone started ringing. The sound was more impossible to ignore than the rockets that had driven me there a couple of hours before. Still half asleep, I listened to the words: "More casualties, Van. We need you in surgery."

By the time I arrived in the operating room, I was alert, with my senses at their peak. I changed immediately to scrub clothes and reported to the head nurse for my assignment. Her short red hair was wild, the front of her scrub dress blood-stained. A mask dangled from her neck. "There's a bad one in the neuro room," she said. "I need you to pump blood in there."

The neuro room was one of the places I usually tried to avoid. Head wounds were so messy and this one would undoubtedly be bad. But even knowing that, I was totally unprepared for the sight that awaited me when I stepped through the entrance.

Leading to the operating table was the largest trail of blood I had ever seen. I tried to walk quickly through it but slipped. When I regained my balance, my eyes were drawn to the gurney, where several people were transferring the wounded soldier from the green litter to the table. Three intravenous lines ran from bags of blood to his body, one in his jugular vein and one in each arm. The lower portion of his jaw, teeth exposed, dangled from what was left of his face. It dragged along the canvas litter and then swung in the air as he was moved from the gurney to the table. His tongue hung hideously to the side with the rest of the bloody meat and exposed bone. When he was on the table, Mack Shaffner, the facial surgeon, dropped the lower jaw back into place. One of the medics kicked the gurney to the side. It rolled across the room and banged into a wall.

I held my breath to keep from getting sick. For a moment, I was glued to the spot. I had already been through six months of combat casualties, plenty of them gruesome; I thought I had gotten used to it all, but they kept getting worse. I didn't think I could handle this one.

But the shout of the anesthesiologist, Jim Castelano, snapped me out of my trance. "The son of a bitch is drowning in blood," he screamed. "Somebody help me get a fucking airway in him." My training and instincts moved me into action for a tracheotomy. I raced across the room and ripped a prepared instrument pack out of the cabinet, quickly removing the layers of heavy cotton wrap from the tray as I placed it on a Mayo stand and rolled it to him. Scalpels, clamps, sponges, forceps, retractors, scissors, metal trach tube.

A gurgling came from the soldier's throat. Jim's hands were quick. "Don't you dare die, you motherfucker." With two fingers, he felt for the space between the cricoid and thyroid cartilage. "Give me a knife, Van." He made a vertical incision to get through the skin, and a horizontal one between the cartilage. Blood spurted from the neck. Then he pushed the scalpel handle into the space and turned it sideways to open a hole. "Trach tube."

I handed him a crescent-shaped hollow metal tube, which he immediately shoved into the hole. He pulled out the tube guide and more blood shot from the opening. There was an ugly metallic coughing sound as the soldier bucked for breath.

"Suction!"

I brought the suction machine and some clear plastic sterile tubing. Jim forced the suction catheter into the trachea. Immediately, red blood and mucus were sucked through the clear tube. Then it stopped.

"Come on, asshole, cooperate!" Jim pulled the catheter out. A long black string of clotted blood hung from the end. With a sponge he wiped it away before forcing the catheter back into the trachea. More blood and mucus. He retracted the catheter once more. "Breathe, damn you!"

A barely audible metallic sound escaped.

"That's it, soldier, come on." We connected the oxygen line to the trach tube and Jim started using an airbag to regulate the boy's breathing.

I immediately moved into position to help Mack, who was already grabbing instruments from the trach tray to clamp off the largest bleeders in the face and jaw. Meanwhile, the scrub technician set up the sterile field of linens and instruments.

Once the largest bleeders were tied off, Mack put on his gown and gloves and began to repair the damage. Now I fully realized what the head nurse meant when she told me I was needed to pump blood: The soldier was bleeding so fast that three IV lines were not enough.

''No blood pressure,'' Jim yelled. ''Keep that blood pumping and get another IV into him.''

I replaced the empty hanging blood bags with new ones and then started a fourth line in his left leg.

''The stethescope is broken. Van, get me another one.''

''Get the crash cart, Van, in case he arrests.''

''Who stole my goddamned tape?''

''Van, more towels for his head.''

In the middle of the confusion, the neurosurgeon who had replaced Bubba came into the room. He looked at the soldier on the table and shook his head. His face was red. ''Who the fuck woke me up for this gork?''

''The brain doesn't look too damaged,'' Mack answered.

''You're wasting your time.''

''We can fix him,'' Max insisted. ''Just give me a chance.''

''Bullshit,'' the neuro guy answered. ''That sucker's going to die and there's not a fucking thing you can do.'' He stormed out of the room.

Mack yelled after him. ''We're going to need your help as soon as we stop the bleeding.''

''You call me when you're ready,'' the neurosurgeon said, ''and not a minute before.'' It was a moment when we all sorely missed Bubba. If he had been here, he would have stayed with us through the night to offer any possible assistance in pulling the soldier through. Unfortunately, not all neurosurgeons were as helpful.

When the circulating nurse arrived, my sole job became pumping blood, while Mack fought against the odds. After a while, I turned it into a routine: Start at the neck, take down the empty bag of blood, slip a new one into the pressure cuff, pump up the cuff, rehang it, and check the temperature in the blood warmer. Then go to the left arm and repeat the process. Next the left leg and finally the right arm. Then start back at the neck and repeat the entire sequence. It took about five minutes to complete the steps at each site, about twenty minutes to make a round of him.

As Mack and the scrub tech clamped and cauterized the blood vessels, little puffs of smoke rose from what was once the soldier's face. The smell of burning flesh filled the room.

Following every second or third time around the soldier, I changed the IV tubing because the blood filters were getting thick with clots. Since we only had two blood warmers, I had to run the other lines through buckets of warm water to raise the temperature. When the buckets started to cool, I changed the water. It was all just another simple job where I could turn off my mind and try to forget that we were working on a person.

But this one was different. The young soldier wasn't about to let me forget.

During one of my circuits around the table, I accidentally kicked his clothes to the side. A snapshot fell from the torn pocket of his fatigue shirt. The picture was of a young couple—him and his girlfriend, I guessed—standing on the lawn in front of a two-story house, perhaps belonging to her parents. Straight, blond, and tall, he wore the tuxedo with a mixture of pride and discomfort, the look of a boy who was going to finish the night with his black tie in his pocket, his shirt open at the neck, and his cummerbund lying on the floor next to the seat. She, too, was tall, and her long brown hair was mostly on top of her head, with a few well-placed curls hanging down in front of her ears. A corsage of gardenias was on her wrist. Her long pastel gown looked like something she had already worn as a bridesmaid in a cousin's wedding, and it fit her in a way that showed she was quickly developing from a girl into a woman. But the thing that made the picture special was how they were looking at each other.

I could see, in their faces, the love he felt for her, and she for him, a first love that had evolved from hours of walking together and talking about dreams, from passing notes to each other in history class, from riding together in his car with her sitting in the middle of the front seat so they could be closer.

On the back of the picture was writing, the ink partly blurred from sweat: "Gene and Katie, May 1968."

I had to fight the tears as I looked from the picture to the helpless boy on the table, now a mass of blood vessels and skin, so macerated that nothing could hold them together. *Gene and Katie, May 1968*. I had always held the notion that, given enough time, anything could be stopped from bleeding. If you kept at it, eventually you would get every last vessel. I was about to learn a hard lesson.

I pumped 120 units of blood into that young man, yet as fast as I pumped it in, he pumped it out. After hours of work, Mack realized that it was futile. The boy had received so much bank blood that it would no longer clot. Now, he was oozing from everywhere. Slowly, Mack wrapped the boy's head in layers of pressure dressings and sent him to post-op ICU to die.

Gene and Katie, May 1968. While I cleaned up the room I kept telling myself that a miracle could happen. He could stop bleeding. He could be all right. Nothing was impossible. *Please, God, help him*. I moved through the room as if in a daze, picking up blood-soaked linens, putting them into a hamper, trying to keep myself busy. Then I saw the photograph again. It was still on top of the torn, bloody fatigue shirt. A few drops of blood were beaded on the edge of the print. I wiped them off and stared.

This wasn't merely another casualty, another piece of meat to throw on the table and try to sew back together again. He had been real. *Gene*. Someone who had gone to the prom in 1968 with his girlfriend, *Katie*. He was a person who could love and think and plan and dream. Now he was lost to himself, to her, and to their future.

When I finished making the room ready for the next head injury—the next young boy—I walked to post-op to see Gene. His bandages had become saturated with blood several times over and the nurses had reinforced them with more rolls of gauze, mostly to cover the mess. Now, his head seemed grotesquely large under the swath of white. The red stains were again seeping through. I held his hand and asked if he was in pain. In answer he squeezed my hand weakly. I asked him if he wanted some pain medication, and he squeezed my hand again. All the ICU patients had morphine ordered for pain, and I asked one of the nurses to give Gene ten milligrams intravenously, knowing that, while it would relieve his pain, it would also make him die faster. I didn't care at that point; I just wanted him to slip away quickly and easily.

The drug went to work immediately. As his respiration slowed and his grip became weaker, I imagined how it would be back in his hometown. Some nameless sergeant would drive an Army-green sedan to the house where Gene's parents lived. The sergeant would stand erect in his dress uniform, with his gold buttons glinting in the morning sun and bright ribbons over his left breast pocket. Perhaps a neighbor would see him walking past a tree in the front yard, one that Gene used to climb before the war; perhaps a little boy would ride his bicycle along the sidewalk and stop near the house to watch the impressive stranger stride confidently up the stairs and to the door. And when the mother and father answered the knock, no one would have to say a word. They would both know what had happened from the look on the sergeant's face.

And Katie? She would probably find out over the phone.

I ran my finger along the edge of the picture before putting it into the envelope with his other possessions. Then I walked outside, sat on the grassy hill next to post-op, and put my head in my hands.

I wouldn't cry, I told myself. I had to be tough.

But I knew a profound change had already come over me. With the death of Gene, and with the deaths of so many others, I had lost an important part of myself. The Lynda I had known before the war was gone forever.

I was off the next day, so I hitched a helicopter ride to Cam Ranh Bay. I had to see Barbara. I had to talk with her, to talk with someone who knew me before all this began. I had to try to make sense of it, to perhaps recall something from our past that could make me laugh, that could make me remember something other than war. I wanted to talk like we did on our cross-country trip, to look back on the pranks of nursing school and to dream about a future when the war would be over and we would each be married, living in our nice houses with our loving husbands and kids.

Was that all a fantasy? You bet your ass it was. I knew now that life would never be like that, but there was no law about dreaming.

When I reached Cam Ranh, I helped the helicopter crew and hospital staff to move some wounded from the chopper. Then I went to find Barbara.

A new woman was living in Barbara's room and she seemed annoyed at me for disturbing her sleep. When I told her I was Barbara's best friend, she told me that Barbara had been transferred to an evac hospital in the Mekong Delta. I got a sick feeling in my stomach as I walked back to the chopper pad. It would be nearly impossible for me to get transportation all the way down to the Delta.

I caught a chopper back to Pleiku that afternoon. I had a feeling I would never see her again.

I didn't cry.

I just felt empty.

December 7, 1969, was the twenty-eighth anniversary of the Japanese attack on Pearl Harbor. It was also my hump day. I envied my father's generation for their "moral war."

> Hi, Lynda, this is your father with the tape recorder again. I'm sure you know that December 7th was one of the most memorable days in history. Early Sunday morning, I got my usual Pearl Harbor Day call from Tom Gladstone. You've heard me say time and again that on the real Pearl Harbor Day, Mom and I were with Maureen and Tom when the news broke. We were at war.
>
> From what we read in the papers and see on television and from the little snatches we get from you, I know things are anything but pleasant over there where you are. I know it's a real sacrifice for you and all these other kids. But I'll tell you one thing: It makes me walk ten feet tall when I tell them that my little gal's right over there at the front.

Although we had spent the previous days under a lot of pressure, my hump day was fairly routine—a few belly wounds, some chest cases, a missing limb or two, and not more than a couple of expectants. I worked a scheduled twelve-hour shift. The time moved quickly.

After work, Jack and a group of friends took me to the Air Force Officers Club for dinner. We watched a Philippino USO show—a rock band and some dancers who were supposed to be sexy—and everyone had a few drinks. I hadn't been drinking for the previous month or so, but that night I had two rusty nails. The second was probably a mistake. I was only half through it when the tears started rolling down my face. By the time I was finished, I was visibly shaken and sobbing quietly. I couldn't stop.

As I looked around the club, all I could see was Gene, the young bleeder we had lost a few nights earlier. *Gene and Katie, May 1968.* Then, when his face was gone, I began seeing all of them—the double and triple amputees, boys with brain injuries, belly wounds, and missing genitals. I could see the morgue and hundreds of bodies strewn haphazardly; the faces of eighteen-year-old kids wracked with pain as they lay dying. There were seventeen-year-old kids who probably hadn't had a chance to make love yet who had lost their penises. There were others who were not old enough to shave who had their faces burned off. There were married fathers who were blinded and would never see their children. Or who were paralyzed and would never be able to throw a ball, run along a trail, or even lift a pencil. They were all with me in that room.

I tried to force them out of my mind.

For a moment, I did.

Then all the images came crashing back on me. I lost control and became hysterical.

My friends tried to soothe me. They could not.

Finally, they took me back to my hooch and left me alone with Jack. He offered comfort. I wouldn't accept it. I became a wild person, sobbing and shaking uncontrollably. "I want my mother. I want my father," I screamed. "I want to go home! Vietnam sucks! We don't belong here! This is wrong! I want Barbara! The whole thing is wrong! I hate it! I hate it! I hate it!" I kept screaming the same things again and again. Each time Jack would approach me, I would kick him away.

He called Coretta for help. She had gone through a similar episode months before and knew what to do. She understood.

When she came into the room, Coretta leaned against the far wall, asking me questions and quietly saying things to comfort me. Eventually, she came close enough to touch me. She sat on the bed and put her arms around me, rocking me and whispering in my ear while I spent the night bawling.

Around five in the morning, I passed out from exhaustion and slept for the next twenty-four hours. After I awoke, I felt numb. I threw away the rhinestone flag I had previously worn on my uniform and found myself feeling nothing.

Christmas in Vietnam. They say the star in the east is only a flare over Camp Enari.

After Christmas, I turned my numbness and sorrow into anger.

> *Dear Mom and Dad,*
> I don't know where to start except to say I'm tired. It seems that's all I ever say anymore. Thank you both for your tapes and all the little goodies in the Christmas packages. Christmas came and went marked only by tragedy. I've been working nights for a couple of weeks and have been spending a great deal of time in post-op. They've been unbelievably busy. I got wrapped up in several patients, one of whom I scrubbed on when we repaired an artery in his leg. It eventually clotted and we did another procedure on him to clear out the artery—all this to save his leg. His name is Clarence Washington. I came in for duty Christmas Eve and was handed an OR slip for Clarence—above-knee amputation. He had developed gas gangrene. The sad thing was that the artery was pumping away beautifully. Merry Christmas, kid, we have to cut your leg off to save your life. We also had three other GIs die that night. Kids, every one. The war disgusts me. I hate it! I'm beginning to feel like it's all a mistake.
>
> Christmas morning I got off duty and opened all my packages alone. I missed you all so much, I cried myself to sleep. I'm starting to cry again. It's ridiculous. I seem to be crying all the time lately. I hate this place. This is now the seventh month of death, destruction, and misery. I'm tired of going to sleep listening to outgoing and incoming rockets, mortars, and artillery. I'm sick of facing, every day, a new bunch of children ripped to pieces. They're just kids—eighteen, nineteen years old! It stinks! Whole lives ahead of them—cut off. I'm sick to death of it. I've got to get out of here.
>
> I'm so glad that Steve finally got out. He was lucky to have made it through a year in this hellhole without getting seriously wounded. I never got to talk to him, but I understand the bitterness in his letters home, now, in a way I couldn't when I first got here.

When I finally got someone in his unit on the phone the other day, they said he'd just left for Saigon to catch his Freedom Bird. With any luck, he's somewhere over Japan about now, and free from this green suck. How I envy him.

I found out a couple of weeks ago that Barbara has been transferred to a unit near where Steve was. I've written her a few times but gotten no answer, and the phone lines in her area are utterly awful, so I haven't been able to reach her. I hope she's okay.

I just heard another chopper come in. I better go. They need me in the OR.

Peace,
Lynda

14

Vietnam Rag

Hello, Lynda, this is Dad. Mom thought it would be a good idea to fill just one side of each tape. I'm going to go along with her on it because this does take an awfully long time. By the time you plop out a half hour of gas on one side, you're not too ready to knock off the other half hour. So we'll probably start sending you tapes done on one side.

I don't want you to think we're cutting you short or anything like that, but we want to get the tapes over there more often. I think it's for your good and our good, too. I can tell by the way you talk that you're kind of getting into battle fatigue. Perhaps one of the most important things for us is more frequent communications rather than lengthy communication. You said yourself that news from home lets you know there's somebody thinking about you.

There are two big questions that have arisen. We ordered the *Arlington Sun* for you quite a long time ago. You never said, either on tape or in a letter, that you have been getting it. Have you? We had them publish on Thanksgiving Day the letter you sent us when you first went to Vietnam, asking us to fly the flag every day. A lot of people have told us they read it.

The other question is, Where are you going for your R&R? We hear all kinds of fabulous tales from people who go. There's Australia and Hong Kong and lots of places like that. Maybe even Tokyo. Please try to take a vacation soon. You sound like you need it.

Hi, Lynda, this is Richard. I got out of the Army about a month ago and since I was up here for Christmas, your dad asked me to say a few words on your tape recorder. I guess there's not too much to say. I'm getting ready to head back to school. I'll be down at Fort Worth, Texas. If you're ever through there, stop by and give me a call. In the meantime, enjoy the war. I'll get off the recorder and let somebody else come in and say hi to you.

Hi, Lynda, this is Arlene. I feel kind of silly sitting here in a room by myself talking to you, but your father insisted. Charlie and I just got back from Hawaii for Christmas. Right now, everybody's sitting in the living room getting up their Christmas cheer. Elizabeth's going to Marymount and she's decided she's going to be a nun. My father talked her into waiting awhile. I can't think of much else to say, so I think I'll go back in and join the party. Merry Christmas and Happy New Year.

Hi, Lynda, this is Cindy Risset. I've spent a couple of marvelous days here with your family before Christmas. I guess you probably know by now I'm engaged to a boy named Claude Bradley. Your family was very good to me at Christmas. I got a nightgown to start my trousseau and a slip and some Jean Naté powder. I hope Christmas is a good one for you in Vietnam and that all goes well with you. Let us hear from you. We keep you in our prayers.

Hi, Lynda, this is Uncle George. We're over at your mother's and we're having a marvelous time. The snow is coming down and it's really Christmas. I guess you know that your parents had your letter about the flag published in the *Arlington Sun*. We all read your piece and thought that what you said was the most wonderful thing. I'm sure it should inspire many Americans to be better citizens and to think more of you poor people who are over there giving everything you have for us to live better here. So, all I can say is God bless you, dear.

Hi, sweetie, this is Aunt Dot. Guess what. It's snowing like mad and it's beautiful. We had the most wonderful surprise this morning. My kids bought us a color television. We miss you lots, honey. I'll keep writing. I hope everything goes well with you and we'll see you real soon. Be a good girl.

Hi, Lynda, this is Uncle Max. We sure do miss you. Wish you could be with us. We're real proud of you. Keep up the good work. When I think of you and the kids over there while we have this lovely Christmas, I can't help but feel a little selfish and a little guilty because you're not here with us. We all hope this thing will be over soon. Incidentally, we're keeping that flag flying every day. So are the people across the street. We're all proud of you. God bless you.

Hi, Lynda, this is Carol, your long-forgotten cousin. I'm sitting here right now with the tape recorder, looking outside your mom and dad's window at the snow. We've had a great Christmas this year but I have to admit everybody's a little lonesome for you. I'm sorry I've been bad about writing letters, but I promise I'll get better at it. John's stationed at Fort Belvoir for his officer training right now. It's hard, but I think he enjoys it. He finished the fourteenth of May. Chances are that he'll stay in the service for twenty years.

Hi, Lynda, this is John. I hear you're going to be back about the beginning of June. Our baby is due then. Between that, my finishing OCS, and your homecoming, this family ought to have one hell of a party. Lynda, I know you're doing a tremendous job over there and it's hard, but keep up the good work. The men are depending on you. I had friends who went over there and aren't coming back. We're looking forward to seeing you again.

Hello, Lynda, this is Mother. Many days have passed since the last words on this tape, which were said on Christmas Day. I hope you enjoyed listening to all the gang. Time has gone so fast and it's New Year's Eve already. We've been partying as usual.

As you can tell by the previous recording, we had a lot of houseguests. That kept me pretty busy and I didn't get to the microphone. We had a great time, but we missed you very much. I think everybody enjoyed sitting down and talking to you by tape. It made them feel like they were a little part of your Christmas.

I'm getting to the end of this tape, so rather than drop off, I'm going to say good-bye now, my sweet. I love you very much. We all miss you and hope to hear from you soon.

Hello, Lynda, this is your dear old dad. It's Saturday night and I have a little time where I can be by myself with the recorder and say a few things to you. This has been a wild week from start to finish as you'll probably know from the other side of the tape and from our letters. We had a hard snow on Christmas. Since then, the ground's been pretty well covered. With the whole crowd being here, Mom's very happy. Incidentally, Mary got bitten by a dog the other night. She's the original hard-luck kid. With all the other visits to the hospital in the past couple of years from her car accident, Mary needs more problems like Custer needed more Indians.

Also, Jean is depressed because of some problems with her boyfriend. Lately, this place seems to get depressed every hour or two. If it's not one problem, it's another. I'm kind of looking forward to retirement and getting up in the country and maybe getting away from some of this. But I strongly suspect that it won't be too long after I'm up there, we'll have some grandchildren with all new problems. Maybe I need this aggravation to stay young. Right now, Mary and Jean are screaming at each other. You can hear them in the background.

I'm going to cut off now. I want to tell you, doll, I love you so much. I want you back and I'm so proud of you. The flag is out front every day. You really won't ever know how much I miss you. Happy New Year. Let's hope 1970 brings good things to you.

Maybe there were people in Vietnam who spent their entire tours motivated by blind patriotism and an unquestioning belief in the American way of doing things. Maybe there were those who could overlook the corruption of the South Vietnamese officials and their rigged elections. And their senseless brutalities against their own citizens. And their soldiers' lack of commitment to the South Vietnamese government. And the total disregard for the value of human life in war.

Maybe there were American soldiers who could forget about the inane regulations that always seemed to get in the way of the job to be done. Maybe they could ignore the petty harassment and make-work details that came during lulls in the fighting. Maybe they could avert their eyes from their buddies who were dying. Or from the young children without limbs. Or from the Vietnamese women who were forced to prostitute themselves to stay alive.

Maybe there were some normal, healthy all-American men and women who could spend 365 days in that crazy environment and never once ask why.

If there were, I never met them.

When we worked nights, we had a group of people who would meet each morning for a party before going to sleep. Unlike the Bastille parties, these were far more sedate. Instead of wild laughter and nonstop drinking, our morning parties usually consisted of candlelight, grass, quiet discussion, and readings from e.e. cummings. Mostly, we talked about our frustrations with the war, Nixon, and the Army. We would close the blackout windows in someone's hooch, sit in a circle around a candle, and try to create our own refuge. We hoped to salvage our sanity. I don't know if all of us, or any of us, succeeded.

Our music was of the plaintive type. Although the night parties involved the sounds of the The Iron Butterfly, Country Joe and the Fish, The Doors, and plenty of acid rock, our mornings were filled with Judy Collins. My favorites were "Pirate Jenny," about a downtrodden washerwoman who rises to command a pirate fleet, and "Marat Sade," the soulful song of an oppressed mass of people who want their rights. Eventually, "Marat" became a theme for the entire 71st Evac and later, it spread to other bases in Vietnam. Sometimes, we even sang it in the operating room when we were tired and depressed and facing too many destroyed young bodies.

One of our main targets for frustration was the attitude of the lifers who tried to appear gung ho and who frequently forced us to perform meaningless tasks. It was made more difficult by knowing that they, too, probably questioned the war in private, but would not voice their opinions because their precious careers might be damaged. Out of our frustration, an anonymous 71st Evac trooper penned the portrait of a "Superlifer":

Able to harass butter bars with a single glance;
Slightly faster than a Montagnard with three
    baskets of banana leaves and a baby san;
Harder to get along with than General Hershey;
As fair as Judge Hoffman with the Chicago Seven;
As discreet as a trip flare at midnight;
As subtle as a drill sergeant in basic training;
As dainty as Baby Huey;
As helpful as lung cancer;
As open-minded as George Wallace;
As appealing as Phyllis Diller;
As welcome in surgery as Lee Harvey Oswald
    in Hyannis Port;
As friendly and outgoing as Howard Hughes;
As lively as a radio with dead batteries;
And about as great a person as you'd ever
    want to avoid!

Most of the original compositions that were brought to the morning parties were more pensive and reflected the true sorrow of the writer. One of the most memorable was another anonymous work titled "Each Day":

Each Day
that year
I would pause
Before the almost too narrow door,
With its neatly lettered,
almost forbidding,
sign:

INTENSIVE CARE UNIT

To hear
The unmistakable rhythmic gush of a respirator,
And the steady beep of a monitor.
Then, I would enter,
and silently pray:

"Oh, God,
Help me to see past the bottles,
    see past the tubes,
    see past the machines,
That I might see into their eyes,
    see into their minds,
    see into their hearts,
And bring them some small part of my healthy self,

That they will still believe
Life is worth the living,
Life is worth the fight."

All of us in the group that met for morning parties must have believed that life was worth the fight, because we translated our frustrations into action. Two of our members had organized the John Turkey Movement and made the media contacts. Others had written numerous letters of protest to President Nixon, congressmen, and their local newspapers. I chose, as my own personal crusade, to attempt to eliminate the petty harassment that interfered with good patient care. The most obvious manifestation of this was the treatment of our enlisted surgical technicians. It wasn't bad enough that they had to put in regular twelve-hour shifts under a great deal of pressure; the lifers also expected them to pull guard duty for a few hours each night, to prepare for regular inspection, to pull K.P., police up the compound, burn out latrines, and in what was probably the silliest requirement of all, to practice marching in formation. What sense could it possibly make to waste time marching already exhausted technicians, when people were dying?

Why?

Even during regularly scheduled operating room times, some enlisted techs were too tired to be effective at the table. During the pushes, they would collapse long before the doctors and nurses, who did not have to perform as many foolish additional duties. Unfortunately, since enlisted personnel were at the bottom of the Army's totem pole, they had no voice in the running of the hospital. I became their unofficial representative. Every time our OR techs had a complaint, they came to me. I would relay it up the chain of command to see if that would bring results. When there was no response, I would go over the heads of the lifers. There was some positive action, but I quickly gained a reputation as a troublemaker. It was a reputation held by the entire morning party group. Since the lifers had all the power, there were repercussions.

When I had been sent to Vietnam, I had been promised that after six months of OJT in the OR I would be awarded the military occupational specialty of surgical nurse, the same specialty I would have received if I had not got sick near the end of the OR course in Texas. The specialty had been one of my reasons for going to Vietnam so soon. It was only a piece of paper in a file, but that piece of paper could have an impact on my life, in a system where promotions, pay, assignments, and dozens of other factors were influenced by that file.

My paperwork requesting the specialty kept getting mysteriously lost every time I filled out new copies. Although I had spent the previous six months doing all the work of a credentialed surgical nurse and had been considered competent enough to work as the OR head nurse on some shifts, the new head nurse was now claiming that I was "lacking in experience." A new hospital directive came down saying that no one could serve in the OR without close supervision unless he or she possessed the documents that certified him or her as a surgical nurse. Those who didn't possess this documentation—I was the only one—would be required to work under the kind of tight supervision that was only available on the day shift. Loosely translated, it meant that I could no longer work nights and would not be able to attend the morning parties with the other rebels. The lifers were using their bureaucracy to harass me and any others who dared speak out against the system. At least five members of the morning party group, including the two who had organized the John Turkey Movement, were separated by transfers to other units, most of which were worse assignments than the Seventy-worst Ejac.

The additional harassment plus the never-ending flow of casualties increased my feelings of bitterness about the war and everything connected with it. The problems carried over to my relationship with Jack.

I had some good times with him. We laughed and played together when we had the chance and we spent countless hours planning and dreaming about our upcoming R&R. But we also argued a great deal.

Jack was also being branded as a troublemaker, largely because of his association with me, and he had become the object of subtle harassment. We were constantly on edge. We took a lot of our frustrations out on each other. He held a lot of resentment against me, and I sometimes acted toward him as if he had been the one to start the war. But we stayed together through the bad times. That counted for a lot.

In spite of our disagreements, I loved Jack. It was not the kind of love I had felt for Carl, who had been far more experienced and almost fatherly. My love for Jack was based more on equality. Although he was older than me, I had been in Vietnam longer and had been able to help him through the early days, as others had helped me when I was an FNG.

And I had enormous respect for Jack as a surgeon. He was good not only in the OR, but also in post-op, where it often counted the most. Sometimes, when a soldier was especially bad, Jack would sit with him through the night, giving the kind of care that made a difference between life and death. However, while those vigils saved lives, they also cost Jack sleep and made him more irritable and argumentative. Our relationship was like a roller coaster. After a while, we were going mostly downhill.

When the casualties slowed and we had free time, Jack and I went with others on Medical Civil Action Patrols, better known as Medcaps. We visited Montagnard villages and provided the people with routine medical care. Although we were always accompanied by guards who were constantly on the lookout for the Viet Cong, these visits to villages did take us partly away from our war. At least on Medcaps, we were not always treating wounded.

The Montagnards, a primitive people who lived almost exclusively in the Central Highlands, were usually short, dark, and sinewy. They resembled Indonesians and Philippinos more closely than ethnic Vietnamese. Frequently compared to the American Indians, Montagnards are believed to have been the original inhabitants of Vietnam who were forced into the mountains by the Chinese immigrants when they took all the fertile farmland and fishing grounds. Their lives revolved around the villages and they lived on dryland rice and wild game, which they hunted with crossbows. When they weren't hunting or farming, they were usually a bit high on rice wine or marijuana.

They were terribly oppressed. They were heavily taxed, cheated in trade, and deprived of even minimal medical facilities when they were sick. As a result, they abhorred the Vietnamese. But they always got on well with the Americans. Our Special Forces units used them extensively as soldiers and guides and found them to be far more reliable than the ARVNs.

Our Medcap visits to the villages usually began with a welcoming ritual that included smoking a peace pipe of marijuana or drinking from a communal jug of rice wine. Unless we smoked or drank with the chief, there would be no medical treatment. Then, when we were finished working for the day, we had to drink again with the chief before we could return to the 71st Evac. By the time we reached our compound, we were usually inebriated.

We also worked with Montagnards at the Civilian Irregular Defense Group (CIDG) hospital, which was located ten miles from the 71st Evac. The hospital was on a Special Forces compound and was run by Chuck Cornwallis, a Green Beret captain who had been in the middle of his internship when he was drafted. As the only CIDG doctor, Chuck was badly overworked and in need of all the assistance he could get. In addition to occasionally providing doctors and nurses, we also helped Chuck by training two Montagnards, Sui Bonh and Nago, to serve as his surgical assistants. By the time their training was completed, Sui Bonh and Nago were even able to perform certain types of surgery themselves during pushes. Fortunately, Chuck was not tied down by the same regulations as the American hospitals. He gave his Montagnard helpers all the responsibility they could reasonably handle, in spite of their lack of diplomas. In fact, before I left Pleiku, Chuck's assistants were skilled enough to hold their own against any school-trained surgical assistant.

Dear Mom and Dad,

I'm sure you have heard about the Civilian Irregular Defense Group over here. They're a big part of the war. Ben Het is actually a CIDG camp. The CIDGs work with and are supported by our Green Berets, who are probably the greatest group of people assembled. Jack and I have been going over to CIDG on our days off to do surgery and help them set up their operating room. Yesterday, the Montagnard personnel there held a party to thank us and initiate us into Montagnard tradition. You've never seen anything like it. During the ceremony, Jack and I each received Montagnard tribal bracelets and we had to drink rice wine with the people. Sui Bonh, the Montagnard I have been training most of the time, asked me to drink with him. I couldn't refuse, or he would lose face. So I drank. When I finished before him, he beamed and said, "Golden-hair Van, you numbah one!" He took the bracelet off his arm and put it on mine. Then we ate a Montagnard feast—very highly seasoned water buffalo, with onions and strange vegetables alternating on wires similar to a shish-kabob. There was also a bland lettucelike leaf and bread in small loaves—similar to French bread. All was eaten with the fingers, of course. It was the first good afternoon I've had in a long time. I have never been so enjoyably drunk in my life. It's an experience I won't forget. As a matter of fact, everything here is an experience. Most of them, I wish I could forget, but I won't depress you now with bad news.

I miss you all.

Peace,
Lynda

The Vietnamese New Year, unlike ours, usually falls at the beginning of February. Called Tet, it's the biggest event of their year and combines all the pomp and celebration of our Christmas, New Year, Easter, and the Fourth of July. It is supposed to be a time for correcting all faults, putting past mistakes behind you, forgiving the offenses of others, and not having enemies any longer. It also marks the beginning of Vietnam's spring. The Vietnamese spend weeks preparing for the festivities.

At the 71st Evac, we, too, spent weeks preparing for Tet. For us, the holiday had an entirely different meaning. We were well aware of the major Tet offensive of 1968 and, although the last Tet hadn't been as bad, we expected all hell to break loose in 1970.

So we used what free time we had to fortify bunkers, order more medical supplies, receive additional weapons training—just in case—and get ourselves mentally ready for what could be the worst period of our lives. One of the medical techs, a skinny short guy, spent the entire month of January in a constant state of anxiety. He had been in Vietnam in '68. The guy never told anyone what he had been through in that Tet offensive, but from the way he acted, we could have guessed. His fear was contagious. By the third week of the month, everybody was jumpy.

Along with the fear and tension that came from anticipating Tet, I had to contend with the increasing harassment from the lifers. I was put on the worst cases and it seemed like someone was constantly looking over my shoulder. No matter what I did, there was always a lifer around to tell me I was wrong. But I wasn't about to crack. Every time one of our enlisted men came to me with a problem, I fought for him. And when I realized that my own certification paperwork could be delayed indefinitely, I filed another inspector general complaint, this one on my own behalf. I was making the lifers furious.

And they were making me a nervous wreck. I was having frequent bouts of indigestion now, and was forever pouring antacids down my throat.

I desperately needed a break. Fortunately, the Tet Offensive of 1970 never materialized. It was a routine week, with casualties slightly fewer than they had been in recent weeks.

My R&R had been approved for the week after Tet—I was going to Hong Kong.

On January twenty-seventh, I was told to report to headquarters. Figuring it was to be one more dig from the lifers, I was prepared to be tough and ignore them once more. I was not prepared for the hint of kindness in their faces.

I was greeted by the chief nurse, who introduced me to a strange woman in civilian clothes. She had a Red Cross armband on her right sleeve. My heart sank as I waited for whatever bad news she was bringing.

"I'm sorry to have to tell you this, Lieutenant Van Devanter. Your cousin, Sergeant Stephen Kramer, died this morning. He was—"

"No," I shouted. "He didn't die! He DEROSed at Christmas! He's home! He's back in the world! I don't believe you! I *won't* believe you! Somebody get me a phone and I'll just call home and they'll set you straight."

I was blindly furious that these assholes could make such a stupid mistake. Wasn't there enough death around without them inventing it?

"It's true, Lieutenant. I'm so sorry. When he was on the plane going back to the States, he became ill. He was put off the plane in Japan and hospitalized there. He had malaria and blackwater fever."

I was growing number and colder by the second, and kept losing parts of what this stranger was saying.

"... evaced back to San Francisco after several weeks in Japan ... comatose on the flight ... malarial encephalitis ... died this morning ... parents with him ..."

I listened no more. It was the last straw. Vietnam sucked so bad it could suck you back down out of the sky. It could suck you all the way back from the world. It was hopeless. You could DEROS, but you could never leave. It was in our very blood, eating away at us, and it would always be there.

Frozen, I spoke to the chief nurse.

"I want a compassionate leave to go home for the funeral."

"I'm afraid that won't be possible, Lieutenant," she replied. "It's not a close enough relation."

If I hadn't turned on my heels wordlessly and stormed out of there at that moment, I don't know what would have happened. I was blinded by white-hot rage. Rage at the war, at Vietnam, at the diseases, at the death and destruction, at the fucking goddamned lifers who wouldn't let me out for Steve's funeral, and yes, I even felt rage at Steve. How could he have fucking died and destroyed my belief that we could ever leave this green slime?

I wanted to scream, to kill someone. Instead, I closed the wall tighter around me. I wouldn't feel anything.

I wrote a letter to Aunt Ginnie and Uncle George and the kids, saying only that I was sorry about Steve. And then I filed his death away with all of my other memories of the year.

15

Vietnam Sucks

I had waited nine months before taking my R&R so I could go on that five-day vacation to Hong Kong with Jack. He became eligible in February.

Dreaming about R&R had helped to keep me sane during the toughest of times. I had sent away for all the tourist information I could get. During our free moments, Jack and I would pore over the pamphlets and talk about all the things we were going to do and see. It would be a perfect vacation. I wanted to see a Chinese opera and ride on a Chinese junk. I anticipated shopping in the open-air night market at Temple Street in Kowloon. And walking along Bowen Road to see the famous Lovers' Stone. And exploring the antique shops on Hollywood Road. And seeing the horse races at Happy Valley. And visiting the Hong Kong Museum of Art. And making some purchases at the Jade Market on Canton Road. But more than anything, I just wanted to get the hell out of Vietnam.

Unfortunately, that proved to be more difficult than I had imagined. For starters, when Jack was not in an operating room, he tended to be achingly slow in whatever he did. He was an extremely difficult person to get moving and had already driven me to frustration more than once. On the day we were to leave Pleiku, I was ready at least three hours before the helicopter was scheduled to depart for Saigon. Jack didn't even begin packing until a half-hour before takeoff and I had to do most of it for him.

"Stop farting around, Jack."

"I'm not farting around. Besides, we've got plenty of time."

"We'll miss our chopper."

"No, we won't."

We missed the flight. I was fuming as we waited on the airfield for another ride to Saigon. I threw some of my most vicious abuse at him and even threatened to literally kill him if he made us miss the connection between Saigon and Hong Kong. I don't think I ever meant anything as much in my entire life.

Two hours later, we hitched a ride with a Chinook that was carrying bodies on the first leg of their return to the cemeteries back in the world. The smell wasn't very pleasant, but I was willing to put up with anything to get away from Pleiku.

We stowed our baggage alongside the corpses and tried to make conversation with the crew chief, in spite of the deafening sounds of the rotor blades. "Ain't nobody ever gets out of this hole," he said. "Vietnam sucks so bad it sucks Freedom Birds right out of the sky. And even if you make it back to the world, you find out the war's already sucked out your brains and your heart."

"I know," I said.

We reached Tan Son Nhut Airport fifteen minutes before our scheduled departure. As soon as the chopper landed, I shouted for Jack to grab his suitcase and run with me. He walked as if in a daze and when we were halfway to the terminal, his suitcase popped open, emptying its contents on the runway. I turned back to help him, but he refused to be hurried. Every piece of clothing had to be refolded and placed in the suitcase properly. It drove me crazy. I became more and more annoyed. I called him every name I could think of. Finally, I grabbed his hand and dragged him after me.

When we got to the terminal, I asked directions three times. We were sent twice to the wrong gate.

At last, we found the correct gate. We were too late. The flight was already rolling down the runway. I dropped my suitcase and sat on it.

"There'll be another flight in the morning," Jack said calmly.

"You son of a bitch," I replied. "I hate you, you bastard." The thought of spending another night in Vietnam was more than I could stand.

But I had no choice.

Furious, I left Jack to his own resources, and I stayed with an old friend from nursing school days, Maureen Donovan, who was stationed at the 3rd Field Hospital in Saigon. After Maureen and I caught up on some old times, she took me to a party at a nearby officers club. I tried to celebrate as if I were really on R&R, attempting to fool myself into believing that I was already out of Vietnam.

By the time Jack and I got on the next plane to Hong Kong in the morning, I was almost at the point of punching him.

When we reached our destination, I didn't want to look at him anymore. I only wanted to get out of my grungy fatigues and into a bathtub. We stayed in separate rooms, and as soon as I entered mine, I called room service to order a double martini on the rocks with a twist of lemon. I stripped off my clothes and started filling the tub. At Christmas we had got stockings from the Red Cross with the silliest things in them. One of the items was a bottle of bubble bath, which was about as useful in Vietnam as pimples. I doubt that there were more than two or three tubs in that entire country. But now, in Hong Kong, I was finally able to use the bubble bath.

I poured half the bottle into the tub and let the bubbles pile so high that they spilled over the side. Then I lowered myself into the boiling water. I felt my tensions draining away.

Ten minutes later, the bellhop knocked at the door with the martini. There was no way I was going to get out of that tub. If possible, I would have spent my entire life in the water under all those bubbles. I shouted for him to come in and he brought the drink into the bathroom. I signed the check, giving him a ten-dollar tip.

During the next three hours, all I did was lie in the water, drink myself into a stupor, and once in a while reach over to flush the john to see if it still worked. Every so often, I would empty half the tub and fill it again with more bubbles and boiling water. I wasn't quite convinced that the running water and flushing toilet were real. They could have been figments of my imagination. Every time I turned the faucet and felt the hot water I giggled. HOT WATER! When the toilet flushed, I laughed out loud.

Later, I tried to scrub away all the traces of Pleiku, feeling like Lady Macbeth, except that there was no visible spot on my hand; it had already penetrated my skin and was on my soul. Of that, I was certain. As hard as I tried, I knew I could not get rid of Vietnam.

In the early evening, Jack called with an apology and a dinner invitation. Through the meal, I struggled to maintain a civilized demeanor. Ours was an uneasy truce.

Later, I walked through the streets with him and almost relaxed. Perhaps a couple more candlelight dinners would have eliminated most of the hostilities that I felt toward him. But not that night. When we got back to the hotel, I wanted to be alone.

Jack had different ideas. While saying good night, he eased his way into the room and then maneuvered me into a position so I was standing with the backs of my legs against the bed. I tried to be nice and tell him that I had no desire to make love with him that night, that I desperately needed to be alone, and that maybe I would feel differently if he just gave me some time.

He put his arms around me and kissed me. At first I was so tired and frustrated and depressed that I was going to let him stay for awhile.

Then the anger overtook me and I exploded. I punched Jack and scratched at his eyes. He slapped my face. I spit at him. He pulled my hair and spit back. Then I kicked him, with all my might, in the stomach. "This is *my room*!" I screamed. "And *my body!* Get the fuck out of my room or I swear I'll kill you."

"Fuck you," he said.

"Jack. Leave. Please!"

He stared at me for a long moment and then left, muttering to himself, "You bitch."

When he was gone, I ordered a couple more martinis and sat in a chair by the window, drinking and crying. I'd had it with Jack, and with Pleiku, and with the war, and with the harassment, and with trying to turn bloody pieces of meat back into people. I'd had it with my whole life. I decided then that as soon as I returned to Vietnam, I would do anything in my power to get transferred away from Pleiku.

Jack called my room and apologized four times.

I hung up the first two times. The third time, I told him to leave me alone. The fourth time he said that he loved me and didn't want to spend his life without me. I told him I'd have to think about that for a while.

During my entire R&R, I didn't go out more than a few times, for some civilian clothes and for some meals. The rest of the time, I sat alone in my room, getting drunk and thinking about Vietnam. Whenever I tried to sleep, I would see Gene and Steve and all the faces of the nameless kids who had died, especially one—a bloody mess of macerated flesh and bone. And along with that face, I would see the inscription on the back of a prom picture: *Gene and Katie, May 1968*.

Why?

I went back to Vietnam at the end of the week, more tired than I had been when I left. As soon as I reached the 71st Evac, I filed for the transfer. It made the lifers happy.

16

Short-Timers

At least five companies were tangling with the NVA at different locations throughout Pleiku Province and all of them were getting trounced. We couldn't empty the dust-off choppers quickly enough. I had taken the last litter out of a Huey and was heading back to the ER when another, billowing smoke, came in low and fast, cutting in front of three choppers that were already stacked up waiting to use the landing pad. As soon as it touched down, everybody who wasn't already occupied scrambled. Hospital personnel and the crew chief off-loaded the wounded while the pilot shut the engines down and carried his copilot to safety. The copilot had been shot in the stomach and through both legs. The pilot also had a couple of wounds, but both of his were in his left shoulder. Everyone bolted away from the chopper as quickly as possible, trying to get a safe distance before it blew. The other choppers headed over to the Air Force compound to unload their patients safely.

Flames shot out from the engine. They were working their way back along the fuel lines to the gas tank. It was only a matter of time. Coretta had what she thought was the last man. She swiftly wheeled him toward the ER, until she heard a loud plaintive moan come from the fiery bird. Everyone else, except the helicopter crew chief, was at least a hundred meters away and sprinting farther by the second.

"That's Jackson," Coretta's casualty said. "He's still in the chopper."

"We've got one more," Coretta yelled to the few free people who were maintaining a safe distance. No one made a move toward the

Huey. Even the crew chief was fleeing the burning wreck without any thought for Jackson. He was practically a blur as he passed Coretta.

"Wait," she shouted. "You forgot one."

The crew chief, feeling safe at this distance, stopped. "He's gonna die anyway," he said.

"The hell he is!" Frustrated, Coretta yelled for someone to take her other casualty to the emergency room. Then she headed back to the chopper.

The crew chief stopped her. "Are you nuts, Lieutenant? It's gonna go up any second. You'll get killed!"

Ignoring him, Coretta returned to the burning helicopter, climbed inside, and dragged Jackson to the door.

"Crazy broad," the crew chief shouted. "You're gonna die."

She tried to lift Jackson from the litter so she could throw him over her shoulders. He was too heavy. She couldn't do it alone.

"Coretta, get away from there," someone cried out.

"Forget about him," the crew chief screamed.

The fire was inches from the fuel tank. It was now only a matter of seconds. The flames rose higher. Black smoke engulfed the helicopter. Coretta wasn't about to give up.

"Stupid!" the crew chief yelled. Yet as he said it he was sprinting toward the chopper. He grabbed Jackson's hands and ordered Coretta to help him throw the guy over his shoulder.

Coretta and the crew chief heaved at the same time. In a split second, they were running back toward the emergency room, accompanied by the cheers of those who watched from a distance.

Then it happened—the chopper blasted into pieces with such force that the concussion shook the walls of the surgical-T.

Neither the crew chief nor Coretta was seriously hurt. And Jackson was on the operating table within ten minutes. They said the odds weren't good, but a thoracic surgeon spent six hours rebuilding the young soldier's chest.

Jackson lived.

The head nurse in the ER put Coretta in for a Bronze Star with "V" device for valor. When it came a month later, it was missing the "V" device. The head nurse was furious and demanded to know what had happened. She was told by the C.O. that they didn't award things like that to nurses. Livid, the head nurse threatened to file a complaint.

"Don't bother; it's not worth it," Coretta told her. "It don't mean nothin'."

As we approached our DEROS—Date of Expected Return from Overseas—we were referred to as short-timers or simply called short. Like those who had ribbed me when I arrived in-country, labeling me an FNG and a turtle, I too played the part of the old veteran. "I'm so short," I would say, "I have to stand on a ladder to tie my bootlaces." I began talking a lot more about what I would do when I got back to the world. One of the first things would be to have a McDonald's hamburger. Then I would buy a brand-new yellow MG. Filled with anticipation, I sent my family a mimeographed letter that was circulating throughout Pleiku:

> TO WHOM IT MAY CONCERN:
> The above-named individual is very shortly returning to the WORLD after spending one year in the combat zone of Vietnam. In order that you may be adequately prepared to communicate with the named individual, it is highly suggested you thoroughly read and digest the following:
>
> Her language will be totally Army-oriented. Please smile appropriately when she utters such terms as latrine, hooch, flak jacket, boonies, grunt, DEROS, Victor Charlie, incoming, Medcap, roger that, and negative.
>
> You must realize she has worn combat boots and fatigues for a year. Please gently remind her of correct ladylike manners. Please do not get hysterical if she continually throws her feet up on the furniture or on the walls.
>
> The first few times she should ride in a vehicle, please remind her to close the car door. Jeeps do not have doors. Do not allow her to throw her feet up on the dashboard.
>
> If she should ask you which unit you are with, or when your DEROS date is, make something up.
>
> If she should turn the shower on and then let the water run for thirty minutes, don't yell about the water bill. She is merely waiting for the water to warm up. When she discovers hot water is a standard item in your house, don't be surprised if she insists everyone take a shower before the hot water system breaks down.
>
> If she insists on putting blankets, flashlights, books, helmet, and flak jacket under her bed, please do not remove these items

until she is thoroughly convinced incoming rockets and mortars are not likely in your neighborhood.

Please be polite as possible when she throws her dirty clothes out in the hall. Please maintain your sense of humor when she calls you "Mama San."

She may spend hours on the phone. Be patient—she is just amazed with its quality and consistency.

Never, under any circumstances, mention the word HELICOPTER.

Please allow her to open the refrigerator at least twenty-six times a day. If she insists on standing in line for meals, gently guide her toward the table. Assure her she does not have to sign for meals.

Her language will be extremely FOUL. She has lived in a world of GIs for a year. Have patience, and if that doesn't work, sign her up for a convent. It is advisable not to let her mingle with relatives or friends for several days.

If you have any green objects in the house, remove them. Never wear any green clothes in her presence.

Never serve meals on a tray of any type. A plate will bring her total happiness.

If she should run around the house half nude, remind her she is back in civilization.

Do not allow her to go shopping alone. She is accustomed to the small PX. She may well buy six bottles of shampoo, twelve bars of soap, and four toothbrushes because you can never tell when the PX will be resupplied.

And NEVER make any loud, sudden noises unless you are prepared to pick her up off the floor.

IN SHORT, THIS KID IS COMING HOME!!!!

"The kid" still had three months to do before DEROS and the last couple of weeks at the 71st Evac were tension-filled, but the end was definitely in sight.

Shortly after I filed my request for a transfer, I was besieged by some of the enlisted techs, who pleaded with me not to leave Pleiku. With me gone, they argued, who would fight for them? It took a great deal of convincing, but I decided to stay. However, when I tried to retrieve my transfer request, I was stopped by the hospital's chief nurse. "No, you don't," she said firmly. "We've been waiting for an excuse to get rid of you, Van Devanter. As far as I'm concerned, you're gone."

I expected to be transferred to some outpost that would be the Vietnamese equivalent of Siberia. Instead, I was ordered to the 67th Evac Hospital in Qui Nhon.

A few days before my move, I had an accident that would keep me out of the OR for at least six weeks: I electrocuted myself. It all started when the lights in FUB-1 went out. We were constantly blowing fuses, so I went to the bathroom to check the fuse box that was on the wall. Because the shower never drained properly, there was always a puddle of water in the middle of the room, right under the box. When I reached up with my middle finger to open the metal door, the current shot through me and I was frozen to the door. My whole body vibrated. I grabbed my right shirt-sleeve with my left hand, and pulled for all I was worth. When I came loose I felt myself thrown to the floor of the shower. When I had caught my breath, and my terror had ebbed, I looked at my hand. My finger was badly burned, and it quickly began swelling.

I went to the ER and got a tetanus shot and one of the surgeons did an incision and drainage of the finger. Unfortunately, it became infected and the infection spread all the way to my elbow within a couple of days. I had to have another I&D. By the time I left Pleiku, my hand was in a cast with the middle finger extended. It seemed an appropriate gesture with which to say good-bye to the lifers who ran the 71st Evac.

For my first six weeks in Qui Nhon, I worked on the medical wards because my infection made me dangerous to surgical patients. We had sick kids and dying kids. There were strange diseases like plague, malaria, blackwater fever, and cholera. A lot of guys were drug overdoses. And there were plenty of FUOs—fevers of unknown origin. People would come in with temperatures of 105 or 106 and we'd never find out what was wrong with them. We'd do cultures and they'd come back negative. All we could do was give supportive care until the fever went down or the patient died.

One patient, on ward eleven, had an FUO that lasted almost three weeks. He had all kinds of catheters and IVs either draining into him or draining out of him. He also had dysentery so bad that it smelled up the entire ward. We had to change his bed and clean up shit five or six times each day. Sometimes he would be calling people who weren't there and other times he would be a million miles away. His brain was fried. He was the most pathetic case I saw in my time at Qui Nhon and he reminded me of Steve. I guessed he must have been somewhat like this case. And I saw others who were in similar circumstances.

However, after Pleiku, this assignment was a piece of cake. Of course we still had patients dying and others coming in who were blown to pieces; there were occasional pushes; the war continued. But we mostly worked in regular twelve-hour shifts and had some free time. Best of all was that I actually felt safe at the 67th Evac.

When I first arrived, I was shocked to find two-story buildings on the compound. It was considered stupid to build anything more than one story high in most of Vietnam because when rockets exploded, they sent shrapnel upward. If it were possible, the people in Pleiku would have had every building well below ground level. But at Qui Nhon, two-story buildings made sense. Why? Because there hadn't been many rocket attacks in the years the hospital had been there. That continued almost throughout my stay.

I lived in quarters that were part of a quadrangle built around a grassy area. If you looked out my door, you could almost forget you were in Vietnam. Doctors and nurses who were not on duty would be lying in the sun or sitting in beach chairs. There was an unreal quality about the entire compound, as if it had been lifted whole from a stateside post and plopped in a vacation area on the South China Sea.

I made plenty of friends at Qui Nhon. We had regular parties, held picnics on an island a few miles from the mainland, and we worked well together. But the intensity I had known in Pleiku was missing. Our parties were fun, but the work wasn't as difficult or intense, and the friendships weren't as close as they had been at the 71st Evac. Perhaps it was the lack of danger. When the threat of death wasn't constant, people didn't seem to need each other as much. Perhaps I was just distancing myself as my time grew shorter.

Although I missed the intensity, I appreciated a lot of other things about the 67th Evac. The lifers here were not as petty as the ones who ran the 71st Evac, and they put patient care before all else. The hospital was as relaxed as a stateside civilian facility. We weren't expected to spend time on military eyewash but merely to heal the sick and wounded.

Soon after I was transferred, Jack was sent from Pleiku to an assignment near the DMZ, to work under conditions that were more primitive than even those at the 71st Evac. Strangely enough, whatever insane tie there was between us remained, in spite of the geographical separation. We began corresponding and spoke regularly of love and commitment. When we got days off, we hitched chopper rides to visit each other. When Jack came to visit me, he joked that he had finally arrived in heaven and he asked to be introduced to God. When I visited him, I was sure I had made it all the way to hell. It was so hot near the DMZ that you felt like you couldn't breathe. One time I looked at a thermometer and it registered 122 degrees in the shade. I told Jack that thermometers should be outlawed on his compound because they only made people feel worse.

The units in this area were always taking heavy casualties and his hospital usually seemed to be in the middle of a push. When my hand had healed, I would spend my days off working in surgery at Jack's hospital so we could be together. The head nurse there never objected. She could always use an extra pair of good hands.

But when the work stopped, Jack and I got on each other's nerves. There were no more blow-ups like the one in Hong Kong, yet after an initial period of politeness, we resumed our bickering over insignificant things. Jack was much easier to love from a distance. He probably would have expressed the same sentiments about me.

Surprisingly, the thing I liked best about my limited time at Qui Nhon was the Medcap work we did at the leper colony. I would visit the place at least once a week with Michael Carlisle, an eye surgeon from the 67th Evac. Together, we'd give routine medical care and perform surgery when necessary. The people were very appreciative, and I enjoyed helping them. However, my first exposure to the lepers was a bit unsettling. There were people with deformed faces, others with hideous growths all over their bodies, some who were missing fingers or toes, and still others who were blind. It was difficult, initially, to look at them without being repulsed. But I learned to see beyond their disfigurements so I could treat them as people. And as crazy as it might sound, the leprosarium was the only place in-country where you could find total peace. That was partly because the colony was geographically isolated; it was in a little valley, surrounded on three sides by mountains and on the fourth by the South China Sea. But mostly, it was because all Vietnamese—V.C., NVA, and ARVNs—were afraid of the lepers. Their fear kept the war on the other side of the mountains.

Run by an order of French nuns, the Lep was beautifully maintained and extremely clean. The architecture was French colonial and the buildings boasted such luxuries as tile floors, louvered windows, and covered walkways. Although the medical supplies were minimal, these women gave the best of care. Their wards were well organized and sanitary, not at all like the filthy, overcrowded ones in the province hospitals I worked at in Pleiku. Here, each patient had a clean bed with clean sheets and regular meals.

Michael had got involved with the lepers earlier that year when he was asked to do an eye operation at the colony. It seemed that there were a lot of problems with the disease eating away the skin and the eyes. When he finished his first case, Michael took a look around and decided he could be of some help to others. He kept coming back. Unfortunately, by the time he got to see many patients, they were too far gone.

It was Michael who taught me that leprosy need not be the horrible disease that many people imagine. He claimed that the biggest problem was that leprosy had got poor press. There was no denying its horrifying results, but if leprosy was treated properly in its early stages, the prognosis was good and the disease rarely fatal.

But people almost never came for treatment in the early stages. The lepers felt that when they went to the colony, it was the end of the line. Moving to the leprosarium meant that a person was in permanent exile. Most of them didn't want to leave their families unless they were forced. Ironically, the disease is not very contagious and the isolation wasn't always necessary. While it is possible to transmit leprosy from one person to another, nine out of ten people have a natural immunity to the virus and the others would require continuous close contact over a long period of time before they could catch it. Some lepers brought their families with them and there were plenty of healthy, active people living in the colony.

Although the Lep was considered safe, to get there we had to drive over unsecured roads. We were required to have guards for protection and it was a job for which the enlisted guys would compete. For them, it meant a day off. While we worked in the OR or on the wards, they would lie on the beach and drink beer. We would finish by early afternoon. Following a sumptuous French meal specially prepared by the nuns, we would spend the remainder of our day swimming or sunbathing. Once we brought along an LFRB—"little fucking rubber boat"—but the waves were so strong that we were unable to launch it properly.

Sometimes, while lying on that beach, I would imagine myself on another beach, the one in Ocean City, New Jersey, and I'd think about what it was like back in the world before all this began. I felt as if I had aged 100 years since the summer after nursing school.

But it wouldn't be long before I could be back on the beach in Ocean City if I wanted. I was counting the days until I stepped on my Freedom Bird. As the number got lower I found home consuming my thoughts. Every day I colored in another space on my short timer's calendar, and the outline of its Snoopy character became more multicolored from my colored pencils.

> Hi, Lynda, this is Dad. My little girl's coming home soon. I can't wait. I don't guess we'll be sending too many more of these tapes back and forth, so I won't be running at the mouth much longer. I can't wait until you get home. We all miss you very much. This is your loving daddy signing off. Good night, Lynda.

"I am going to spend every cent I made this year," Mickie said.

"Me, too," I replied. "We'll have one huge shopping spree."

"I don't care what we do," Coretta said. "As long as we don't see any casualties for a whole week."

Near the end of our tours, the three of us wangled five days of leave and we were determined to have an exotic vacation—*without men*—before we had to return to the world. We chose Bangkok, Thailand. It was a trip that had been in the planning for months, starting while I was still at the 71st Evac. With Mickie and Coretta going back to the world in a matter of weeks, and me returning just after them this would be our last chance to sample some good times in an Asian country that wasn't at war.

Everything went perfectly. The flight connections were on time; the official briefings in Bangkok were short—you're a representative of your government, don't get into trouble, and be ready to go back to Vietnam in five days—and the hotel was perfect.

We got a room in a place that was off the beaten track, a few miles from the business district. From our window, we could see farmers working in rice fields and children playing happily along the sides of the road. There were no closets; instead we had oversized teak wardrobes which were positioned between the beds to allow each person some privacy. It was a dorm-style atmosphere, but the place had one feature that was an absolute requirement—a bathtub. It was an old deep clawfoot tub that stood in the center of the bathroom, a perfect tub for soaking.

We drew lots to see who would get to take the first bath. I won. I filled it with boiling water and bubbles that rose higher than my head, sitting in the luxurious warmth until Coretta and Mickie got tired of waiting and nearly broke the door down to get me out.

We had decided to share a room so we could save money to buy more souvenirs. Like most tourists, we spent the bulk of our time shopping. The biggest decision we had to make was whether to buy pure bronze or nickel-plated flatware. Nickel-plated doesn't tarnish. I was being pure: I decided on bronze. Years later, after hundreds of polishings, I would come to regret that mistake.

I bought presents for everyone in the family: a good camera for my father, jewelry for Sue, Jean, and Nancy, pearls for me, and a princess ring made out of nine different precious stones for my mother. I wanted something special for Mary, so I found a jewelry maker and designed a ring that had an emerald set diagonally between two diamonds. It took him only three days to have it ready.

For myself, I bought clothes. I'm the kind of person who, when I see something I like, usually decides to buy more than one. I figure if I like something, I can't go wrong with a half-dozen. That's exactly the number of sundresses I had made from the same pattern. I found the style in a tailor's window as I was walking through Bangkok. It had an empire waist with a low-cut top and a flap of material over the front that gave it a wrap-around effect. I fell in love with it and ordered four in cotton and two in Thai silk.

Unfortunately, the hemlines were very short. I never stopped to think that the styles might change. I had expected to be wearing the sundresses for the next five years, at least.

When we weren't shopping, we were visiting all the tourist sites and telling ourselves that we were getting a quick education in the culture of Thailand. We went to TIMland—Thailand in Miniature—where we saw hundreds of exhibits and demonstrations of the life lived by the Thais. The place was a Thai version of Disneyland and it was probably designed specifically for the GIs on R&R who wanted a minimum of culture with their girl chasing. There was Thai boxing, a sport that involves the hands as well as the feet; cockfighting; pottery-making; doll-making; and school children singing songs. We watched some women in brightly colored costumes as they did a very stylized dance called "Dance of the Fingernails," a Thai folk custom for which some women grew nails that were at least three or four inches longer than the norm. The three of us rode on elephants, and Mickie and I had our pictures taken with boa constrictors around our necks. Coretta passed on that one; "Ain't no snake gonna wrap itself around my gizzard," she said.

Whenever we took a tour, we were always one step behind the crowds, which made the time more enjoyable and less harried than is the case with most tours. We traveled daily by boat and saw a life that was centered on the canals. As we floated downstream, we viewed shacks built over the water and people using the waterway for dozens of purposes. The canal was the highway for some to get to work. For others, it was the way their grocery stores came to them, the merchants pushing long skinny boats along with long poles. Most surprising was to find people in various stages of undress using the canal as their bathroom. It was not unusual to see one man defecating in the water and, a few feet away, a woman washing her hair in that same water.

The canals also held the floating markets, which were collections of boats and a few stationary buildings on the edge of the water. Although the floating markets had started out to serve the needs of the Thais, by the time we saw them, they were far more tourist-oriented. Inside, each shop looked similar to millions of other tourist shops around the world. They sold items like spoons, postcards, and plastic bags that had printed on them, in English: "Souvenir of Bangkok."

The most interesting part of the vacation was the tour of the various temples around the city. We visited the Temple of the Emerald Buddha, the most famous in Thailand, which is located near the Grand Palace, the former residence of the King of Siam. The actual Emerald Buddha was a mere thirty-one inches high. It had been carved from translucent emerald-colored jasper and sat on a high, elaborately decorated altar.

We also saw the Temple of the Golden Buddha, which houses a 25,000-pound statue of gold that had been cast in the thirteenth century; the Temple of the Reclining Buddha, which contained a resting statue that was forty-six meters long with mother of pearl at the feet; and the Temple of the Great Relic, which was on the same site as one of the largest Buddhist universities in the country.

My favorite was the Temple of Dawn, which was on the west bank of the Chao Phraya River, the River of Kings. Sometimes referred to as the "Teacup Temple," the Temple of Dawn was inlaid with millions of pieces of Chinese porcelain and, according to legend, had been built by immigrants who wanted to thank Buddha for ensuring their safe passage by boat from China through storms and other hazards. The temple was a tribute to survival over adversity. As I walked through it, I could appreciate the emotion that had gone into building the structure. I identified closely with those men and women who had survived. I, too, was a survivor. Like them I had triumphed —nearly a year of death and destruction would soon be over for me. It was merely a matter of weeks, now.

On the last day of our vacation, we were at the hotel's front desk paying our bill when we saw the huge banner headline on one of the English language newspapers: "U.S. INVADES CAMBODIA." At first, we thought it was somewhat humorous to be reading "the latest news." After all, we had spent the past year treating American soldiers who had been wounded while they were over the fence. For us, there was nothing newsworthy about soldiers in Cambodia.

Then Coretta read the first few paragraphs. "It says we're sanitizing the sanctuaries," she said. "If Uncle Sam's putting out a story like this, things in Cambodia must be real bad. But it does say that American casualties are minimal. I hardly believe anything I read in the papers, but I hope they're right.''

When we arrived in Saigon, we immediately hitched a ride on a chopper heading for Pleiku. I was going to hitch another chopper from Pleiku to Qui Nhon. But when we descended toward the helipad at the 71st Evac to let off Coretta and Mickie, we saw a line of body bags that seemed as long as a football field, some stacked two and three deep. There were so many wounded that some wouldn't fit in the emergency room. At least fifty were on litters on the ground outside the surgical-T.

I didn't get the next chopper to Qui Nhon. Instead, some calls were made and I stayed in the 71st Evac's operating room for the next forty-eight hours. When I left, everyone was still working at the same pace.

Some weeks later in Qui Nhon, I handled my final case in Vietnam. The soldier had only a couple of small frag wounds of the left forearm and we did him under regional anesthesia. He was awake during the operation.

''You, my friend, are my DEROS patient,'' I said proudly. ''My Freedom Bird is leaving tomorrow.''

''Tell me you're the last person *I* am going to see in Vietnam,'' he said. ''Then you'll catch my interest.''

When DEROS day arrived, I was probably more nervous than I had ever been. I couldn't hold down any breakfast and my hands were shaking. I also had a nasty hangover from the night before, when everybody from the OR had thrown me a DEROS party. I'm not sure what I was more afraid of—going home, or getting on the Freedom Bird.

There was a rumor going around that the Viet Cong snipers had a nasty habit of shooting Americans as they walked up the ramp to their Freedom Birds. Whether it was true or not was irrelevant. I believed it. And so did everyone else in Vietnam.

But I tried to block the worries from my mind. I spent the helicopter ride from Qui Nhon to Saigon forcing myself to think about all the good times that awaited me back in the world. I was going home. My year was over.

We waited in Saigon for a few hours while papers were processed and GIs were assigned to flights. I looked around to see if I could recognize anyone, perhaps someone who had come over with me a year ago. They all looked like strangers. I wondered about the two men who had sat with me on that trip—the young draftee out of college and the lifer sergeant. Did they make it? I would never know.

When I got on the plane, I was, once again, the only woman. Some guys were whispering to each other, but mostly, the plane was filled with silence. I don't think there was a soul on that flight who wasn't sure that we were going to be shot down before we could get away from Vietnam. *Vietnam sucks so bad, it sucks Freedom Birds right out of the sky.*

The stewardesses welcomed us and checked to see that our seat belts were fastened. They seemed younger than the ones who had brought us here a year ago. Were they really younger? Or were we older? As we taxied down the runway, the voice of the captain came over the intercom. "Men, I want to welcome you to your freedom flight. It's all over now. You can say good-bye to the land of Viet Cong. So just relax and leave the driving to us. We'll be home before you know it."

"Maybe," my seatmate, a tired sergeant said. "But we're not out of Vietnam until we clear the airspace. I can still feel the suction."

As the jet took off, I was filled with the most exhilarating sensation of my life. It was a feeling of lightness, like the weight of a million years had been suddenly lifted from my shoulders. And there wasn't anybody on that plane who didn't experience that rush. Yet, we were still silent. Later, when the pilot told us we were officially out of Vietnam airspace, there was a collective sigh of relief.

"Did we make it?" someone in the front yelled.

"Yes!" we all shouted in unison.

"Does it suck?"

"Hell, yes!"

"Is it going to suck us back?" he screamed.

"Hell, no!" we answered.

"Can you feel it?"

"No!"

"Can you hear it?"

"No!"

"What can't you hear?"

"Vietnam."

"What does Vietnam do?"

"Vietnam sucks!!!" We cried out with one voice. Then everybody cheered at the top of their lungs. There was laughter and hugging and tears in spite of our lack of familiarity with each other. Colonels and sergeants and privates all joined in. We were the lucky ones. We had made it out alive.

But as soon as we realized we were safe, there was a vague uneasiness that came over us. We wondered what we would face back in the real world. Would it be the same as we had imagined? Would we be able to adjust? Would our friends and families still know us? Still love us? Or had we changed too much? I wondered if what happened to Steve would happen to me. I grew nervous as we passed over Japan.

However, the uneasiness was fueled by something more important than the anticipation of facing the world again. We were all feeling guilty and sad. We had left friends in Vietnam. Each person on that plane suspected in some part of his or her heart, that we all should have stayed behind to help them survive.

Now that we were gone, who would look out for our friends?

17

Welcome Home, Asshole!

Soldier, rest! thy warfare o'er,
Sleep the sleep that knows not breaking,
Dream of battled fields no more,
Days of danger, nights of waking.
—SIR WALTER SCOTT

When the soldiers of World War II came home, they were met by brass bands, ticker-tape parades, and people so thankful for their service that even those who had never heard a shot fired in anger were treated with respect. It was a time when words like honor, glory, and duty held some value, a time when a returning GI was viewed with esteem so high it bordered on awe. To be a veteran was to be seen as a person of courage, a champion of democracy, an ideal against which all citizens could measure themselves. If you had answered your country's call, you were a hero. And in those days, heroes were plentiful.

But somewhere between 1945 and 1970, words like bravery, sacrifice, and valor had gone out of vogue. When I returned to my country in June of 1970, I began to learn a very bitter lesson. The values with which I had been raised had changed; in the eyes of most Americans, the military services had no more heroes, merely babykillers, misfits, and fools. I was certain that I was neither a babykiller nor a misfit. Maybe I was a fool.

There are those among the poets, philosophers, and psychologists who believe that the root of all unhappiness is unfulfilled expectation. Many people, they argue, have unrealistic expectations. If you learn not to expect too much, their logic goes, you won't be disappointed. Therefore, you'll be happier. Perhaps they're right. Perhaps if I hadn't expected anything at all when I returned to the States, I would not have been disappointed. Maybe I would have been contented simply to be on American soil. Maybe all of us who arrived at Travis Air Force Base on June 16 had unrealistic expectations.

But we didn't ask for a brass band. We didn't ask for a parade. We didn't even ask for much of a thank you. All we wanted was some transportation to San Francisco International Airport so we could hop connecting flights to get home to our families. We gave the Army a year of our lives, a year with more difficulties than most Americans face in fifty years. The least the Army could have done was to give us a ride.

At Travis we were herded onto buses and driven to the Oakland Army Terminal where they dumped us around 5 A.M. with a "so long, suckers" from the driver and a feeling that we were no more than warm bodies who had outlived their usefulness. Unfortunately, San Francisco International was at least twenty miles away. Since most of us had to get flights from there, wouldn't it have been logical to drop us at the airport? Or was I expecting too much out of the Army when I asked it to be logical?

I checked into commercial buses and taxis, but none were running. There was a transit strike on, and it was nearly impossible to get public transportation of any kind. So I hung one of my suitcases from my left shoulder, hefted my duffel bag onto my right shoulder, grabbed my overnight case with my left hand and my purse with my right, and struggling under the weight, walked out to the highway, where I stuck out my thumb and waited. I was no stranger to hitchiking. It was the only way to get around in Vietnam. Back in 'Nam, I would usually stand on the flight line in my fatigues, combat boots, jungle hat, pigtails, and a smile. Getting a ride there was a cinch. In fact, planes would sometimes reach the end of the runway, then return to offer me a lift.

But hitchhiking in the real world, I was quickly finding out, was nowhere near as easy—especially if you were wearing a uniform. The cars whizzed past me during rush hour, while I patiently waited for a good Samaritan to stop. A few drivers gave me the finger. I tried to ignore them. Some slowed long enough to yell obscenities. One threw a carton of trash and another nearly hit me with a half-empty can of soda. Finally, two guys stopped in a red and yellow Volkswagen bus. The one on the passenger side opened his door. I ran to the car, dragging the duffel bag and other luggage behind me. I was hot, tired, and dirty.

"Going anywhere near the airport?" I asked.

"Sure am," the guy said. He had long brown hair, blue eyes framed by wire-rimmed glasses, and a full curly beard. There were patches on his jeans and a peace sign on his T-shirt. His relaxed, easy smile was deceptive.

I smiled back and lifted my duffel bag to put it inside the van. But the guy slammed the door shut. "We're going past the airport, sucker, but we don't take Army pigs." He spit on me. I was stunned.

"Fuck you, Nazi bitch," the driver yelled. He floored the accelerator and they both laughed uncontrollably as the VW spun its wheels for a few seconds, throwing dirt and stones back at me before it roared away. The drivers of other passing cars also laughed.

I looked down at my chest. On top of my nametag sat a big gob of brownish-colored saliva. I couldn't touch it. I didn't have the energy to wipe it away. Instead, I watched as it ran down my name tag and over a button before it was absorbed into the green material of my uniform.

I wasn't angry, just confused. I wanted to know why. Why would he spit on me? What had I done to him? To either of them? It might have been simple to say I had gone to war and they blamed me for killing innocent people, but didn't they understand that I didn't want this war any more than the most vocal of peace marchers? Didn't they realize that those of us who had seen the war firsthand were probably more antiwar than they were? That we had seen friends suffer and die? That we had seen children destroyed? That we had seen futures crushed?

Were they that naive?

Or were they merely insensitive creeps who used the excuse of my uniform to vent their hostility toward all people?

I waited a few more hours, holding my thumb out until I thought my arm would fall off. After awhile, I stopped watching people as they hurled their insults. I had begun noticing the people who didn't scream as they drove by. I soon realized they all had something in common. It was what I eventually came to refer to as "the look." It was a combination of surprise at seeing a woman in uniform, and hatred for what they asssumed I represented. Most of them never bothered to try to conceal it. "The look" would start around the eyes, as if they were peering right through me. Their faces would harden into stone. I was a pariah, a nonperson so low that they believed they could squash me underfoot; I was as popular as a disease and as untouchable as a piece of shit.

While I stood there alone, I almost wished I was back in 'Nam. At least there you expected some people to hate you. That was a war. But here, in the United States, I guess I wanted everything to be wonderful. I thought that life would be different, that there would be no more pain. No more death. No more sorrow. It was all going to be good again. It had to be good again. I had had enough of fighting, and hatred, and bitterness.

Around 10:30 A.M., when I had given up hope and was sitting on my duffel bag, a passing driver shouted three words that perfectly illustrated my return to the world:

"Welcome home, asshole!"

A few minutes later, an old black man in a beat up '58 Chevy stopped and got out of his car. He walked with a limp and leaned forward as if he couldn't stand straight. His clothes were frayed and his face deeply lined. He ran his bony fingers through his gray-black hair, then shook his head and smiled. "I don't know where you're going, little girl," he said. "But I been by here four times since early morning and you ain't got a ride yet. I can't let you spend your whole life on this road." He was only headed for the other side of Oakland, but he said he'd rather go out of his way than see me stranded. He even carried my duffel bag to the trunk. As we drove south on 101, I didn't say much other than thank you, but my disillusionment was obvious.

"People ain't all bad, little girl," he said. "It's just some folks are crazy mixed up these days. You keep in mind that it's gotta get better, cause it can't get any worse."

There were hundreds of GIs at the San Francisco Airport, waiting to get home. Some had waited for more than twenty-four hours. They had spent the night on benches and on the floor, using old field jackets for blankets and duffel bags for pillows. Some who had tried to save money by flying "Space Available" found themselves bumped. A few walked around in a daze, as if they couldn't believe that they were finally out of Vietnam.

I quickly went to a ladies' room and stripped off my fatigues and jungle boots, for the last time, I realized. I donned my green summer cord uniform, fixed the brass and ribbons, and ran a brush through my hair. I looked down at the pile of dirty fatigues and boots for a second. It almost seemed that they *were* Vietnam. I stuffed them into the duffel bag, yanked it closed, and went out to find the nearest airline with the next flight to D.C.

"Can you hear it?" a corporal asked me while we waited in line to book our flights. On his uniform he had the crossed rifles of the infantry and three rows of ribbons. In his eyes, I could see a lifetime's worth of sadness.

" 'Nam still sucks," I answered. "But I can't hear it anymore."

"Sure you can," he said. "Everybody does. It never stops."

I was one of the lucky ones in San Francisco. I got a seat on a direct flight to Washington that was leaving within an hour. The corporal, who was trying to get to some backwater town in Louisiana, found out he would have to wait until midnight before a seat would be open on something going his way. And with layovers, he wouldn't get home until the next night.

When I called my parents' house to give them my arrival time, I could barely contain my excitement. My mother answered the phone. Her voice cracked when I told her I was coming home.

"I'll make a pan of lasagna," she said.

"I'd like that."

"Lynda, I want you to know . . . " She was fighting tears. I closed my eyes. I could almost see the quiver of her jaw as my mother, who had always been so proper, struggled with her emotions while she tried to get out the words. " . . . I want you to know that . . . that your father and I missed you. We missed you very much."

"I missed you too, Mom."

I had a quick drink in the airport and another on the plane to make me sleep. I was exhausted; hadn't slept in more than twenty-four hours. As we were passing over the Midwest, I began to doze. But before I was able to reach a deep sleep, I saw an image that startled me awake. It was the bloody, blown away face of the young bleeder into whom I had pumped blood six months earlier. *Gene and Katie, May*

1968. He was wearing his tux and dancing with Katie, but his face was all exposed meat and bone. Blood was running like tears down the area that was once his cheeks, and it was drip-drip-dripping onto Katie's exposed shoulder and inching down her back, staining her gown. I tried to warn her that she was ruining her dress, but the words wouldn't come out. Then finally, I made a sound, a low moaning that took every bit of strength I had. Katie turned to look at me. Her face, too, was blown away.

She laughed.

I screamed.

The elderly businessman next to me touched my shoulder. When I opened my eyes, I was drenched with cold sweat and was shaking. He asked the stewardess to bring me a blanket, which I clutched tightly to my chest. It was a few minutes before I realized where I was. By that time, I'm sure they all thought I was crazy.

"It was only a bad dream," I said, still shivering.

Although the nightmares had started early in my tour in Vietnam, they had gotten progressively worse during the last few months, especially after that long fruitless operation on Gene. On the way back from 'Nam, I had spent a few days in Hawaii, partly because I thought this might be my only chance to visit the islands and partly because I wanted to decompress before facing my family. Although the days in Hawaii were enjoyable—as soon as I arrived, I had a McDonald's hamburger, french fries, and a Coke—the nights were pure hell, with the dreams coming one after another, until I was afraid to go to sleep.

I tried drinking myself into oblivion; that was only effective about half the time.

When I had asked Carl about the bad dreams, he had shrugged my questions off. "Of course you'll have nightmares," he said. "Everybody in this hole does. It's part of the price we pay."

"But when will they stop?"

"I don't know. Maybe when you get back to the world."

That was one of the few things about which he was wrong.

I ordered another drink from the stewardess and tried reading a magazine. I couldn't concentrate. My mind kept bouncing back and forth between my life in Vietnam and the world I would face when I got home. I wondered about the soldiers I had worked on: What about the guy who had fallen into the pungi pit last week? Had he survived? And the guy I had saved from the expectant room a few weeks earlier?

Did he make it? Or the chest cases? How many of them lived? Were they in Japan now, or already in graves back in the world?

I worried a lot about Jack. How was he doing up at the DMZ? Had the casualties let up yet? Did he miss me? Would he get through the rest of his tour safely? Or would I get a letter telling me that something had happened? Or if something happened, would anybody in his unit even know enough to send me a letter? Would they find my parents' address in his wallet?

My biggest worries came not from the life I had left behind, but from the life that was ahead of me. I knew that this year had changed me drastically, probably more than I realized. My parents would be meeting an entirely different Lynda than they had said good-bye to only twelve months ago. They told me they loved me and missed me, but would they love me when they got to know me again? Would they even like me? What would I do if they didn't like me? How would I ever fit in?

I tried a couple more drinks to help me forget all the worries, but again the alcohol did no good. I stayed sober and anxious. By the time the pilot announced that we were approaching National Airport in D.C., my hands were shaking, my heart pounding, my palms sweating, and my throat dry. I had a headache that wouldn't quit and a lump in my throat that I thought would choke me to death. I had trouble breathing. It felt as though someone were sitting on my chest.

My parents are waiting. They're on the ground.

The plane began its descent. I gripped the arms of my seat. Sweat beaded up on my forehead and rolled down the side of my face. I grabbed a Kleenex from my purse and wiped it off, my hands shaking the whole time.

As I looked out the window trying to find some familiar landmarks, the pilot's voice came back over the speaker system. "We're in a bit of a traffic jam," he said. "The tower hasn't given us clearance to land yet, so we're going to circle. We'll be in the air another twenty minutes. Relax and enjoy the scenery."

Relax? My stomach was tied in knots. I felt like I would throw up. I wanted to go to the bathroom, but the overhead sign told us to keep our seat belts fastened. I opened a barf bag in case I needed it.

The plane descended lower. A few clouds floated past. They were soft, white, and fluffy, kind of like I had always pictured the floor of heaven. I wiped more sweat from my forehead and squeezed the armrests tighter. My heart was pounding so loudly I thought I might explode. I felt like I was going to pass out.

We came lower and went into a sharp turn. "We're on the final leg of our approach to Washington National," the stewardess said. "Please make sure your seat belts are buckled, seat backs are up, all tray tables in the full upright position, and any carry-on luggage securely stowed under the seat in front of you."

When we broke through a thin layer of clouds, I could see all the landmarks that I had come to know as a child. There was the Washington Monument, where my friends and I had climbed to the top singing folk songs while one of the boys played a guitar; the Capitol, where we had gone with our civics class to listen to the senators and congressmen debate the Civil Rights Act in 1964; the White House, where an embattled and untrustworthy president now resided; and the Pentagon, that enormous sandstone building where generals made decisions that would affect my life and the lives of more than a million others in uniform.

I took a deep breath and felt the tears welling up as the plane's wheels screeched against the runway. The pilot reversed the engines to bring us to a stop. My ears popped from the pressure. *I can't cry,* I told myself out of habit. *I have to be strong.*

Then it hit me that I didn't have to be strong all the time any more, that maybe now I would be able to start relaxing, that now people's lives were no longer dependent on me holding things together. There would be no more calls in the middle of the night. No more helicopters bearing wounded young boys. No more rocket attacks. No more monsoons. No more Viet Cong. No more seventy-two-hour stretches at the operating table. No more trying to turn pieces of meat and bone back into human beings. In a few more minutes, when the plane stopped at the terminal and I walked down the ramp, I would be home.

We taxied off the runway and slowly made our way toward the building. There was another slight delay while we waited for a departing plane to leave our gate. The stewardesses, in their bright, cheery way, welcomed us to Washington, gave us the local time and temperature, and suggested that on our next trip, we fly their airline. I was a tightly wound spring about to snap, and as each moment passed, I got tighter and tighter. It seemed like we'd never get there. By now my heart was racing faster than the speed of sound and my body was shaking uncontrollably. As soon as we came to a stop, I grabbed my carry-on bags and jumped over my seatmate. People in front were moving into the aisle. I pushed past them all.

I wanted to scream with frustration as I waited an interminable length of time for the man outside to hook up the ramp so the stewardess could open the door. I stared at that door, and silently cursed it for being there. It was the last obstacle between me and home. I wanted it moved.

Now!

Suddenly, it was open.

And at the other end of the ramp, I saw two anxious faces.

I broke into a broad smile.

They both smiled at the same time.

Then I laughed.

I heard my mother call first. "Lynda," she said in a special way, pronouncing each syllable slowly and crisply as only she could. Unencumbered happiness was in every tone of her voice.

I burst through the door and ran down the ramp.

Then I heard my father's voice. "My little girl's home," he said.

I couldn't run fast enough. In a moment I was in his arms, laughing and crying as I hugged and kissed my father and mother. I felt the strength from those protective arms and I wanted to melt into them. I wanted somebody to pick me up and hold me like a baby. I didn't ever want to be strong again. I wanted to be somebody's child. My father's child. And my mother's child.

The three of us squeezed each other so tightly it's a wonder we didn't all turn blue. I couldn't stop the tears and neither could my parents. For that moment, I felt loved more than I ever had in my entire life. Finally, I stepped back and looked at them. "You don't know how great you both look," I said.

They laughed. "You look great, too," they said.

After a few more moments, my mother hugged me again. I noticed something about her face. She had been worried. Now, she seemed relieved. "At least they fed you over there," she said. "You've put on a little weight, haven't you, dear?"

There were problems that first day. To start with, my parents and I waited at least a half hour at the baggage claim area—me hugging and kissing them, and laughing and crying while my father kept his eye out for my duffel bag and suitcase. Hundreds of bags from three different flights went past us. None were mine. My father, who had experienced the same predicament a few times in his own travels, led the way to the man at the baggage claim counter. Dad quoted from FAA regulations and spoke with such authority that the counter man was intimidated. But it was to no avail. The man couldn't produce my bags at that moment. They could have been misrouted on any one of the flights leaving San Francisco. He promised to do all that he could—which was probably nothing.

"Look, my daughter just got back from Vietnam. You have all her clothes. She has nothing but this uniform. You've got to help her."

"I'm sorry, sir."

Fortunately, I had carried everyone's presents and a few packets of slides in my shoulder bag and overnight case. I borrowed a pair of Bermuda shorts and a top from my mother so I didn't have to stay in uniform. The style didn't suit me, but I was too heavy to fit into my sisters' clothes.

My mother was pleased with her princess ring; my father immediately began taking pictures with his new camera; my sisters were just as happy with their presents. But the one who seemed most thrilled was Mary. When she opened her small package and looked at the ring, her mouth dropped. "It's absolutely beautiful," she said. "I love it." For the remainder of the evening, she almost constantly stared at the ring, except for a brief time during dinner when I forgot where I was and said, "Mary, pass the fucking salt."

Forks and knives dropped. The room was deathly silent, except for Mary's laugh as she tilted her head and studied me. My mother almost had a coronary.

Mom got up from the table, trying to appear calm, but obviously shaken. "Lynda," she said. "Come with me to the kitchen. I need your help with something."

As I followed her out of the room, suddenly realizing what I had done and feeling sheepish, I overheard my father: "What is so funny, Mary?"

"Didn't you hear her say—"

"Mary!" He cut her off before she could get the offensive word out once more. "I fail to see any humor in the situation."

I got some of the same treatment in the kitchen. "I don't know what kind of language you used in Vietnam," my mother said patiently, "but around this house that word is not to be spoken."

"Yes, ma'am."

When we got back to the dinner table, neither Mary nor I could look at each other or we would have burst out laughing. She went back to eating her lasagna, staring at her ring, and trying to control the urge to howl with amusement.

I hadn't really known Mary very well during the previous years. She was so much younger than I was, and between nursing school and the Army, I had spent the last four years as more of a visitor than a family member. We had exchanged letters a few times during Vietnam, but they were mostly newsy and gave little indication of her personality, except for one, which was written in the fall. It asked me to tone down the "God and country business" in my letters because it was starting to make my sisters "a little nauseous." I found out later that Mary and my other sisters had got involved in the peace movement, but none had told me because they didn't want me to think that they were against me. Although their activities had caused some tension at home, they felt vindicated when my last letters had turned against the war and the people who were running it. "It was nice to learn that you were human and not some patriotic automaton," Mary later said.

I'd always had a special feeling for Mary and I think a lot of it had to do with her attitude toward life. In many ways, she was the family rebel. It's not that she was a bad kid. She never got in trouble with the law or did anything that most people would consider really wrong. But she usually managed to ask questions that most people would have preferred to leave untouched. While we had all taken paths toward more traditional careers—college or nursing school—Mary wanted something that was totally unacceptable in our middle-class world. She was going to be an actress and a singer. They were the same dreams I had held as a small child, but had discarded by adolescence. Mary was talented and strong-willed enough to achieve them. I never doubted her.

I liked the way she challenged the forces that hold many families together. She loved my parents as dearly as they loved her, but she refused to be motivated by guilt. If she thought something was right for her, she would do it. If she thought it was wrong, she wouldn't. No amount of threatening, coaxing, or arm twisting could change her mind. For that I had to respect her.

I also admired her in other ways. Although she was only seventeen at the time and had many of the personality tics of a teenager—giggles, shyness, quick changes of temperament—she seemed to see certain things with a maturity beyond her years. When she talked about serious topics, she could be levelheaded and insightful. When someone close to Mary was hurt, she was always the first one to offer help. She had a sensitivity that was unequaled in most girls her age.

Part of it may have come as the result of an ordeal she endured when I was in nursing school. She had been given a ride home on a snowy day. The roads were slippery and another car slid into the vehicle. Mary went through the windshield. The next few years were difficult ones for her. She had numerous surgeries and felt undesirable at an age when most girls are beginning to test their social wings. Although the hardships may have slowed Mary down, they didn't stop her. By the time I was back from Vietnam, she was not only extremely popular and very pretty, she also had some solid friends who would stand by her through anything.

During the next few years, we would renew our acquaintance and come to be best friends. She always tried to help me—even when no one really could.

After we finished the lasagna that first night, I set up the slide projector to show pictures of Vietnam. I wanted to tell my family what it was like, to make them understand. I wanted to share with them the times when we worked through pushes and the times when we laughed. I wanted them to know how much I had changed and how I had learned that life could be so different than any of us had ever imagined. I wanted them to be a part of every moment, good and bad, so there would be no distance between us, so they could understand the person I had become.

My father got the projector and I filled the tray with slides while Mary and Jean set up the screen. The first slides were pictures of the compound. I showed them the Bastille and the banana trees, the Bernard J. Piccolo Memorial Peace Park and the pool. And there were pictures of Bubba and Slim and Coretta and Mickie and Carl and Jack and me.

Then came the casualties. I didn't notice anything different in the beginning, but when the slides got bloody, everyone became extremely uncomfortable. They tried to stop me by making little jokes to get me off the topic. But I didn't understand. I figured they were just putting me on, teasing me. I continued, flipping through more gory pictures of the OR.

"Lynda," Mom said quietly, "isn't there something a little less gruesome you can show us?"

I didn't understand. "It was an ugly year," I said.

She got up, touched my shoulder, and looked at me with sadness. I could see that those pictures had given her an idea of how much I had suffered. It hurt her to know that. "I don't think you really want to show those slides," she said sorrowfully. "Maybe it would be wise to put them away."

Perhaps she was right, but the realization hurt me more than bullets or rockets or napalm ever could. I wanted to grab the people I loved by the shoulders and say, "Listen to me! Look! This is what I've gone through! I'm one of you! This is life! Please let me talk about it!"

If I had done that, I know they would have sat and politely listened. They loved me and wanted to see me happy. But would they really have understood the pain? Was it fair to expect anyone to understand unless they had been there?

I gathered my slides, put them back in their boxes and carried them up to my room, where I stored them in the back of a closet. I had learned my lesson quickly. Vietnam would never be socially acceptable. Not here, not anywhere in the world.

I felt a deep emptiness inside, a longing for someone who might understand. I didn't belong in this place. These people loved me, but I didn't belong with them. Maybe I was no longer suited for the world. Maybe others who had taken repeat tours were right—"Vietnam sucks out your heart and soul until there ain't nothin' left."

I drank as much as I could hold and when I went to bed, I passed out. *Attention all personnel, Pleiku airbase is under rocket and mortar attack. Take cover.* When I woke the next morning, I was under the bed. I searched for my flak jacket and helmet. They weren't there. I had left them in Vietnam. I went back to bed and slept some more.

Later that evening, after I woke, Mary came upstairs to visit with me. "I'd like to see your slides," she said. "I want to know what it was like for you."

"It sucked, Mary. That's all you need to know. The rest is too ugly."

For the next few days, we called the airline every morning, but my bags hadn't been located. I spent most of that time sleeping and smoking and sitting in my room, looking out the window at the trees below. It had always been a special room. When I was a little girl, it started out as the attic. But as the family grew, the need for extra bedrooms grew, too. When I was eight, my father took three-quarters of the attic, pushed a double dormer out the back and a single one in front, and made what was probably the largest bedroom in the house. It had pine paneling, built-in drawers, a desk, a window seat and a massive window that offered the best view of any room we had. When it was first built, it had been Nancy's room, and at one time it was my fondest wish for Nancy to grow up and move out so I could move into that room. During those years, it had always been off limits to the rest of us. But when Nancy left, Jean and I took possession.

As an adolescent, I spent countless hours sitting at that window, watching the scenery and daydreaming. From the spring through the fall, I could feel like I had my own little world up there. When the leaves came to the trees, they blocked out almost all the houses below, and in October, the different colors shone so brilliantly that it could take your breath away. I had missed that room when I was in Vietnam. It was a place where I imagined I would find some tranquillity. But when I finally got there, I realized that it would be years—perhaps a lifetime—before I would ever find that kind of peace again for more than brief moments.

That initial period home was probably harder on my parents than it was on me. I could see in their eyes that they wanted badly to help me, to do something to make me happier. I was very difficult to communicate with. They tried to get me out of my shell, but they couldn't. Probably no one could have helped.

It had to be tough on the two of them. They had said good-bye a year earlier to a happy-go-lucky all-American girl who thought she could grab the world by the tail. Now in that girl's place they had a very sad and bitter young woman who did little but brood. I sometimes wonder if they were blaming themselves. Perhaps it would have been easier for them if I could have told them that the mistakes were mine, not theirs. They had raised me as well as possible. How could they have known that Vietnam would turn my world upside down? And if they had tried to stop me from going to war, I probably would not have listened.

The only time I left the house that first week was on Sunday, to go to Mass. Although I had stopped going to church years before, except for a few occasions in Vietnam, there was one hard and fast rule in my parents' house: You attended Mass. I wore my uniform and sat in the back because I didn't want anybody to see me. When I got home, my bags were waiting. It was time for me to move on.

18

You're in the Army... Still

I had orders to report to Walter Reed Army Hospital to work as an OR nurse when my leave was up. Although the hospital was within commuting distance of my parents' home and they would have been happy to have me stay with them, I knew I couldn't live there anymore. Too much of me had changed. So during the second week of leave, I bought a yellow MG convertible with $2500 in cash that I had saved in Vietnam and I found a two-bedroom apartment in Alexandria that I shared with another nurse Penny Foreman, who had been in Pleiku during part of my tour. Our downstairs neighbors were three guys who were also Vietnam vets, and we all spent a lot of time drinking, smoking pot, and talking about 'Nam. Penny was engaged to one of them. They planned to be married in September after she got out of the Army. My two years would be up at the end of October. I couldn't wait.

I had only been in the apartment a few days and was alone one night when I got a telephone call from someone whose voice was totally unfamiliar:

"Lynda?"

"Hello?"

"Hi, I got your number from your parents."

"Yes? Can I help you?"

"It's me, Lynda," he said. "J.J. I worried about you all year. Are you all right? Were you hurt?"

"I'm okay."

"Nobody's okay," he said. "Not after 'Nam."

"Maybe not," I answered, "but I'll survive."

We were silent for at least a full minute. I asked myself if I still felt anything for J.J., but all I could find inside was the emptiness. Yet maybe we stood a chance together if we tried. I would understand him more since, I, too, had seen the war and knew what it did to people. And he would understand me. He had always been good to me.

But I told myself I was still in love with Jack. Perhaps I really was.

"How was it?" J.J. asked.

"Exactly like you said: It sucked."

"Lynda, I miss you. I'd like to see you again."

"That wouldn't be a good idea," I said. "I'm involved with another man." It was the last time I ever heard from J.J. The memories of him that I kept were good ones.

Some people who knew I had been to Vietnam weren't satisfied with "It sucked" as an answer to "What was it like?" They would nag me so much for more information that I was convinced they were interested. However, as soon as I got past the surface travelogue material, they would stop me, saying, "Oh my God, that's too awful." They didn't really want to know; they just wanted a summary in twenty-five words or less.

Those who met me for the first time were astounded to learn that the Army actually sent women into a combat zone. Their amazement was usually followed by an insensitive statement like: "Any woman who'd go to Vietnam would have to be a fool." Maybe I was a fool for going, but they didn't have to rub it in.

There was also an underlying assumption by every man that I would leap into bed at the drop of a hat. In fact, one even asked the question that was on so many minds: "How many guys did you fuck in 'Nam, honey?" The correct answer was zero; I didn't fuck anyone. I had made love with two men. I told the idiot who asked that it was none of his business.

After a while, I decided it was easier to simply deny that I was a Vietnam vet. There was certainly nothing good in being one, so why broadcast it? I buried the experience as deeply as I could.

But at night, it was still in my dreams.

Dear Lynda,

. . . I'll be coming back to the world in the middle of September.

Will be stationed at Fort MacArthur until I get out. Should be visiting you after I see my family . . .

Sincerely,
Jack

Dear Jack,

. . . I can't wait to see you. Since I'll be getting out of the Army on 31 October, I can move to Los Angeles, too. I'll find a job and we can live together. . . .

Love,
Lynda

I had thought that the people running the 71st Evac at Pleiku were too concerned with military Mickey Mouse, but as soon as I started at Walter Reed I had reached the pinnacle of Army bullshit. One of the largest medical facilities in the country, and perhaps the largest military medical facility in the world, "Walter Wonderful" was so topheavy with rank, I'm surprised the buildings didn't tip over. It had been named for the doctor who conquered malaria during the construction of the Panama Canal and the hospital had a reputation for being in the forefront of medical research. Any doctor or nurse who was planning to make the military a career had to have an assignment to Walter Wonderful in their files. The medical professionals were largely majors, lieutenant colonels, and colonels; the patients were frequently generals, congressmen, and other VIPs.

A first lieutenant in that atmosphere was considered somewhat lower than a worm, which created plenty of difficulties for me. I had spent my time in Vietnam becoming technically competent and working in the capacity of a first assistant surgeon. At Walter Reed, I was treated as a totally inexperienced nurse with absolutely no say in the running of the OR. I was assigned to the hemorrhoid room where, as we would say, it was "one asshole after another." I was told by the head nurse of the OR that I should not think that my experience in Vietnam meant much back in the States.

"This is still the Army, Lieutenant, and that doesn't mean anything here."

I might have been able to accept my lowly position in the hierarchy. A person can put up with almost anything for a few months. But I couldn't accept the inequality in patient care.

In Vietnam, every soldier who came through the OR was treated as well as anyone else. We gave all people the best we could, regardless of rank. At Walter Wonderful, everything was based on rank. When a lower enlisted man was brought in for surgery, he'd be handled roughly and told to "Get your ass onto the table." When the generals came in, the situation was entirely different. They were patted and puffed into place for fear of giving them the slightest pain.

One day, we had just finished with a corporal who had been manhandled; he was followed by a two-star general, a real jerk who ordered people around right up until he was put to sleep. All the others in the OR fawned over him. I kept my distance. After he was anesthetized, we turned him onto his belly and raised his fat backside into the air. I scrubbed him and draped him and then brought over my Mayo stand. "Isn't it amazing?" I asked rhetorically. "They all look the same from down here."

My timing wasn't the greatest. I hadn't realized that the OR chief nurse had entered the room and was standing behind me. She was not thrilled by my attitude. By the time she finished jumping in my shit, I felt like I had a new asshole of my own.

Dear Lynda,

. . . I don't think living together would be a good idea. I'm not sure we could do it without fighting all the time. . . .

Sincerely,
Jack

Dear Jack,

. . . I'm sorry that we fight so much. It's probably my fault. I promise if we live together I won't fight anymore. I love you. I miss you and want to be with you.

Love,
Lynda

At the apartment, Penny and I always kept the linen closet stocked with beer. The price was low at the PX and I could go through a six pack without batting an eye. I never appeared drunk to anybody else, but the alcohol usually served its intended purpose—it numbed me. On nights when Penny was working, I'd sit alone with the lights turned out, a candle burning, and music playing. One wall was almost totally glass, with floor-to-ceiling sliding doors leading to a small balcony. I kept the curtains apart because I had this thing about being able to look at open space. It probably came from spending an entire year not being able to see out of the operating room or out of my hooch in Pleiku. I didn't want to feel closed in anymore.

I'd find a song on an album and play it over and over again, not even letting the record finish before I'd move the needle back to the beginning. "The Draft Dodger Rag," as it was most popularly known, by Country Joe and the Fish, was repeated so many times that the record should have worn itself out. But it didn't.

For it's one, two, three what are we fighting for?
Don't ask me, I don't give a damn,
My next stop is Vietnam.
For it's five, six, seven, open up the pearly gates,
Well, there ain't no time to wonder why,
Whoopee, we're all gonna die.

I tried to find Barbara. Each time I'd contact another classmate from nursing school, I'd hear the same reply. Nobody knew where she was. I tried the people who handled the Army nurses' records, but they had nothing on her, which meant, according to the administrative officer, that she was either transferred to another branch, discharged, or dead.

The one person who I thought might have the best chance of knowing anything about Barbara was Gina. The three of us had been such good friends in nursing school. I also thought that since Gina never did the socially acceptable things, I might talk with her about surviving in the world after Vietnam. If nothing else, perhaps we could have a party and laugh about some of the good times.

Although we hadn't corresponded since her wedding, I knew that Gina and her husband, Ken, were living in his family's beach house in Wildwood, New Jersey, for the summer. So early one Saturday morning in July, on the spur of the moment, I put the top down and took the MG to Wildwood. Instead of the untamed girl I had known from nursing school, I found a sad, broken woman in Gina. The two years since graduation had not been good to her. There had been problems with the marriage and the things that had happened during the past six months had made her life intolerable. She had got pregnant the previous October and had been happily on her way to a big Italian family of her own. Although she and Ken had argued during the first year of marriage, the pregnancy had seemed to calm them both down. They were happy. But circumstances conspired against them.

First, Gina's mother died in January. She took it hard. Then, in March, her father died, too. It was quick and painless. He had a stroke while he was sleeping. In April, Ken lost his job, and near the end of May, Gina had her baby.

It was born dead.

She and Ken spent the following weeks hardly speaking, each silently blaming the other—and themselves—for the death of the baby. Things got so bad they split in the middle of July, a few days before I made my surprise visit.

I found Gina crying on her back porch. She had lost so much weight that I almost didn't recognize her. Her face was drawn and her eyes bloodshot. She tried to compose herself when she saw me, and for a while, the tears stopped. But they came back again when we talked.

We spent the afternoon drinking beer and walking the beach, each trying to share her pain, yet only half listening to the other.

"He hasn't had anything to do with me since the baby," she said. "I don't understand why."

"I had these kids coming in with arms and legs blown away," I said. "And the V.C. mutilated the dead."

"I wanted that baby so much, Lynda. The doctor doesn't think I can have another."

"There was this one kid whose face was destroyed. His name was Gene. I wanted so badly to save him."

"It's not my fault the baby died. Is it?"

"I had thought I could save every GI that came through the OR. Crazy, isn't it?"

"If he loved me, Lynda, wouldn't he at least hold me?"

"You try to fight the emptiness," I said. "But after you've seen so many kids die, you can't. Maybe it's really true, Gina, it just don't mean nothin'."

We tried to wash away the tears. That evening we went out for dinner and then walked the boardwalk, pacing back and forth past the crowds of people and the barkers in the stands until late at night when most of them had gone home. It was as if we both hoped we could walk away our anguish; maybe only a few more steps and we would again be innocent girls playing practical jokes between classes. We walked back onto the beach, took our shoes off, and stood ankle deep in the cool water, looking out toward the darkness.

"I guess I expected too much," Gina said. "I did blame Ken, but it started a long time ago. I blamed him for not being a superman. That poor guy didn't stand a chance. I thought he could do anything. If something broke, he could fix it. If the weather was bad, he'd be able to change it. If something was wrong, he'd make it right. I hated him because he wasn't a magician. And all the while, he just wanted me to let him be human. Maybe we can try again."

"Gina," I said, "I haven't heard a word from Barbara. Do you have any idea where she might be?"

"No, Lynda. I'm sorry."

"Me, too," I said. "More than anyone will ever know."

While I was walking through D.C. one day, I got a handbill from a guy in an old fatigue shirt and boonie hat. He was a member of the Vietnam Veterans Against the War and they were holding a meeting in a church basement that night. All Vietnam vets were invited.

When I showed up at their meeting, the room was packed. It was so hot and stuffy that I had trouble breathing. I couldn't hear the speaker very well, but one thing was clear: They were planning a march on the White House to demonstrate against the war. That was something I definitely wanted to be a part of.

During the next couple of weeks, I debated with myself about joining VVAW. From the John Turkey Movement in Vietnam, I knew that there were regulations against participating in protests while on active duty. I didn't need any more trouble. But I decided that the possible consequences were worth the risk if we could convince the government to pull out even one day sooner.

I tried to persuade Penny and the guys downstairs to join the march. "What if the people at Walter Wonderful find out we were in it?" she asked.

"Who cares?" I said. "What are they going to do to us? Send us to Vietnam?"

I returned to that church basement alone on the morning of the march, wearing my fatigue shirt and boonie hat along with a pair of jeans. I didn't talk with anybody, but I listened to the things the other vets were saying about the war and how we should be out of Vietnam immediately. I was in total agreement. As I made my way through the room, I could hear guys talking about their tours and some of the things they saw in 'Nam. I felt at home with these men. They had been through the same experiences as me and they were doing something to stop the war so no one would have to go through it again.

There were only a few women in that room. They seemed lost. Some clustered together; others, like me, stood alone, not yet knowing anyone well enough to feel comfortable. When we moved outside to line up, I took a place near the front. However, one of the leaders approached me. "This demonstration is only for vets," he said apologetically.

"I am a vet," I said. "I was in Pleiku and Qui Nhon."

"Pleiku!" he exclaimed. "No shit! I used to be with the 4th Infantry. You must have been at the 71st Evac."

"I worked in the OR."

"You people did a hell of a job," he said. "You folks saved my best friend's life." He smiled at me for a few moments while I shifted awkwardly under his praise.

"Do you have a sign or something I can hold?" I asked.

"Well," he said uncomfortably, "I . . . uh . . . don't think you're supposed to march."

"But you told me it was for vets."

"It is," he said. "But you're not a vet."

"I don't understand."

"You don't look like a vet," he said. "If we have women marching, Nixon and the network news reporters might think we're swelling the ranks with nonvets."

"I can prove I was in Vietnam."

"I believe you," he said. "But you can't be a member of our group. I'm sorry."

If I had stayed and argued with him, I might have changed his mind. But when I looked around, the other women were leaving. I guess I didn't want to force the issue. If they didn't want me, why bother?

Dear Lynda,

. . . In regard to living together, let's talk about it when I come to visit. . . .

Sincerely,
Jack

From the day I made my remarks about the general's backside until the time I got out of the Army, I was never quite a favorite of the chief nurse in the OR. She talked to me frequently about my nonmilitary attitude. When she said I wasn't conducting myself as an Army officer, it was supposed to be a reprimand. I took it as a compliment. It meant that I didn't look or act like a lifer. I was proud of that.

During those last few months, I did everything I could to lessen my identification with the military. I started by refusing to wear my hat when I was outdoors. Most of the other military people either didn't notice I was without one, or they ignored me. Occasionally, an MP would stop me. When he asked me where my hat was, I would simply tell him I had lost it in Vietnam. If he tried to pursue the matter, I walked away. Later, I started wearing a sweater over my white nurse's uniform whenever I was out of the hospital so I could hide my first lieutenant's silver bar and the branch insignia. Without those, I looked like a regular civilian nurse. I felt good about that. It was a sign that the Army was losing a certain amount of control over my life. I couldn't wait until I was able to eliminate all their control. I wanted to be free.

But freedom wouldn't come until fall; I still had a job to do.

Besides the hemorrhoids, I was given other cases that were every bit as undesirable. I never objected to the work. I kept telling myself that I would do any job they gave me as long as they let me out on Halloween. I could take any crap they dished out.

Any crap but the gynecological case I was assigned to near the end of August. The surgical slip had listed it as an abdominal hysterotomy, which meant that we were going to open the uterus. In those days we didn't do pre-op visits and there was no diagnosis on the paper. I assumed that we would be going after tumors. It was an erroneous assumption.

After we got the patient ready, I pulled my Mayo stand over and began handing the surgeon his instruments. For the first couple of minutes, it went like a routine hysterotomy. Then he asked for the specimen bowl. I handed him a small stainless steel bowl half-filled with saline. He dropped the specimen in and I took the bowl from him. When I looked down, I was shocked.

I couldn't move.

Instead of a fibroid tumor or other unnatural growth, what I saw was a perfectly formed infant floating in amniotic fluid. It had fingers and toes. It was a boy. I touched it through the sac material and fluid. There was a pulse. The baby moved.

"What should I do?" I asked the surgeon.

My question annoyed him. "You're a nurse; aren't you?" he answered sarcastically. "Put the bowl on the back table and keep handing me instruments."

"But the baby. We haven't got a pediatrician here. Should I get one to resuscitate?"

"Don't you dare."

"The baby will die if—"

"That's not a baby," he insisted.

"But—"

"It's a fetus, a five-month fetus."

"But it's alive."

"This is an abortion, honey," he said with irritation. "It's a hysterotomy to remove something from the inside of the uterus. That something is a fetus. Don't you call it anything else and don't you dare call any pediatrician. That's an order. Now give me a suture."

I was thoroughly confused. No one had warned me about this. If I had known—

"Nurse," the surgeon said, "you're not listening. I said I needed a suture."

It was a baby. If we didn't get a pediatrician immediately—

"Suture, dammit!" the surgeon screamed. "What the hell is the matter with you? Are you trying to kill this woman?"

I put the specimen bowl on the back table and handed him a suture for the uterine wall. As I watched him put the woman's belly back together, I wanted to scream. I wanted to grab the baby and run to find the nearest pediatrician so we could keep it alive. But I kept handing sutures. I didn't know what else to do.

When there was a break, I turned around to see the baby quietly dying. With a scalpel, I poked around the amniotic sac. Then I poured saline over the boy as I said, "I baptize you, in the name of the Father, and of the Son, and of the Holy Spirit, Amen." I didn't know what else to do.

Within a few moments, the boy was no longer moving. Five minutes later, he was dead.

As soon as we finished the case, I walked out of the OR and stormed unannounced into the office of the OR chief nurse. "Don't you ever assign me to another case like that,'' I shouted at the colonel. ''You didn't even have the decency to warn me.

''I am hereby categorically refusing to scrub any more abortions. That is my right, and I am taking it. And while you're at it, don't pull that kind of sneaky trick on anyone else, either. It's immoral and unethical.''

The colonel was furious with my attitude, but legally I was on solid ground, so there wasn't much she could do. I suppose I was lucky I didn't get an Article 15 for the way I hollered at her.

They never assigned me to an abortion again.

The young man came back into the dream as he had so many nights before. He was wearing fatigues and a boonie hat, but the clothes were all bloody. There was a large hole where his belly and chest used to be. He had no arms and legs and his face was blown away. He whispered something that I couldn't hear. He wanted me to come closer. Struggling against my inclination to run, I put my head so near to the spot that had once been his lips that I got blood on my cheeks. The soldier kept whispering one word:

Why?

The following Friday, another OR nurse Susan Thomasina and I decided to finish off a terrible week with some cheap drinks at the officers club happy hour. We could use some happiness. Susan was heading for Vietnam in two weeks and wanted me to tell her what to expect. When she asked me what it was like, I told her the truth: ''It sucked.'' When she asked for more information, I said, ''It sucks so loud that you can hear it ten thousand miles away.''

''Would you go back?'' she asked naively.

''Do I look crazy?'' But I knew that answer wasn't totally accurate. I missed a lot of things about Vietnam, things that I couldn't articulate. It had been a terrible year, hadn't it? Yet why did I find myself thinking about it so much? Why couldn't I get it out of my mind? There had been an intensity there. We had lived each day to the fullest, regardless of what that day brought. Now it was hard to readapt to a world where people concerned themselves with meeting the mortgage, playing bridge with friends, and figuring out what they were going to watch on television that night. There had to be more purpose than that in life.

I missed Bubba and Slim and Coretta and Mickey and Carl and Jack.

And the Bastille.

And the Bernard J. Piccolo Memorial Banana Tree.

And the Elizabeth L. Piccolo Memorial Banana Tree.

And the Bernard J. Piccolo Memorial Peace Park.

And the morning parties.

And even, as much as I hated to admit it, the surgical-T. At least there we found ourselves doing more important things than operating on six rectums a day five days a week.

I sat at a corner table with Susan and the two of us knocked back a pitcher of beer in a half-hour. Dinner was cheese and crackers from the complimentary snack tray. Near us was a large table filled with men. They called for us to join them. We politely declined. Neither Susan nor I was in the mood to be very sociable.

Our second pitcher, the waitress informed us, had been paid for by the men. We thanked them but again declined their offer of company. A few minutes later, one of them, a tall, lanky, handsome warrant officer came to our table. He had only one arm.

Originally, I hadn't noticed anything different about the group, but now when I glanced at it, I saw that everyone was missing at least one limb. Some, as many as three. One had no arms. The man next to him was feeding him beer. They were all from Ward I, the amputee ward, at Walter Wonderful.

"You don't have to be afraid of us," the man said. "We don't bite."

"We've had a bad week," I said. "We're not good company."

"Maybe we can cheer you up."

"Maybe another time."

He started to walk away, then hesitated and turned back. "It's because we're cripples," he said bitterly. "Isn't it?"

"That has nothing to do with it."

He shrugged, only half believing me, and returned to his table. Fifteen minutes later and a few beers bolder, five men got up from the table. Before we knew what was happening, we were shanghaied. It was all in great fun and everyone laughed, but by the time we were sitting with them, being introduced around, I was nettled. Sue and I really had wanted to be alone.

Sue took it like a trooper and in a few minutes was joking with the guys. When the subject got to Vietnam, she told them that she was going soon and that I had recently returned. Encouraged by what they felt was a receptive audience, the men began telling us how angry they were. They were being discharged within the next week and each said he wanted one more chance.

"If only I could kill one more gook," one of them said.

"I'd like to zap a few of those zits," said another. "Ten for each friend I lost."

A guy in a wheelchair agreed. "I'd give anything to be able to douse every dink between Saigon and Hanoi," he said. "And when I got there, I'd fuck Ho Chi Minh's old lady."

"He doesn't have an old lady," someone else interjected.

"Then I'll fuck his sister and make him watch."

"Ho Chi Minh is dead," I reminded them. They ignored the comment. As they got more and more graphic in their descriptions of what atrocities they would perform if only they could get one more shot at "the little slants," I blocked their conversation and withdrew into my own thoughts while I drank the beer. It tasted flat.

"Wouldn't you like to kill a few of those slimy yellow bastards, too, Blondie?" one of the guys said to me.

I tried to avoid the question and made an innocuous comment about the war not being good for anyone. That was a mistake. They all started firing questions at me. Wouldn't I love to see every one of those "fucking Vietamese jerkoffs" blown to shit? "No." Shouldn't we napalm "all the gooks?" "No." Wouldn't it be fun to watch them fry? "No." Shouldn't we kill all the women first so they couldn't reproduce any more "baby gooks"? "No." "What's the difference between a truckload of dead baby gooks and a truckload of bowling balls?" "I don't want to know." "You can't unload the bowling balls with a pitchfork." "Please stop it." "Don't you think we should nuke the whole country?" "No." "Is nuking maybe too good for them?" "No." "Wouldn't you love to see every one of those 'gook cunts' suffer?" "Why don't we castrate all of them?" "Don't you want to go back one more time?" "Just one more chance?" "One more opportunity to blow their shit away?" "Don't you—"

"Stop it," I yelled.

"Wouldn't you love to cut their guts out, Blondie?"

"Stop it. Stop it."

"Wouldn't you—"

"Why?" I screamed. "How can you—"

"Maybe collect a few of their eyeballs for—"

"Stop it!" I grabbed one of the men by the shirt. He had no legs. "Look at you," I shouted. "Look at what they did to you." I turned to another who was missing his left leg and right arm. "Look at you! You stupid fucking bastards! How can you want to go back for more after they've already done this to you?"

It was the wrong way to deal with the situation. It immediately escalated into a shouting match and then into a brawl, with beer mugs being thrown, a few people swinging, and everyone screaming. When the dust cleared, I was the only person ejected from the club. I sat in my car staring ahead at nothing for a half-hour, shaking, totally confused, angry, and sad. Finally, I just became blank, and drove back to my apartment. I found Mary sitting on my steps.

"I didn't know if you'd be home," she said.

"It's nice to see you," I said as I climbed out of my MG.

"I figured maybe if you weren't doing anything tonight we could—" When I walked toward her, she stopped.

"They threw me out of the officers club, Mar."

"Oh my God, Lynda," Mary exclaimed. Then, as I walked up the steps, she did something for which I would never be able to thank her enough. She put her arms around me and pulled me close, trying to take away some of the pain. For that, I loved her.

Mary hugged me so tightly that I felt like a baby. The tears came in a river. She sat me on a step, brushed my hair back with her fingers, and in between my sobs, she got me to tell her about the evening. When I stopped twenty minutes later, she wiped my tears away. Then she put her fingers under my chin and lifted my face so we could look into each other's eyes.

"Lynda," she said, "don't you see what those men were doing? It's precisely because they lost something so tangible in Vietnam that they have to believe they lost it for a reason. And if they lost it for a reason, they have to say that they would be willing to go back and do it again. They have no choice."

"Why, Mary?" I asked. "Why does anybody ever have to go to war at all?"

"I don't know," she said. "I just don't know."

That summer was when my parents were planning to build a cottage in the mountains. It would eventually be enlarged when Daddy retired, but for now, they wanted someplace more comfortable than a trailer for their weekends. I looked forward to going with them again, since the mountain had been the scene of so many happy childhood memories.

But when I got there, it was different from the way I had remembered it. There was something about the mountain that made me feel almost like I was at home—my real home. I walked the trails, breathed the fresh air, and looked up at the sun. I napped on a bed of moss, watched deer in the field, and listened to the birds singing. Each time I went back there, I found periods when the emptiness would be gone. They might last only a few seconds, or a minute, but they offered hope.

I tried to figure out what it was about the mountain that gave me those feelings. Why was I so strongly attracted to this place? Why did I feel myself wanting to come back every chance I could get?

Then one Saturday night during a rainstorm as I sat alone under a poncho on the side of a hill, I realized what it was: The sloping hills, the trees, the valley below, and the red mud—they all reminded me of Pleiku.

I was lying in a ditch during a rocket attack. The explosions came closer and closer. Then I was in the OR being chased by bloody deformed casualties who were losing arms, legs, and guts as they ran after me. Ahead was the door leading to the ER. If I could make it to that door I could get free. I ran harder, but as I came closer my legs felt like they weighed a ton. Then the floor started opening up and I was slogging through mud up to my knees. I was sweating and crying and frantic. I pushed ahead with everything I had. I reached the double doors and struggled with them, for what seemed like an eternity. Finally, they opened. But I wasn't free. Hundreds of bodies came from the other direction, trapping me in the middle of walls of bloody flesh. There was nowhere for me to go. I tried to scream. Nothing would come out until, at last, I shouted one word that woke me:

Why?

Every few weeks that summer, I would start once more to talk with my parents; if not about everything that happened in Vietnam, at least some of it. I was a stranger to them. I had seen and felt things that I wanted them to understand. And I'm certain they wanted to understand, too. But each time I brought the subject up, I dropped it immediately. I didn't want to hurt them and I knew that if I went into all of it they would be devastated. My father probably thought I was trying to sweep it under the rug. "Sometimes it's better," he said, "if you forget about a bad experience and simply put it behind you. Maybe God doesn't want us to understand everything."

I swallowed my frustration and tried to make believe that Vietnam never existed. Occasionally, I was successful.

Jack DEROSed in September and he came to Washington a week later. In many ways, it was like a honeymoon. There were only good times. We saw the sights, ate in fancy restaurants, and came together with so much emotion that I was sure he loved me and would want me with him for the rest of his life. The best part was that there was no more bickering or fighting. Maybe it was because the pressure was off. I took him up to the mountain and introduced him to my parents. They both liked him immediately.

I was sure then that I loved Jack. He would have fit in perfectly with my family and I would have been ecstatic if he had asked me to marry him. I wanted to make a home for the two of us, to have his children, and to share the good times and the bad. He was the only person who I thought could understand me. Although we both looked normal on the surface, Vietnam had set us far apart from others. I figured he needed me, too. I could make him happy. I wanted the chance.

We didn't discuss living together until the day before he was scheduled to leave. He had thought about it long and hard, he said. He cared about me in a way he never cared for anyone else. The good times we had shared in Vietnam were precious to him. But in the end, he told me, he didn't think we could work it out together.

"I'll make you happy," I pleaded.

"I don't think anyone could make me happy," he answered.

"Can we at least stay in touch?" I asked.

"Of course."

Dear Jack,

. . . I know I can make you happy if you please give me a chance. . . .

Love,
Lynda

Dear Jack,

. . . Can't we just try? I promise things will be good. . . .

Love,
Lynda

Dear Jack,

. . . I've never wanted or needed anybody more than you. . . .

Love,
Lynda

"Hi, Lynda."

"Jack! Oh, God, you don't know how good it is to hear your voice. I miss you so much. Thank you for calling. I think about you all the time. How are you doing in L.A.?"

"Fort Mac is still the Army. It sucks."

"Jack, I—"

"Lynda, why don't you come to L.A.?"

"You mean it? I don't know what to say. I'm so—"

"I've got an apartment. You can live with me. We'll try it out."

"Oh, yes! Yes! Yes! A thousand times yes. I love you, Jack."

"When do you ETS?"

"Thirty-one October. I can be there in November."

On the day I was discharged, the director of nursing services, a lifer colonel, tried to talk me into reenlisting. I told her, in no uncertain terms, where she could shove those reenlistment papers and what she could do with them when they got there. Finally, I was free. It was all over. As I drove off the Walter Reed compound for the last time, an MP at the gate saluted. I returned the salute, by giving him the peace sign. When I drove past the Pentagon, I gave it the finger.

I arrived in L.A. in the second week of November and found Jack studying day and night for his surgical board exams, which he would take on December 15. The apartment was a two bedroom in San Pedro, around the corner from the post, and it was designed in a way that made it impossible to get much privacy when two people were there. I did my best to avoid disturbing him. I tiptoed around, making as little noise as possible, did the cooking and cleaning and ran errands for him. When he needed help studying, I would quiz him. I immediately found a job as a ward nurse in a community hospital and, although I wasn't crazy about the work, I was content to do it until a position opened up in the OR.

Soon after I settled in, the arguments started again. We would fight about the silliest things. I didn't understand what was happening, but things weren't going well. He insisted that I do things his way. I insisted he do them my way. Instead of one of us compromising, we continued our disagreements until they escalated into full-scale arguments and one of us stormed out. There were plenty of other scenes like that and all of them were over petty issues. Neither of us was happy.

Jack decided that the night before his boards, he would stay in a motel a block from UCLA. The exams were to be given at the university. Since we lived thirty minutes from Westwood, I didn't think his plan made sense, but I said nothing and prepared myself to spend Friday night in Westwood with him. When he realized that I didn't completely understand his intention, he sat me down. "Lynda, I want to be alone that night."

Slightly embarrassed, I shrugged. "Okay, sure."

"It'll be better that way," he said. "I'll be able to concentrate on last-minute studying."

"I understand," I said. "That's fine."

But that wasn't all he had to tell me. As soon as he got that issue settled, he dropped a bombshell. "I don't think this is working out," he said. "After I finish the boards, you should find a place of your own."

"I love you," I said. I was too shocked to cry.

He sat on another chair and leaned forward. "I'm sorry, Lynda, but I don't love you."

I got a sick feeling and felt like I was going to puke. Then the pain started deep in my gut. He mumbled some things that I didn't hear. There was a buzzing in my head and his face was out of focus. Jack was all that was left of my world. He was all I had. What about the good times? Didn't they count for anything? Didn't he understand that I needed him? What would I do without him? I struggled for breath. "But—" I said.

"Listen, Lynda," he said. "I don't even know if I have the capacity to love *anyone*. Since Vietnam, I feel like an empty shell. Nothing has any meaning."

"I can change that," I argued. "I can help you."

"I don't want your help."

"Jack, please—"

"I'm sorry, Lynda," he said. "I'm really sorry."

I ran back to my parents for the holidays. They welcomed me with open arms. I needed them. I needed someone. When I cried to my mother, she tried to patiently explain that I shouldn't have gone to L.A. expecting the relationship to work, when it had been so stormy in Vietnam. Although she was right, I didn't want to hear that. "If it's not going to work out," she said, "there's no way you can force it." My father was even more to the point. "You've got to let go," he said. "Try to forget Jack. There are other men who can make you happy."

Maybe I thought that my parents would be able to make me stop hurting. But then, maybe it was hopeless for me to ever expect them to understand.

How could they understand me, when I didn't understand myself?

But I was angry for awhile, upset because they offered wisdom instead of immediate relief from the pain. They were my parents! Why couldn't they kiss the hurt and make it better? Wasn't that what parents were supposed to do? Why didn't they have magical powers? How dare they be human, too!

I had come back to Arlington thinking I might stay, but I knew I had to live my own life away from my family. I thought I would only hurt them if I remained and let them see how desolate I felt. When I left, I had the feeling that I was going into exile. I didn't belong with my family. I didn't belong with Jack. I didn't belong with anyone. I felt alone and afraid. I had never felt so alone before. But, as I had done so many times in Vietnam, I told myself I had to be strong to survive.

19

The World?

I returned to my job in the community hospital near L.A., rented an apartment in a house in Manhattan Beach, and then began a slow descent into the depths. I desperately needed people but it seemed impossible to meet anyone outside of work. The people at the hospital were almost all twenty to thirty years older than me and married. I had almost no friends, I didn't fit anyplace. I wanted to belong somewhere and to belong with someone. I found myself thinking frequently about the comradery I had felt in Vietnam, the strong bonds we had all forged. I wanted to be back in a group like that, but none were available—except in 'Nam, and there was no way I was returning to the war.

I kept calling Jack, trying to convince him to take me back. He said no. I shifted my tactics and tried a softer sell. I'd invite him for dinner and make all the foods he loved; I would buy and make little gifts that I would take to his apartment. It gave me an excuse to see him and ask the question again. He always said no. Sometimes we had fun together; they were probably the toughest times because I would always think there was some hope. I was wrong.

"Don't you understand," Jack would say, "I don't have the capacity to love anyone. It has nothing to do with you."

"But—"

Within a short time after we separated, Jack received notification that he had passed his surgical board exams. He phoned to tell me that and to say that he was moving back to Eugene to set up practice.

"I'm sorry it didn't work out, Lynda."

"Me, too."

"I wish you the best."

"You, too."

I never saw or heard from Jack again.

I began "hitting the scene," and was in a different bar every night, becoming a person I hated. The lines I heard were all the same: "You're looking pretty tonight." "You seem awfully sad tonight." "Like to dance?" Everybody was a first name. I don't think I ever got a last name from anyone, although I usually asked. None of them ever asked about me. They were only there for themselves. I would try to get to know them but they didn't talk. If I tried to find out who they were, what they did for a living, where they came from, there would be a series of one word answers, reluctantly given. And if I asked a question too many, they would walk away without so much as a good-bye. They wanted to be anonymous, didn't want anyone "getting into their space."

I was seeking someone with whom I could connect, someone who would talk and listen, hold me and open himself up. I was obviously going to the wrong places, but there seemed nowhere else to meet people. It was like eating at Howard Johnson's: You may not like the food, but when you're on the highway and hungry, where else are you going to go? I was starving.

It's not a very pleasant time to talk about; however, it happened. In searching for someone, anyone who could make me feel loved, who could take away some of the emptiness, who could give me a reason to keep living, I did a lot of things I would have never considered two years earlier.

We would meet in a bar, hold an innocuous conversation for maybe an hour, and then the guy would make the suggestion: "It's getting loud in here. Why don't we go back to my place and talk?" I would follow him to an apartment, be offered some cheap wine in a dirty glass, and after a few minutes of directionless conversation, we would get to that inevitable moment of silence when he would gaze into my eyes and say, "You're so lovely." Then he would reach over, put his arm around me, pull me close, and kiss me.

And each time I went through it, I convinced myself that it wasn't empty. *Maybe this one will love me*. I told myself that maybe he was serious. Maybe he really did think that I was special.

He would always promise to call. I would usually allow myself a few days of waiting by the phone before admitting the truth.

Occasionally, if I fell asleep in front of his simulated gas-operated fireplace, I might have nightmares of Vietnam. When I would wake screaming and crying and sweating he would be annoyed. That wasn't part of the script. Never once did any man offer to hold me after a nightmare. However, a few asked me to leave so they could get a decent night's sleep without being interrupted by "a crazy broad."

I felt used, stupid, degraded, dirty, depressed, despairing, and disgusted. But I kept going back. Hoping. *Maybe this time.*

I attributed much of my unhappiness to my job, so I transferred from the ward to the hospital's emergency room. ER didn't begin to touch any of my expectations. I was bandaging cuts and handling cases so routine it was hard not to get bored. Most people used the ER as a clinic. I had thought it would be more like a shock trauma unit or else like the ER in 'Nam where you needed every bit of your medical training to do a good job. I wanted some kind of work that was challenging, although I couldn't say exactly what that might be. I wanted the intensity I had felt during the war, the feeling that I was spending every waking moment with my brain in gear and my physical endurance being pushed to the limit. I missed that rush of adrenalin that came whenever I had heard choppers in 'Nam. I also missed the respect. Nurses in stateside civilian hospitals were looked on merely as handmaidens to the doctors. It was a bitter pill to swallow.

I worked the intensive care unit, the coronary care unit, and the recovery room, but didn't find anything more than fleeting satisfaction.

When I got back to working as an OR nurse around 1971, I ended up with mostly routine cases until I started working with Dr. Arthur Bradley Weston, a highly respected but difficult vascular surgeon. A forty-year-old genius in his field, Dr. Weston was so fanatically precise that he had a reputation as a prima donna. The first time I scrubbed with him, he gave me the third degree and demanded to know what right I had to be working in *his* OR. When I told him that I had been assigned to him, he stormed out to the nursing superviser and demanded one of his regular nurses. "I can't work with somebody who doesn't know me," he said. "I won't have a nurse who's not experienced."

"Dr. Weston, you're going to love her," the supervisor said. "She'll be just fine."

Her reassurances failed to convince him. He ranted and raved and even stamped his feet. Finally, the supervisor had had enough. "Look, Dr. Weston," she said. "You're not going to get anyone else and that's final. All the others have scrubbed today. Lynda's one of the best. Give her a shot. If she doesn't prove herself, I promise you'll never have to work with her again."

We kept reference cards on each surgeon and I had studied Dr. Weston's carefully. Before the operation, I quickly ran through a list of questions with him to better familiarize myself with his procedures. When he started cutting, I had the exact instruments he needed in his hand before he got a chance to ask for them. He was shocked. He had never expected that kind of treatment. By the time he was in the belly, he had relaxed and was conversant. During the next few months, Dr. Weston began insisting on having me at his table. He taught me a lot.

I looked forward to the cases he brought in. His toughest were the people with ruptured aortic aneurisms. The aorta is the vessel that carries blood from the heart to the rest of the body. As the largest and longest blood vessel, it has branches to all organs and limbs. An aneurism is a bulge in the artery's wall, a weakening of the artery that's comparable to a soft spot on an inner tube. Sometimes blood can clot in the aneurism and close off the aorta. Other times, the aneurism can rupture. When it goes, if it's not fixed within minutes, the patient will die. By the time the aneurism ruptures, there is little hope.

The patients with ruptured aortic aneurisms were usually the ones who showed up in the ER one day with gut pain. They would look flushed, pale, and sweaty. At times they'd arrest in the ER and you'd lose them. Those who didn't crash were immediately rushed into surgery. Their bellies were swollen and shiny. By the time we opened the peritoneum, there would be an explosion of blood and clots. That was the point at which many crashed. The blood pressure would drop through the bottom. Until that moment, it would have been kept up by the pressure on the belly. We had to work like hell. Everything in the OR had to be planned right down to the most minute detail. A hesitation of seconds could cost a life. It was as close to 'Nam as I had gotten in the OR.

Once we were in the belly, we had to locate the aneurism and clamp it off immediately before we lost the patient. Then there would be only a short time from when they were clamped until they had to be unclamped. If the blood flow was stopped for too long, the patients could lose kidneys, the liver, the legs, the intestines, or all of them.

As soon as Dr. Weston got into the belly, he turned into an artist. His hands were swift and accurate. Every suture had to be in exactly the right place. He worked effectively under even the worst pressure. But he wasn't infallible. Sometimes it took too long when it was a difficult case. And sometimes the patient developed ischemic bowel and would eventually die. However, the losses weren't his fault. His record was better, probably, than any other surgeon in southern California.

Not all cases were like Dr. Weston's aortic aneurisms. Most were hernias, hemorrhoids, D & Cs, gall bladders, and appendectomies. I got the OR routine down so pat that I could do it in my sleep. I was bored and unhappy with handing instruments to surgeons who talked real estate while their arms were buried in someone's belly. My nursing supervisor offered me a chance to change the work by becoming the head OR nurse on the evening shift. I took it.

Evenings were times when we were either very busy or very bored. There never seemed to be any middle ground. When I had no cases, I spent a lot of time hanging around the ER, as I had done on so many slow nights in Vietnam. But on the busy nights, I hardly had time to think.

The cases would usually be things like motorcycle crashes, industrial accidents, or terrible car wrecks. We got the traumatic amputations, crushed bodies, and massive burns. The OR crew also took turns being on call for the night shift so sometimes I was awakened out of a sound sleep to go in and work for hours on people whose bodies were mangled. It could get ugly, but in many ways it was satisfying work. Yet I was starting once more to become unhappy with my job. Something was missing. I didn't know what that was.

There was another problem with the OR on evenings: After particularly bad cases, when I went home to sleep, I would dream about Vietnam. I spent many nights seeing the faces of kids who had died on my table. One stood out above all of them. His face was blown away and it was nothing more than a mass of blood and bone. *Gene and Katie, May 1968*. He would call to me until I screamed and woke up. If I went back to sleep, he would call me again. I spent a lot of nights pacing the floor and drinking until I could fall into a dreamless sleep.

But the odd thing was that I never connected the dreams with the work I was doing at the time.

In the bar scene, every guy had his own routine and the routines varied depending on which group the guys belonged to. The Manhattan Beach guys were macho; El Porto guys were into partying; Hermosa guys were younger and did more dope; Marina Del Rey guys were plastic.

Marina Del Rey had to be the World Capital of Plastic. In the movie, "The Graduate," when some guy pulled Dustin Hoffman aside and said, "Benjamin, I want to talk to you about one thing—plastics," he had to be thinking about Marina Del Rey. All the guys were bankers, businessmen, or stockbrokers, and when they went out at night, they assumed completely new identities. But when you got back to their places, the apartments were all the same: wall-to-wall sliding glass doors opening onto the marina. Tacky wood veneer cabinets in the kitchen. Wall-to-wall shag rug, white textured drapes, glass and chrome furniture, and Naugahyde couches. They all had king-size beds with velvet spreads and long low dressers. There were little breakfast bars with chrome stools to divide the kitchens from the living rooms. And their refrigerators all contained a six pack of beer, a bottle of cheap wine with a Safeway price tag on it, and a jar of mayonnaise. They had grungy towels in their bathrooms and all the rooms looked like they hadn't been cleaned in months.

The irony was that when you'd talk with a Marina Del Rey guy in a bar, you'd think that he had class coming out his ears. And when he brought you home, you'd be expecting to drink vintage wine out of pure crystal, not Gallo from a jelly glass.

But none of it mattered, so long as the man stayed and talked with me. If he stuck around for an hour I was grateful. I showed my gratitude by going with those plastic men to their plastic apartments. If I didn't there were hundreds of other girls who were willing. *Maybe this one.*

Opening lines:

Hermosa Beach: "You look really groovy tonight."
Marina Del Rey: "You are so lovely."
Manhattan Beach: "I really get off on you."
Translation: "Come with me."

They were mostly people I saw only once, except for a few. One guy down the street I had originally met in a bar came back to my place whenever he was bored. Of course, whenever he came knocking at the door, I was too desperate for company to tell the creep to get lost. I'd offer him a beer or a glass of wine, we'd sit in my living room, and he'd tell me what happened at work that day.

And there was this married doctor who wasn't getting enough attention at home, so he'd sneak over to my place occasionally. I'd make him a nice dinner, buy a good wine, have the candles lit, and play soft music. I would comfort him.

And later, there was another doctor, a divorced one who was sending all his money to his ex. I convinced myself that he cared, until he dumped me for the hospital sexpot.

And another.

And another.

And another.

I thought a lot about suicide. I had it planned very clearly. Things were perfectly organized. I was going to do it painlessly and quietly so I didn't leave my family with a mess. From Vietnam, I knew that Darvon was an effective way to do the trick since there wasn't any antidote. At the time, Darvon wasn't a controlled substance, so it was easy to get. I had a stash that would have knocked over an elephant.

I always planned the suicide for a Friday night at the start of a weekend, so nobody would notice until Monday. By the time they missed me, I'd be long gone. I would sit at the dining room table, count out fifty Darvon, then throw in some codiene, and a few Libriums and Valiums to make sure I had a good mixture. That way, if someone did chance upon me and try to resuscitate me, they wouldn't be able to figure out what was in me until it was too late.

But I always chickened out in the end. I would simply get dressed and head for another bar to find another guy who would tell me I was special.

Although I stayed at the same hospital, I bounced between so many jobs that it seemed like no job could last more than a few months. When I was unhappy with the OR routine, I was offered a chance to get involved in hemodialysis. I knew nothing about dialysis, but it was something new and different. I jumped at the opportunity.

In simple terms, hemodialysis is a way to sustain life when the kidneys can no longer filter the body's waste products from the bloodstream. A machine replaces the function of the kidneys and the patients are usually hooked up to the artificial kidney two or three times a week. Without the machine, they would die a slow and painful death. These days, with the machine, they can live a normal, healthy life. However, that wasn't the case at my hospital in 1971.

As late as 1960, there were no kidney doctors. Dialysis was hardly heard of, and nephrology was still in its infancy. Internists managed patients who were dying of the buildup of toxic wastes in their bodies—terminal uremia. They gave sedatives and painkillers to get people through convulsive seizures on the way to certain death. During the following years, some doctors started specializing in kidney diseases. They were called nephrologists, and they experimented with patients to keep them alive. As a result, an efficient artificial kidney machine was developed. The patients were hooked to the machine with needles and plastic tubing. The blood was pumped from their bodies to the machines, where microscopic waste particles were filtered out through semipermeable membranes. Once the blood was cleaned, it was returned through the plastic tubes.

Shortly after I got involved in hospital dialysis, I learned to hate it. The dialysis took place in a very isolated section of the building that had been designed as a lab. There were no windows and the room was filled with glass-fronted supply cabinets. It was depressing. Yet it wasn't the surroundings that caused my dislike for the procedure. It was the fact that the patients were doing so badly. Theirs seemed a futile existence. They weren't living; they were merely hanging around, waiting for death. Eventually, nearly all of them died from complications, except for one woman who committed suicide because she didn't want to suffer anymore.

I didn't know then that the problem wasn't dialysis; it was outmoded methods of treatment. Our patients were forced to live on tiny amounts of a few foods and wheat starch bread because that was the one food that supplied calories without leaving potassium and other wastes in the body. But the bread provided few vitamins or nutrients. Also, the patients were dialyzing off water-soluble vitamins every time they went on the machine. We didn't know to replace them. As a result, the patients suffered from bone disease and malnutrition. It wasn't until much later that I realized our methods were not the best.

I spent my working time watching people fall apart piece by piece. It made me more depressed than I had been when I started.

"Hey, baby, haven't I seen you around?"

"I come here sometimes."

"What's your name?"

"Lynda Van Devanter. What's yours?"

"Bob."

"Do you have a last name, Bob?"

"Last names are such bullshit, baby. You look so lovely tonight."

"Thank you."

"Let's go back to my place and talk."

"Okay, Bob." *Maybe this one.*

There weren't enough dialysis patients for a full-time nurse, so I worked part-time in the ER again. After a while, I got so sick of dialysis that I trained another nurse to take my place. She lasted a couple of weeks before she quit. I was forced to go back because nobody else would do it.

"Well, hello, good-looking. I'm Jim. Who are you?"

"Lynda."

"What do you say we go back to my place, Lynda?"

"Sure, Jim."

During my time at the hospital, Ken Nugent, a doctor who was friendly with Jack, kept trying to convince me to go to work with him at a privately run dialysis unit in L.A. I put him off, saying that I was getting out of dialysis at the first opportunity. When I told him it was depressing, he said it didn't have to be. When I told him I hated to watch people die slowly, he said they could live their entire lives on artifical kidney machines.

"What kind of lives?" I asked.

"Happy, healthy, and productive ones," he said. I succumbed to his nagging and visited the unit.

When I walked into the pleasant-looking room filled with machines and beds, I saw people playing chess, watching television, talking to each other, laughing and eating lunch. And lunch wasn't wheat starch bread. These people were eating things that were unheard of for my dialysis patients—Der Weinerschnitzel, Mr. Pizza, and Taco Bell. And they were healthy.

I went to work at Ken's unit two weeks later.

There are two types of dialysis patients: acute and chronic. In acute cases, the kidneys are temporarily out of commission because of injury, infection, or toxic substances. Dialysis is used until the kidneys recover. However, in chronic renal failure, dialysis is necessary for the patient's entire life, or until he or she receives a transplant. Chronic patients have permanent, irreversible damage. Those were the people Ken's unit took care of.

Sometimes chronic patients become acute, when their blood chemistries get far out of line, but if they follow a normal, slightly restricted diet, take the proper medications, and dialyze regularly, most patients have no problems.

I devoted my life to those patients. For a while, they got me out of myself. I was taught to dialyze the correct way and found that it wasn't any more difficult than it had been to do it wrong. When the unit opened an evening shift, I was assigned there as the head nurse.

From the start, I had problems with my supervisor, Marge Inman. She was one of the most efficient dialysis nurses I had ever met and she had a knack for teaching others. I learned a lot from her. But she had problems in dealing with the staff. One minute she would be smiling at you and you'd think that everything was rosy; the next minute she would jump in your case. For some reason, Marge developed a dislike for me. Sometimes it reached the point where, in her eyes, it seemed I could do no right. And later, it seemed that every time she wanted to talk with me, it was to chew me out.

In the absence of any other friends, I became close to my patients —Marge would have said too close. The ones who came to the evening shift were people who were more active and who were trying to work, go to school, and enjoy life. They didn't want to be tied down by their disease, so I tried to help them develop as much independence as possible. When I worked days, I came to know a number of patients who used to "plug in, turn on, and drop out." Some would lie down and put a sheet over their heads as soon as they got on the machine. The sheet wouldn't come off until dialysis was over. It was almost as if they were dead for those hours on the artificial kidney. They didn't want to see what was going on. They didn't want to know. They were afraid. They wanted to space out and let somebody else be responsible. It was a classic form of denial.

Those who came to the evening shift wanted to learn more about their disease. They had a million questions and I made sure that they got answers. I taught them how to put themselves on and take themselves off the machine. I explained how the artifical kidney functioned, what was going on with their bodies, and how they could recognize problems. Eventually, some even inserted their own needles.

Those who took responsibility for themselves always seemed to do better than those who let the nurses and technicians handle everything. I felt strongly that dialysis need not be an overwhelming experience that dominated every aspect of their lives. But some of the other nurses weren't crazy about my ideas, especially when word got back to the daytime patients. The day nurses didn't want patients learning too much about the machines. I felt it was because that would eliminate some of the medical mystique. Whenever I pulled duty on their shift, they insisted that I not rock the boat.

But I believed that the arguments against patient independence were more rationalization than anything else: "We've always done it this way." "It's more trouble than it's worth." "It could be dangerous."

The attitude of many professionals was that the patients might make a fatal mistake. There was a certain amount of validity to this concern if the patients were totally unsupervised. However, if professionals were around, mistakes could be corrected easily before they became a problem. Yet a lot of nurses refused to give the patients any responsibility at all. They treated the patients like children and wanted things to stay the way they were. "My kidneys failed," said one patient, "not my brains."

If the patients knew their machines and knew their bodies well enough they might not agree with certain decisions made by the nurses. Some nurses hated the idea that their authority could be questioned by a mere patient. They were not crazy about my instituting the new program on evenings, but when the doctors saw how smoothly things were running, they gave my shift their stamp of approval. It had been a worthwhile fight.

It wasn't too many months before this job, too, became routine. Yet we had fun on evenings and that made things more bearable. One of my patients was an artist. He did pictures of trains for us. Another was a lady-killer and we enjoyed laughing at his exploits. Then there was Timmy, who had to be the biggest coward I'd ever seen. He was deathly afraid of needles and would scream every time one was inserted into his vein. This was a thirty-year-old man! We had started a new program of tipping the machine's coils to try to give the patients more of their blood back at the end, and the first time I did it, he panicked. The procedure had already been done with hundreds of other patients and it produced absolutely no side effects. But we couldn't resist the opportunity to play with him. "Don't worry, Timmy," I said. "You'll only feel dizzy for a few minutes." True to form, he immediately convinced himself that he was too dizzy to move. He suffered only until we told him we were joking. Even then, he doubted us. Another time, when everybody was reading *Jaws,* one of the technicians brought in a small toy shark and put it in the clear plastic tank that held the dialysate for Timmy's machine. We waited anxiously for him to look but he didn't. I got his attention. Then, as I talked with him, I moved around his chair until I was standing in front of the tank. When I moved again, he saw the shark. His scream was so loud it was probably heard a mile away. But we really loved him, and he knew we were teasing him in fun. In time, even Timmy began doing things for himself.

The closest friend I made was Gail Cinelli, a five-foot-one-inch wisp of a woman who was two years older than I was. She had short black hair, bright blue eyes, and weighed no more than ninety-seven pounds soaking wet. Although Gail had a master's degree in library science from UCLA, she hadn't been able to land a library job because most employers were afraid to hire someone on dialysis. Gail had the wrinkles of an older woman, but the cheeriness in her face and the sparkle in her eyes made up for them. Her father was a lawyer and her mother was the owner of three successful boutiques in L.A. The two of them lived in Malibu in a house they had built themselves. Gail lived in Redondo Beach in a huge apartment she shared with three sorority sisters.

Gail had been on dialysis from the time she was eleven and had come close to dying more than once. She'd had three transplants, none of which lasted longer than six months, and her experiences had been so bad that she swore she would never have another. Dialysis was far more agreeable to her.

Although Gail was one of the first people I saw when I had come to visit the unit with Ken, and she was also one of the first evening patients, we didn't become fast friends until the spring of '72. I called her Hawkeye. It was because she was always watching everybody's machine and could pick out a problem from the other side of the room. We talked about all kinds of things—our childhoods, men, our relationships with our parents. Everything except Vietnam. I never discussed that with anyone. That would have been socially unacceptable—or at least that's what I thought.

Gail wondered whether she would ever get married and whether she would have kids. We both loved kids, but she didn't know if it would be fair for her to marry anyone because of the dialysis. She felt it might be too big a burden.

Sometimes, when I had a day off, we would have lunch with her mother or go sailing on her parents' boat. It was a close family, filled with love. They seemed so open, so willing to talk about anything with Gail. They were the most supportive people I'd ever met.

Shortly after we became friends, Gail and I began planning to take a vacation together. She had never been to the East Coast and wanted to see it. I would be tour guide and nurse on the trip. We called the National Association of Patients on Hemodialysis and Transplantation (NAPHT) for the names of people along the way who would be willing to let us use their home machines to dialyze Gail. Her parents offered to pay my expenses and give me a salary for the two weeks. I told them I was doing it for friendship, not money.

On the Fourth of July weekend, Gail and I took a plane to Boston, where we stayed with my sister Nancy. We visited Lexington and Concord, Louisa Mae Alcott's home, the Salem Witch House, and the House of the Seven Gables. We went out to dinner most nights and had a terrific time.

Gail dialyzed in the home of a man who lived outside Boston. I set up the machine and after she got hooked up, we talked with him as if he were a long-lost friend. One of the purposes of dialysis was to remove excess fluids from the body. If the fluids were not removed, the person could die of pulmonary edema. Starting with that first dialysis, I began to experience what I jokingly called a sympathetic reaction to Gail. As she took off water, I found myself making an embarrassing number of trips to the bathroom. Sometimes, when we reached the end of her time on the machine, I would have lost more water weight than she had. I realized, finally, that all the coffee I was drinking during those long hours of talking during the dialysis was acting as a diuretic on me. When I cut back on the coffee, I cut back on the water loss. Gail laughingly wondered if coffee could do the same for her and cure her kidney failure.

A few days later, we went to New York, where we took an elevator to the top of the Empire State Building, walked through Central Park, went for a ride in a horse-drawn carriage, saw a play, and shopped at Saks, Macy's, and Gimbel's. We dialyzed Gail out on Long Island and became friends with the family who owned that machine.

Next, I took Gail to my home. When we visited Washington, my parents went out of their way to make her feel welcome. I borrowed my father's car to drive to Yorktown and Jamestown after Gail and I did the tourist routine in D.C. We saw the Corcoran Gallery, the Smithsonian, the White House, the Washington Monument, and the Capitol.

There were times when I wanted to talk with my mother and father. I wanted to tell them that I was afraid, that there were things happening inside me that I didn't understand. To tell them that I didn't really like myself anymore, in spite of my ability to maintain a composed exterior. To tell them that I felt myself sinking deeper and deeper into a depression that I didn't comprehend. To tell them about the times when I truly wished I were dead. But I never could seem to find the right words. I didn't want to give them cause to worry about me. The problems were mine, not theirs.

When my father asked me how I was doing, I said I was fine.

In the beginning of the second week, I took Gail to a home in

Silver Spring where the people allowed us to use their artificial kidney machine. It was a different model from the one we had been using. Since I was still relatively new to dialysis, I had no idea that the size of the dialysate tanks differed. I mixed the solution in the proportions we had been using back in L.A., Boston, and New York. That was a mistake.

Gail did fine for the first three hours on the machine, but in the last hour, she started feeling sick. As time went by, she felt worse. I took her off and rushed her to George Washington Hospital. They immediately did blood tests and found that her sodium and chloride were too low. When the doctor explained my blunder, I felt ashamed. I hated myself for being so stupid. They gave her some broth and she began feeling better, but she was still very tired.

We returned to California three days early, partly because Gail was so tired from the vacation and partly because she needed to recuperate.

A couple of months later, Gail began getting slowly ill over a period of a few weeks, until one night when she was at the unit, she spiked a fever and started throwing up. We took her off the machine and got an ambulance to rush her to my old hospital, the nearest one. After they admitted her, they found that the level of toxins in her body was well above the danger point. When the doctors examined her, they discovered a narrowed area in the grafted vein that we used to dialyze her. It had been narrowing for a long time, making the problem almost impossible to spot until it became critical. The vessels were blocked in such a way that we had been unwittingly redialyzing the same blood again and again, while the toxins continued to build up in the rest of her system.

Gail desperately needed to be dialyzed that night. The doctors were afraid that if something wasn't done immediately, she might slip into a coma. The hospital had the equipment, but nobody there was qualified now to use it. I hurried there and set up the artificial kidney while Gail was in the OR having a shunt put into her other arm. The shunt was made of two pieces of Teflon tubing connected in the middle. One end was attached under the skin to a vein, the other to an artery. It provided quick access to her blood so she could be dialyzed immediately.

As soon as Gail came out of surgery, I hooked her up to the machine. Mrs. Cinelli and I sat next to her bed through the night. By morning, she was much better. "If there's anything I can ever do for you," Mrs. Cinelli said, "please don't hesitate to ask."

Marge refused to pay my wages for that night. She said that when I left the dialysis unit, I wasn't working for her. If I wanted payment, she said, I would have to take the matter up with the hospital. Of course, the hospital took the position that I should be paid by my unit.

When Mrs. Cinelli learned of my plight, she offered to give me the salary. I refused. It wasn't the money; it was the principle.

In the middle of August, I sank into the deepest depression I had experienced up to that time. I began crying day and night for no reason. I just felt so awful. I didn't know what was going on with me. I had an overwhelming physical feeling of being oppressed. Everything seemed so dark. It was as if the sun never came out, although in reality it was always shining in southern California. I felt like there was an enormous weight on top of me. It became an effort to get out of bed or to take a step. I started calling in sick a lot and spending entire days in bed. I didn't eat and I couldn't fall asleep. I wouldn't even put my clothes on. I'd stay in my nightgown or wear a T-shirt all the time. I wouldn't read or watch television. I would merely lie around all day crying, with the covers over my head. When night came, I would drink myself into oblivion.

When I went to work, I didn't talk much. I gave monosyllabic responses. My technical skills were still quite proficient, but I wasn't communicating with the patients as I always had. Some of them asked me what was wrong. All I could say was I didn't know.

"Is there anything I can do to help?" someone would ask.

"I don't think so," was my answer.

"Come back to my place, baby."

"Will you hold me? Please?"

"Sure, baby. Anything."

"Okay."

My body felt like a mass of exposed nerves that all hurt. The emptiness inside was so big that I thought it had consumed me. It was as if I didn't really exist. I was so small and getting smaller all the time. It wouldn't be long before I would disappear.

In September, the people at NAPHT asked me to come to a big dialysis convention in San Francisco. It was a major effort, but I forced myself to attend. When I arrived, I learned that they had selected me as NAPHT's first nurse of the year. They wanted to do an article for their newsletter. Why had I been chosen? I was never too sure. I think it had something to do with the trip Gail and I had taken in July. They said it was an encouraging experience for all dialysis patients and it showed them that they didn't have to be limited because of their reliance on an artificial kidney.

I told myself they had made a mistake. How could *I* be honored by any group of people?

The woman who interviewed me was someone I had met in New York during the trip. She insisted that I meet another reporter who was covering the convention. That reporter was Bill Blackton. Little did I know that this shy, handsome man would someday become my husband.

It would be romantic if I could say that Bill swept me off my feet with hearts and flowers and that he made buzzers and bells go off in my head. It would also be a lie. That wasn't Bill's style.

He was slight, very unassuming and soft-spoken, but I began to see that behind the shyness was a man who was very quick and smart, with a wonderfully dry sense of humor. It had been so long since I'd laughed that I had almost forgotten how. Bill made me laugh. It had been at least a full month since I had spent a day without crying. Bill gave me one of those days.

We went to Fisherman's Wharf that evening and had dinner at Scoma with a small group of friends. Bill persuaded me to try the abalone with garlic butter. It was the first time I had ever tasted the shellfish. I loved it.

Afterward, we walked along the edge of the water, talking and holding hands. There was something about him that made me feel peaceful. He wasn't trying to impress me or get me into the sack. He merely enjoyed my company. He liked me for who I was and not for anything I could give him other than good conversation. He listened to what I had to say and made me feel that my thoughts were important. And best of all, he let me see inside him. I liked what I saw. I liked it a lot. After a year of one-night stands with sleazy first-name characters from the meat market, Bill Blackton was refreshing.

We stayed together chatting until very late, and when we said goodnight at my hotel, he didn't even try to kiss me. I saw him a couple of times the next day between meetings and loaned him some pamphlets on dialysis. When it was time for him to leave, we walked together to the bus terminal. I stayed with him until departure time.

Bill lived in Encino, only twenty miles from Manhattan Beach. "We'll have to get together," he said.

"I'd like that."

By the time I returned to my hotel room, I was crying again. I felt desolate. The next day, I was so depressed I could hardly marshal the energy to attend the meetings. The following day I returned home.

I waited, but Bill Blackton didn't call.

By October, I started missing days of work. When my phone rang, I didn't answer it. Sometimes, I was lucky when I got the energy to go to the bathroom.

I hated myself and despaired of ever feeling anything different. I didn't have to kill myself with Darvon or any other pills. The life I was living was a slow suicide.

One day, after I had been missing from work for an exceptionally long period, I got a surprise visit from Gail's mother. She yelled out to me, and I tried to ignore her knocking at my door, but finally, I realized that if I didn't answer it, Mrs. Cinelli would probably break the door down. When I let her in, she took one look and said, "Lynda, you're coming home with me."

I spent the next few days being mothered. Mrs. Cinelli made me eat some healthy meals and forced me to get some fresh air. She walked me on the beach and hugged me and tried to talk with me. I told her how empty I felt and at times she seemed to understand. But I didn't know where that emptiness was coming from. I never really thought that it might have anything to do with feelings that had started in Vietnam. Mrs. Cinelli didn't know that I was a vet and I wasn't about to tell her. She might think I was crazy. Besides, Vietnam was already more than two years in my past. It was over.

She wanted to call my parents, to let them know that I needed help. If she had called, they would have come. But I wouldn't let her. I didn't want them worrying.

Mrs. Cinelli convinced me to see a psychiatrist and by the time I returned home I felt strong enough to go back to work. I was still crying in the morning and through the night, but I was able to get through the working hours, for the most part, without tears. That felt like an accomplishment.

A week later, I had my first appointment with the shrink. I had been crying before I went and my eyes were bloodshot. My complexion was gray. I walked into a walnut-paneled room with a thick carpet and overstuffed chairs to be met by a similarly overstuffed man sitting behind an enormous desk. "I just want to make one thing perfectly clear right from the beginning," he said immediately. I hadn't had a chance to sit down yet. "I don't give professional discounts."

I spent two hours and ninety dollars with him. He told me I was merely another neurotic woman. That wasn't what I needed to hear.

But for some reason, I was regaining control over the tears. I was still mostly waking up in tears and going to sleep in tears, but now I was making it through entire days without crying. I took it as a good sign. Perhaps the depression was lifting. Maybe it would be finally over.

Dear Lynda,

Enclosed are the materials I borrowed. Thank you very much. I had a good time with you in San Francisco. We'll have to get together again.

Sincerely,
Bill Blackton

In December, the tears came flooding back. It seemed as though the harder I tried to pull myself out of the depression, the deeper I sank. It was like quicksand. I was thinking almost constantly about suicide and I counted out the pills more than once. But whenever it came time to swallow them, I couldn't make myself do it.

I was too afraid of dying.

Dear Lynda,
I'd like to wish you a Merry Christmas and a Happy New Year. We'll have to get together soon.

Sincerely,
Bill Blackton

In January, Marge gave me my annual review. It was the worst rating I had ever received. She told me I was too involved with the patients and had lost my objectivity. She said that crying at work was unprofessional and that my performance was totally unacceptable.

''Are you firing me?'' I asked.

She shifted uncomfortably. ''There might be a better way of saying that, Lynda.''

''What do you mean?''

''I'm asking you to resign,'' she said.

I felt like the floor had dropped out from under me. My patients were all that I had. They were my only reason to keep going, the only people who really cared whether I lived or died. I struggled to stop my voice from cracking. ''If that's the way you feel,'' I said, ''you can have my resignation right now.''

20

Acting Normal

When I lost my job at the dialysis unit, I went back to bed and stayed there. Sometimes from nearly morning until late at night, my feet wouldn't touch the floor. I hardly concerned myself with even the simplest functions of life such as eating, bathing, or brushing my teeth. After the money ran out, I got food stamps and collected unemployment, but couldn't look for work. I had neither the energy nor the self-confidence to hold down another job. I saw myself as a failure. I could barely comb my hair; how would I care for patients?

I called a psychiatrist I knew professionally and asked if he could help me. I told him that I was in terrible trouble and so deeply depressed that I wasn't sure I would survive. Since I had no money, he referred me to the Los Angeles County Outpatient Adult Psychiatric Clinic. There treatment was free.

My case was assigned to Franklin Watts, an intern in clinical psychology who would be finishing his degree in six months. During our initial period, I was so bad that Franklin saw me three times a week. I liked him. He seemed to be genuinely concerned for my health. He made it easy to talk about everything. Everything except Vietnam. If I had brought the war up, he probably would have listened, but by that time, I had been so conditioned to hold it in that even the most sincere questioner would not have got a word out of me. Besides, I couldn't tell my shrink I was a Vietnam vet; I didn't want him to think I was that crazy.

Shortly after the therapy started, I got my first call from Bill Blackton. He had two press tickets to see Evel Knievel jump over fifty cars at the L.A. Coliseum. At the time I was crying all day, every day, and didn't think I would be able to go on a date, but for some reason I said yes.

From the moment Bill's little red VW pulled up in front of my house on the day of the jump until long after he left, I didn't cry. Not even a single tear. It was my first dry-eyed day in months. Bill and I were different in so many ways, however, I couldn't help but like him. I forgot the emptiness for a while. In fact, I even laughed. I had a good time. Bill was one of the funniest people I had met. Yet he wasn't frivolous. When he talked seriously, he talked about things that really mattered. In the weeks that followed, we began seeing a lot of each other. Miraculously, whenever I was with him there were no tears.

Bill was working the morning and afternoon drive shift at KFI as a traffic reporter for the radio station's "eye in the sky," Bruce Wayne. While Bruce worked out of the plane, Bill stayed in the newsroom monitoring about fifteen radios that carried communications from the Highway Patrol, LAPD, the fire department, L.A. County Sheriff, and other agencies. Every five minutes, Bill would transmit that information to Bruce, who would then add his own observations from the sky before giving the report to the commuters. On weekends, Bill volunteered at KPFK in North Hollywood, a listener-sponsored station, where he did the afternoon news reports.

The more I learned about this man, the more interesting he became. Unlike the guys I had been meeting in the past year, Bill Blackton had depth, personality, a last name, and a history, all of which he was willing to share. Born in New York City, Bill was one of two children of musical parents. His father was a conductor and arranger who had worked on Broadway and for movies, and his mother had been a professional pianist until Bill's older sister was born. Bill had grown up in both New York and L.A., living mostly in apartments and rented houses. From 1957 to 1972, he resided permanently in New York City, and through most of his school years, he attended the Riverdale School for Boys. He told me about learning to swim with Meredith MacRae in Arizona while their fathers were filming *Oklahoma* and about the kinds of pranks he would pull on teachers and his friends in high school. At one time, Bill had memorized the telephone numbers of a half dozen phone booths in midtown

Manhattan and he and his friends used to call the phones to play tricks on the people who might answer. He still remembered the number of the booth at 47th and Broadway. He had a mind for details and knew enough esoteric facts to fill a trivia encyclopedia. But more than anything, Bill Blackton knew how to show me a good time. I hadn't enjoyed myself as much with anyone since Carl.

There was, however, one thing that made me think twice about continuing to see Bill: After a few dates, he informed me that he had been at the convention not only as a reporter, but also as a dialysis patient. He told me so I might have a chance to change my mind before we got too serious. I had promised myself that I would never get romantically involved with a patient, but by then, it was too late. I was beginning to fall in love with Bill.

He had first learned about his kidney problem in October of 1964, when he was a freshman at Swarthmore College and started feeling run-down. The campus doctor made a diagnosis of simple anemia. Later, when Bill didn't get better, he visited his family doctor in New York for some tests. It was then that he learned he had kidney disease.

Bill continued to get sicker until March 1965, when he began dialysis. "If I hadn't gone on the machine, I would have died," he said.

Bill was one of the fortunate ones. In 1965, dialysis was not widely avalable. Since there were so many people who needed to be dialyzed and not enough machines to handle everyone, some hospitals had life and death committees to decide who would receive treatment. Those who didn't qualify were, in reality, being handed death sentences. It was a very trying time for the Blackton family.

During the following years, Bill attended Columbia University while dialyzing for sixteen hours a night three times a week at a hospital unit similar to the one at which I had worked. Later, he had a transplant, but his body rejected the new kidney and he went back on dialysis. Finding the transplant experience very disconcerting, Bill preferred dialyzing. Now he had his own machine in the house in Encino that he shared with his sister and brother-in-law and he knew as much about it as even the best dialysis nurse.

While living in New York, Bill had started a newsletter for dialysis patients and had entertained the thought of becoming a clinical psychologist. But after a while, he decided to pursue other opportunities. "My philosophy," he said, "is to put as much distance as I can between me and the machine. I want my life to be as normal as possible, not totally centered around dialysis."

When Bill learned that I was unemployed and in a financial bind, he offered me part-time work as his personal nurse. He said that because his job forced him to wake up at 3:30 A.M. every day, he had been accidentally falling asleep during dialysis and needed someone just to watch the machine while he napped. He paid me ten dollars each time I came to the house. After a couple of weeks without a single nap, I knew that the offer was mostly charity. I kept coming to visit during dialysis, but I stopped taking his money.

We talked a lot when Bill was on the machine. He shared all the intimate details of his life and I shared as much as I could. I found the courage to tell him I had been to Vietnam—he said it made me more interesting—and after a couple of months, I even showed him some pictures. The photos were of people I had worked with. My stories were mostly trivial. I never said anything about the kids who died, the rocket attacks, or the nightmares. I didn't want to burden him.

Bill made me feel like I was important. He told me he believed in me, and, over time, he helped me to start believing in myself. In many ways, he was a lifeline. He gave me reason to go on. He said he felt like he could talk with me about anything. I wanted to be able to talk with him about anything, too. But there were some things I just couldn't let myself mention. One was the fact that I was going to a therapist. I thought that if Bill knew, he wouldn't have anything to do with me. I was wrong.

With Franklin, I was working on my inability to maintain relationships. It seemed like I was always picking the kind of men who didn't want to get serious. When one would want to get involved, I would push him away, in spite of my desperate craving for love. It was totally illogical. I found myself starting to repeat the pattern with Bill. I discussed the situation in great detail with Franklin, but was unable to change. Finally, he suggested that I ask Bill to come into therapy with me.

"I can't do that," I said.

"Don't you think he'd be willing?" Franklin asked.

"I haven't even told him I'm *in therapy*!"

"Now you can tell him."

It took a lot of worry, but I eventually built up enough courage to broach the topic. Bill immediately agreed to join me. "It doesn't mean you're crazy because you're getting help," he said. "It's admirable that you're trying to face the problems."

On January 27, 1973, the United States signed the Paris Peace Pact. It was ten years and hundreds of thousands of lives too late. By March 29, American ground troops were out of Vietnam. All that remained were some advisors. When I saw, on television, the arrival of the first POWs, it was difficult to feel anything but emptiness. Their cause had been such a hollow one.

I dreamed that night about Vietnam and woke up in a cold sweat. It was a new dream: *Thousands of American mothers were walking in the streets of Saigon, carrying the bloody bodies of their dead sons. Above the wailing, screaming, and gnashing of teeth, one word was constantly repeated:*

Why?

That spring, I learned how to hold on to a relationship. Franklin was my guide. Each week I would visit him once alone and once with Bill. Franklin assured me I was making progress. I gave everything I had to therapy. I was so determined not to fail in this new relationship that I never really took the time to ask myself whether Bill and I were right for each other. He was a good man who treated me specially. What more could I ask?

I managed to bury the emptiness deep enough so I could live a normal life. I stopped drinking, lost weight, and started taking better care of myself. When the pain would occasionally bubble to the surface, I'd push it back down again.

By the time Franklin finished his internship in July, my tears had subsided and I had convinced Bill, in spite of his initial reluctance, to move to the beach. I told him often that I loved him, almost as if I was trying to make it real by saying it so frequently. He was hesitant to speak of love. "To tell someone you love them is to make a lifetime commitment," he said. "It's not something to take lightly." Those sentiments were not the ones I wanted to hear, but I was willing to wait until he could say he loved me, too.

In May, when my father came to L.A. on business, I spent an evening telling him that I felt like nobody loved me.

''Your mother and I love you dearly,'' he said. ''I'm sorry you haven't been able to see that.''

''I'm so confused, Dad. Sometimes life just feels so empty.''

''I wish there was something I could do to change it,'' he replied. ''You know I'd give anything to see my little girl happy.'' He held me all evening on his lap, hugging me tightly to his chest and rocking me while I cried. He would have sacrificed his life if it would have eased even a fraction of my pain. But nothing would have helped, and my father was wise enough to know that. Yet knowing that didn't stop him from hurting, too. He wondered if maybe I wouldn't be better off living closer to home. I told him I couldn't go home. Not yet.

Bill met my father during that trip and the two of them got along very well. Dad was concerned that I might be setting myself up for more heartache by getting involved with a dialysis patient, but he could see that Bill was a good person and a positive influence on me. He said he wished, with every part of his soul, that Bill would be able to remove my unhappiness and fill my life with meaning. I had the same wish. It was probably too much to ask from any person.

In the middle of the summer, the local hospitals started to receive a lot of patients with short-term severe kidney problems. Unfortunately, they didn't have anyone on staff who was qualified to handle acute dialysis. I was asked to work as an independent contractor. I began in September of 1973 and soon felt like I had found my niche. Other than surgery in Pleiku, acute dialysis was probably the most intense task I had ever faced. I stayed with it for six years. It was exciting in the beginning and it was challenging to the end. When I did acute dialysis, I was usually taking care of the sickest patients in the hospital who were having dozens of other procedures performed on them. Then they had one more thing added—dialysis. Every moment that these people were on the machine, their lives hung in the balance. One mistake on my part could have ended it all. In fact, I had more control over the patients' lives than the doctors did, because I was constantly at the bedside and I mostly worked alone. The other professionals looked on me with respect. It was the first time I had felt that kind of esteem since leaving Vietnam.

My patients ranged in age from teenagers to very old people, and with all the time I spent dialyzing them—some at least eight hours a day for months—it would have been difficult not to establish emotional bonds. One of my favorites was Debbie Roershak, a tiny blond fifteen-year-old girl who, if luck had not been with her, surely would have died. Debbie had been brought into the emergency room one night with a flulike syndrome that had been causing her to vomit for a couple of days. The ER staff examined her thoroughly, did a blood count and chest X ray, but found nothing. They gave her some Tylenol and medication for her nausea and told her parents to bring her back if she didn't get better. The next morning, Debbie was worse. She was dehydrated and lethargic. As the ER nurses were admitting her, she arrested. When they resuscitated, they noticed that her belly was becoming rigid. X rays showed a ruptured diverticulum, which is a little outpouching in the wall of the bowel. She was rushed to the OR for immediate surgery. While on the table, she arrested two more times.

Debbie survived that surgery, but it was only the beginning of a four-month ordeal. She developed gas gangrene, septicemia (an infection in the bloodstream), respiratory problems, and kidney failure. When I first dialyzed her, I found a very sick little girl on a respirator with a tube coming out of almost every body orifice. Her weight was down to seventy-five pounds and her level of toxins was so high that she had to be dialyzed on the most efficient equipment I had. But Debbie was a classic case of everybody pulling together as a team to keep someone alive who, by the odds, should have no chance at all. She had two terrific surgeons and the best staff in town: a nephrologist, respiratory physician, cardiologist, ICU nurses, physical therapists, occupational therapists, and a dialysis nurse.

Debbie's setbacks forced her to return to surgery a few times, but eventually, she started getting better. After a while, she developed a syndrome we used to call "ICU-itis," which is an extreme disorientation some people experience when they are catastrophically ill and in a restricted environment without any input from the outside world. They stop feeling normal tactile sensations, they don't hear normal sounds, and they fade in and out of reality all the time. As soon as Debbie developed these symptoms, we moved her to a room with a window, got her a television and a radio, and did our best to orient her to time and place when we were with her. I bought her a goldfish and hung it in an IV bottle above her bed so she could see it at any time. She named him Sunshine.

Since Debbie had a tracheotomy and couldn't talk, and contractures in her hands made it very difficult to write, I had developed a tap board—a paper with the letters of the alphabet taped to the back of a clipboard—so she could communicate. She was an atrocious speller, but we usually managed to figure out what she was trying to tell us. One day at the end of June, I went into her room to dialyze her and found her crying. When I asked what was wrong, she tapped out F-I-R-E-W-O-K. I didn't know what she was saying.

"Fire?" I asked, figuring she was confused again. "Where is the fire, Debbie?"

She shook her head no, and tapped out F-I-R-E-W-O-K once more. I wracked my brain, then called in another nurse to help me decipher Debbie's code. Finally, it hit us: "You mean fireworks?" I asked.

She nodded like crazy.

"You want to see fireworks on the Fourth of July?"

She nodded again.

By this time, she was off the respirator, but still on dialysis, oxygen, and IVs. After some checking we learned that no fireworks would be visible from the hospital. However, we weren't about to give up. When her mother told us that she took Debbie to Redondo Beach every year for the display, we scrambled to grant the little girl her wish. We got the doctors to okay us moving her and we rented an ambulance with oxygen. One of the dayshift nurses and a physical therapist volunteered to accompany Debbie to Redondo Beach, and the owner of the Portofino Inn offered a free hotel room with a view of the water. When it was over and she was back in the hospital, Debbie tapped out one of the most heartfelt T-H-A-N-K Y-O-Us in history.

Behavior regression is a common occurrence in children and adults who are extremely ill for long periods of time. Debbie was no exception. She sometimes acted like a three-year-old. Our worst problem came after she had recovered somewhat and her trach was removed. Debbie refused to eat because her throat hurt so badly. We begged, pleaded, and cajoled. We got her favorite foods and made all kinds of promises. Nothing did any good. "I know it hurts," I said. "But if you don't eat, you won't get better." She was surviving strictly on nourishment from the IVs until we got her to the point where she would drink milkshakes. However, she still wouldn't take any solids and would throw a tantrum if we tried to force her.

One day, I'd had enough. She was sitting in her chair when dinner arrived. She asked to go to bed. I told her she would not be able to unless she ate something. I set a hamburger in front of her and ordered her to take a bite. She shook her head no. It was a test of wills, and I wasn't about to lose. I informed her that she would not be able to go to bed until she swallowed a bite. Debbie was furious. She picked up a fork and threw it on the floor. Then she threw a spoon across the room. She lifted the hamburger and cocked her arm.

"If you throw that on the floor," I said, "I'm going to put it back on the plate and make you eat it dirty."

She silently glared at me. After a few minutes, she started pouting while she watched me out of the corner of her eye. She was so cute, I had to bite my cheeks to keep from bursting into laughter. Finally, she reached down with her little hands, picked up the hamburger, studied it for a moment, and then took the tiniest bite I've ever seen. After she had bitten off the mouse-sized piece, she looked back at me and smiled. I had to laugh. She had me beaten. I had only told her to take a bite; I hadn't specified how big a bite.

Two hours later, when she was back in bed, Debbie tapped on her board P-E-N-U-T B-U-T-E-R S-A-N-W-I-C-H. Her spelling hadn't improved with her illness, but it was clear that she was getting better. I got it for her immediately. It was a turning point in her recovery.

A week and a half before Debbie left the hospital, her kidneys started functioning again and she went off dialysis. It felt good to know that I had been part of saving such a promising young life.

Not all patients brought as much gratification as Debbie. In the six years I worked with acute cases, I found myself frequently confronted by death. There was Betty, the old woman who looked like a bag lady and watched soap operas all afternoon. One day in the middle of a dialysis treatment, she put her head on my shoulder and cried, "I'm so tired." The next week, she was dead.

And there was Anthony, the short, rotund owner of a Los Angeles furniture store who contracted an unrecognizable disease during a visit to Peru and was spiking fevers of 105 when his kidneys shut down. We thought we had him pulled through and were going to stop dialysis in a few days when he died of a heart attack.

And Daniel, a small Japanese man who had heart problems and

had dropped to ninety pounds before his kidneys failed. He expired on the operating table when the surgeons were repairing a bad aortic valve.

And Michael, one of the ruptured abdominal aortic aneurism cases who survived the surgery, but didn't survive the complications.

And Tricia.

And Scott.

And Millicent.

And others.

As each new year came, it brought more death with it. My feelings were mixed: In many ways, I hated the job, but a part of me loved it. No other work outside of Pleiku had required that kind of commitment. I was using all of my skills, and I began to realize that I really was an extremely competent nurse. The doctors I worked with recognized my ability and frequently consulted me for my advice or suggestions on patients. I was beginning to feel respected, something else I hadn't felt since Vietnam.

I felt needed. I was on call twenty-four hours a day and frequently had to go to the hospital in the middle of the night to take care of a patient. However, the intensity was double-edged. When the stresses got bad, I would again be faced with the nightmares that had haunted me since Vietnam—the surgical-T packed with bodies, missing arms and legs, rivers of blood flowing through Pleiku, and the voices constantly crying, "Why?" I was sometimes able to go through periods as long as three or four months without a single nightmare, but they always came back.

Coast Guard helicopters used to fly over the beach near my house and each time I heard those familiar rotor blades, I would become irritable, pacing back and forth like a caged animal, sometimes shaking long after the choppers had gone. The stomach problems I'd had, beginning in Pleiku, had finally become an ulcer, and I would often turn irrational without a moment's notice. I'd go on tirades for no logical reason. I was filled with rage over even the most insignificant things. I didn't understand any of it. I only wished it would stop.

When the last Americans were evacuated from Saigon in 1975, while the Viet Cong and NVA rockets bombarded Tan Son Nhut Airport, I watched the television reports and saw the Marine helicopters taking people from the roof of the embassy to U.S. warships anchored off the coast in the South China Sea. The media were calling it "the end of an era," but it was only the beginning of another round of bad dreams and sleepless nights for me.

In spite of my emotional problems, my life with Bill was, on the surface, very conventional. Some saw us as the perfect couple and we had all the outward manifestations of a good life. I owned my own cute beachhouse, which I had purchased shortly before meeting him. We went for long walks along the Strand, a stretch of sidewalk next to the beach running from El Porto to Torrance. We had Sunday brunches at the Surfboarder in Hermosa Beach and afternoon picnics by the ocean. We became acquainted with a wide variety of people and did the kinds of things that are supposed to make for a fun life.

In the fall of 1973, Bill decided that it was okay to tell me he loved me. He said the words one day as I was leaving for work. During that entire week I was elated. I told myself that because it had taken him so long he meant it more sincerely than most people.

Yet I couldn't help but wish that Bill had been a little quicker in expressing his love.

It took me two years to convince him to marry me. I was the one who actually proposed. Although he said yes, he didn't seem like he really wanted to make the commitment. While I waited for him to give me a positive sign, I felt the faint stirrings of resentment. Finally, one morning as he was walking out of the bathroom, after our wedding was in the planning stages, he looked at me and said, "Lynda, will you marry me?"

Our ceremony was a beautifully intimate candlelight affair held just after Christmas, 1975, at my parents' mountain home. They had just finished enlarging their one-room cabin into a spectacular three-bedroom house with views of the Shenandoah mountains and valleys from every window. I invited Mickie, Coretta, and a few other old friends from Vietnam, along with all the members of my family. Coretta was married with a small baby and another one on the way. Mickie was engaged to a Marine veteran whom she had met at a peace rally in 1972. They had heard that Bubba was fulfilling his promise to become "just possibly the second best neurosurgeon in North America." He was teaching in a medical school in Boston and was supposedly doing well, in spite of a devastating divorce that had taken place within a year of his return to the world. Unfortunately, while

Bubba had been in Vietnam, his wife had found someone she loved more. Slim was still in the Army, now as a major stationed in Germany, and the others were all scattered through the United States. Nobody had heard from Carl Adams or Jack, although Mickie had heard that Jack had a thriving practice in Oregon, and had never married. I thought of him with sadness, and with hope for his happiness.

I thought also about Barbara that night and wished that she could have been there to share these happy moments. But it was as if she had disappeared without a trace. I felt as though I would never know what happened to her. I missed my friend.

The minister, who was a jovial three-hundred-pound hulk of a man and also the local mail carrier, performed the rites. We said vows we had written ourselves, and I sang Paul Stookey's "Wedding Song" with Mary, while another friend played guitar. Bill's father played Bach on the piano for the processional. My father gave a reading from Saint Paul and then spoke eloquently about love. When I kissed Bill, I told myself that our marriage would last forever. With the valley spread before us, and the snow all around, it was a scene out of a storybook.

But even during that most joyous of celebrations, I knew inside that the emptiness was never far away. It lurked in a dark corner of my soul. Waiting.

The early years of our relationship were not easy ones for Bill. When I became irrational, I could be a very difficult person to live with, and when I woke up screaming from the nightmares, he was frustrated with his inability to help. But Bill had other problems besides me.

In '73, Bill was promoted from the KFI traffic assignment to a job as a newswriter. The next year, the writers all unionized. That move brought a substantial pay increase for about a month. Then the radio station management decided they no longer needed news-writers. Bill was laid off and spent most of the next year looking for work. He occasionally landed some free-lance assignments, but it wasn't until 1975 that he found another steady job in radio, producing documentaries for the Public Affairs Broadcast Group.

Before too long, my pressures from being an independent con-tractor at three separate hospitals became overwhelming. By 1975, I had trained others to assume my duties at two hospitals and I was working on the staff of the third. It cut down on my hours—for awhile.

Occasionally, I would doubt whether Bill and I were suited for each other. I tried to make things work, but I felt that he would sometimes take me for granted. We wanted different things, physically and emotionally. In many ways, my outgoing personality overpowered him and kept him from growing in areas where I took the lead. By the same token, I found myself wishing for someone who was more demonstrative and less cautious in expressing feelings. Often, when I wanted to hold him and be held, he wanted to be left alone. In situations where I jumped, he took his time, carefully studying the hazards. And when I stayed up nights crying, he usually slept soundly.

But Bill was my safe harbor. I always knew that he would be there, that he believed in me and was proud of me. He was somebody to hold onto, an anchor. I never considered what life might be like without him.

One Christmas, when I wanted a calculator and he had no money, he made me an abacus. He used to make a lot of things for me: a hat rack, a wooden box for my cassette tapes, a drying rack for drinking glasses, and a colorful banner with a combination of both our names —Van Blackton—which hung outside our beach house for years. Once when we visited Santa Barbara overnight so he could do some interviews for a documentary, he made a huge heart in the sand below our motel window. It said, "Bill loves Lynda."

We took a lot of trips together. He brought me to New York to show me all the places where he had lived and played as a child. I brought him to Washington to show him the softball field, my old school, and the view from the window of the house on Edison Street.

We went together again to San Francisco, had dinner at Scoma, and retraced the steps we took on the day we met. Then we rented a car and drove north to Muir Woods, where we walked among trees that were hundreds of feet high. The sun was shining in little sparkling rays and the wind was blowing through my hair. We walked out on a parapet overlooking the ocean north of Muir Woods and Bill told me how happy he was. As I leaned against the railing, I felt good. The times like that made life worthwhile and gave me hope. Later that evening, on the way back to San Francisco, we stopped at the Warehouse, a building filled with small shops in Sausalito. I fell in love with a special music box. Although it was too expensive, on my next birthday I found it on my bed in Manhattan Beach wrapped in pretty paper with a bow on top. There was also a note from Bill: "Happy Birthday, Lynda. I love you."

Yet the emptiness was still inside me. It floated to the surface and I pushed it back down.

We went to Hawaii twice over the years and stayed with my cousins, who were stationed in the Army there. Bill and I climbed the hill behind their house and looked out on Pearl Harbor. We went to the bars in Waikiki and sunned ourselves on the beaches. When we visited Maui, we stayed with a friend who lived in a deserted section of the island. She led us on an expedition through the jungle to an isolated blue pool that was fed by an icy-cold stream and a waterfall, surrounded by huge lava rocks. Bill and I kissed underwater and floated on our backs, letting the waterfall massage our stomachs. We laughed and sang and had a wonderful time.

We also visited the Seven Sacred Pools with the same friend and she showed us an underground tunnel that she used to swim through when she was a child to get from one pool to another. When the challenge was presented, I immediately accepted it, while Bill sat on the side and watched. I measured the tunnel a few times and then marked the distance from the top of the water to the tunnel entrance, pushing myself down to see how long it would take to reach bottom. I submerged three or four times, holding my breath, making sure I had enough lung capacity. I checked the tunnel carefully: It was a narrow passage, less than three feet in diameter. There was no way I would be able to use my arms. I would have to kick myself through it. But I could see light at the other side.

Finally, I took the plunge. When I reached the tunnel, I pushed off hard, propelling myself into the entrance. I started to kick and kept my hands at my side. At the halfway point I was swept with a feeling that I wasn't going to make it. I panicked. I could die here, I thought. In a split second, I went through a dozen emotions, the dominant one being fear. I tried to see behind me to determine how far I was from the entrance but I immediately realized that there was no way to propel myself backward. The only thing to do was to keep moving forward and hope.

I kicked and moved a few feet.

I hit my shoulder on a rock.

Some more kicks. A few more feet.

My lungs felt like they were going to burst.

More kicking. More distance.

My vision became blurred.

Kick. Kick.

My head pounded

Kick, dammit, kick!

Suddenly, I was through.

I shot to the surface coughing and gasping for air. When I realized I was alive, something inside of me told me that if I could get through that tunnel, I could do anything. Bill jumped into the water to congratulate me. He was shaking.

"Are you cold?" I asked.

"No, just scared," he said honestly. "I was afraid you weren't going to make it."

We had a highly successful burn unit at the hospital where I performed dialysis. The physician in charge was Garson Schachmann, and, when it came to dealing with burns, there was nobody who could touch him. The man had a mind like a steel trap. It took that kind of mind to keep these patients alive.

One of the biggest problems with burn patients is that their fluids and electrolytes can go out of balance at the drop of a hat. If they're not kept in perfect equilibrium, the patients will develop renal failure. In the days before burn units were established, failing kidneys accounted for the most common complications in burns. But at our hospital's unit, the only time anybody ever went into renal failure was when 90 to 95 percent of their bodies were covered with third degree burns. I got through my first few years without ever having to dialyze a burn patient. That was fine as far as I was concerned. But in 1978, my luck ran out.

Marty Cole, a thirty-five-year-old computer salesman from Eugene, Oregon, was my first burn patient since the OR in Vietnam. Although he had a wife and family in Eugene, he had been staying in a local hotel when a fire broke out. He was in bed at the time. Marty heard the commotion outside, went to the door, and was foolish enough to open it. The fire exploded through his room, blowing him across the floor until he was hanging outside the window with every part of his body, except his face, charred beyond recognition.

By the time I dialyzed Marty, the doctors had already been working on him for several days. He had a shunt in his left elbow and when I unwrapped it, I almost threw up. He was just a piece of meat with tubes hanging out.

Marty was terribly catabolic, which means that he broke down his own tissues faster than he could build them up. It was a common problem with severe burn patients. The toxic waste products of those broken-down tissues got into his system and pushed his poison level so high that they made it nearly impossible to keep his system clean. As a result, I had to dialyze him every day for long hours on a very efficient artificial kidney. I couldn't ever leave his bedside. He was so brittle that I had to constantly evaluate vital signs, IVs, cardiac monitor, respirator, and the gauges on my machine. I also got involved with dressing changes and debridements, which was when the dead tissue was scraped off. It was a stinking, painful, rotten job and it took so long to get the dressings changed that when we'd finish, it was practically time to start over again.

All this was performed in an isolated sterile environment. I wore a sterile gown, gloves, mask, boots, and hat, and my only communication with the outside world was through a little porthole on the door.

Then there was the problem of clotting. Ordinarily, a dialysis patient would be given medication to keep the blood from clotting in the machine. Clots could be dangerous. But anticoagulant drugs couldn't be given to burn patients like Marty because all of the exposed surface capillaries could make the patients ooze blood from all over. As a result, I spent my working hours in terror, monitoring clotting times constantly, and praying that the dialyzer wouldn't clot. When it did, I would scramble to change it.

But the worst part of working on Marty was the odor. I had almost forgotten how disgusting a burn patient could smell until he came along. It was like sticking my head into a sewer on a hot day in August. I found myself smelling the oppressive stench of burned tissue and pseudomonas long after I'd finished my shift. What was more unusual was that the putrid scent was mixed with the petroleum-like odor of napalm. Marty hadn't been exposed to napalm and neither had I since Vietnam. There was no reason to be smelling it now.

Nobody else did. But napalm and pseudomonas were with me twenty-four hours a day: in my clothes, in my hair, in the food I ate, in the sheets on my bed. I couldn't escape the oppressive stink. I tried scrubbing myself with strong soap and the most fragrant shampoo I could buy. It didn't work. I tried covering myself with perfume. That left me smelling pseudomonas, napalm, *and* perfume, in an even more sickening combination. I went to a store and tried on new clothes. They had the stench, too. Even the ocean breezes were polluted with pseudomonas and napalm.

Every night when I went to bed, I saw dozens of burn patients, all on operating tables in the surgical-T at Pleiku: *Pseudomonas was everywhere. Soldiers and Vietnamese ran into the OR with napalm oozing down their backs carrying flames with it as they screamed in agony. They pressed against me, smothering me with burned and decaying flesh until I was scratching at them, tearing away hunks of meat so I could get some fresh air. But they wouldn't let me go.*

Bill would usually be awakened by my scratching and thrashing. When he would ask me what was wrong, I'd tell him it was just a bad dream. Nothing more. He would try to hug me, to offer some comfort. I'd push him away. *He smelled of pseudomonas. His kisses tasted of napalm.* I began staying awake again, drinking until I'd be able to pass into a dreamless sleep—if I was lucky.

The drinks reeked of napalm.

Sometimes the telephone or my beeper would wake me out of a nightmare. I was always on call and there were nights when I would have to go into the hospital as many as three different times to handle a problem. Other nights, rather than waste the valuable sleep time commuting, I'd simply stay at the hospital. During one period, I was at the hospital for a solid week. Bill came to visit and brought me flowers. He never complained when I wasn't home, or when the beeper would go off in the middle of a movie, a romantic dinner, or even a moment of lovemaking. But he was worried about me and was constantly after me to get more rest.

Meanwhile, our marriage was deteriorating.

My sister Mary lived in our downstairs apartment for a time. She had come to L.A. to take acting and singing lessons while holding down temporary jobs to support herself. She worried about me as much as Bill did. Mary was constantly yelling at me to slow down and take better care of myself, yet I rarely listened. She tried to get me to talk with her about the problem. How could I talk about the problem when I didn't have any idea what was causing it? Mary and I did, however, spend some nights talking until the sunrise, but I could never quite explain to her the emptiness I felt inside.

"Lynda, if you keep up this pace, you will kill yourself," she said.

"I can't stop now," I replied. "People are depending on me. If I screw up, they could die."

When I had started dialyzing Marty, the doctors were trying to save his legs, although both were so blackened and deformed that they were beyond help. The docs finally gave up and amputated above the knees. More nightmares soon followed: *I was back in Pleiku. This time the bodies were no more than slabs of meat without arms and legs. Every time I walked outside the surgical-T, it was raining blood. It was sticky and clotting all over my arms, face, hair, and fatigues.*

Each day I'd tell myself that I couldn't go back to the burn unit again, but when I'd return to Marty, I'd put on such a pleasant face that nobody would have ever suspected that I was starting to sink into another depression—nobody except Bill and Mary.

As time passed Marty kept getting worse. Then for a while, he started to improve. It looked like he might pull through. The doctors took him off the respirator and I would talk with him as I sat by his bed monitoring the artificial kidney. He told me about his kids and how much he loved them; and his wife, and the good times they'd had. His oldest boy was a Little League pitcher. I told Marty how my father had called me "the talking catcher" in my softball-playing days. Marty wanted to see his son pitch again. He wanted to see his two daughters grow up and get married. He wanted to live.

A week after Marty had started talking, he went downhill again. This time it was for good. The stench of pseudomonas and napalm got worse almost by the hour. Each dressing change became uglier than the last. Finally, Marty died on a rainy Sunday afternoon.

For me, the foul odor stayed. It was driving me crazy.

I walked through the double doors of the OR in Pleiku and saw thousands of soldiers packed in like cattle. They were all bleeding, some with their guts hanging out, others with their arms blown off, still others without heads. Two were playing catch with a bloody foot that had fallen from a comrade's leg. As I tried to back out the door, I felt a hand grab my arm. When I turned, I saw a young man with his face blown away. In his other hand he was holding a picture. On it was written, "Gene and Katie, May 1968."

It was early in 1978 when I started having what I came to refer to as my "semiannual nervous breakdown," when I would feel as if the walls were caving in and I had to get away. I would go off alone to Santa Barbara for a few days and stay at the Miramar. It was an R&R. I would get a nice room with a fireplace and ocean view, and I would treat myself to long walks on the beach, cozy fires, and ice-cold martinis. Dinner would be at the San Ysidro Guest Ranch, which had a beautiful restaurant that sat in the hills above Santa Barbara. I'd dress up, put on a silk blouse and the pearls I'd bought in Bangkok, and I'd buy myself the most expensive item on the menu, along with champagne. After the meal, I would return to my room where I would sit all night in front of the fire, reading, watching television, and getting blitzed. It helped.

And when I went back home, I was ready, if not always anxious, to return to battle.

My relationship with Bill was heading steadily downhill, but I couldn't quite put my finger on the reason. I was unhappy with so many other things in life that maybe they all combined to sabotage the marriage. Sometimes Bill seemed indifferent to me.

At times, when we were having fun, I'd reach for his hand and he'd pull away. But each time I had another doubt, I'd force it into a dark corner with my emptiness. And when the doubts would spring back to the surface, I'd cover them with a flurry of activity that looked like love. We threw good parties, went caroling at Christmas, and took daytrips to romantic spots near L.A. as I convinced myself anew that everything was fine.

K.C. Davis, a twenty-two-year-old phone repairman, was my second burn patient in 1978. He had been electrocuted while on a telephone pole and had fallen twenty-five feet into a puddle of oil. An electrical charge ignited the oil and K.C. was charred. His smashed face made him look like a monster. He had a massive head, skeletal traction on his legs and skull, and his right arm was amputated. There was not a single piece of surface skin on his entire body that hadn't been burned. The kid was as close to a Vietnam casualty as any I'd ever had.

"He cannot live," I thought. "If he does, he'll be a monster forever. Nobody will be able to repair that face." K.C. reminded me so much of Gene that every time I looked at him, I would see my young bleeder in Pleiku. After I'd finish working on K.C., I would go home and dream about Gene. Sometimes, in the nightmares, Gene and K.C. would blend into one person and at other times, they would be separate. I started thinking about Gene during all my waking moments. I tried to force him out of my mind, but he kept coming back. And I kept seeing that damned blood-stained prom picture: *Gene and Katie, May 1968*.

The stench of pseudomonas and napalm became unbearable. My ulcers started bleeding and I was constantly in pain. I began thinking about suicide again, wondering if I could make it look accidental so no one else would be hurt. Soon the tears returned.

They came slowly in the beginning. At first I cried only late at night after particularly bad dreams when I was afraid to go back to sleep. But it wasn't long before the crying became more frequent. After a while, I was bawling every night before I went to bed, and in tears every morning when I woke. Yet I was still holding it together at work. I had to be tough. They needed me.

Bill didn't know what to say or how to help, although he tried in so many different ways. He would come home and find me sitting on the back porch in tears. "What's wrong, Lynda?"

"I don't know."

"What can I do?"

"I don't know."

"Do you want anything?"

"I don't know."

Although I was controlling the tears better than I had in the worst days of '72, I felt myself sinking into a deeper depression. I had a constant sense of impending doom. Every aspect of life was oppressive. I was afraid I might be going crazy. I'd scream at Bill for no reason and push him away when he tried to hold me. The next minute I'd wonder why he didn't come closer. I hated him for not being able to remove my tears. Why couldn't he? Why couldn't somebody? I needed help.

Each time the emptiness came bubbling back to the surface, it became harder to cover. I was sinking fast into a black muck. I wished I were dead.

K.C. died three months after I had begun dialyzing him. He was followed by Jeraldo Rivas, a factory worker who had got third degree burns on 99 percent of his body when he was caught in an industrial accident. He kept having problems in the middle of the night and my beeper was going constantly through the end of 1978 and the early months of 1979. Once more, I started sleeping at the hospital, partly to save the commute and partly to get away from Bill. I felt my marriage turning into a hollow shell.

Jeraldo was in constant pain. When we made a dressing change, he would writhe in agony. The last day I saw him was a Saturday afternoon. He was so bad that the doctors had lines of Dopamine running into him to keep his blood pressure up. The reading was barely 50/20. He had cardiac and respiratory irregularities and his lungs were so full of fluid that the respirator was only of limited value. Jeraldo was sure to die, but the doctors were determined to keep him alive as long as possible.

I begged them to let me take him off dialysis.

''No way,'' one of the doctors said. ''His potassium is eight. We've got to get it down.''

Eight was a lethal level. ''Let the potassium go,'' I said. ''Let the poor guy die in peace.''

When Jeraldo's heart went into an arrhthmia, I found the doctors at the desk. ''He's going to arrest,'' I shouted through the small window. ''When he does, I want a no code order.'' A ''no code'' meant that we would not try to resuscitate him; we would simply let him go. The doctors wouldn't give the order. ''We'll cross that bridge when we come to it,'' they said. I was furious.

They were down in the cafeteria when Jeraldo went into ventricular fibrillation, which is when the heart stops contracting and just quivers. That's the point at which a code is normally called. I yelled to the nurse outside to get the doctors for a ''no code.'' But when Jeraldo's heart fibrillated, I really had no choice. I had to resuscitate him. To do otherwise would have been unethical.

He had no skin anywhere, so I began closed chest massage directly on his muscle tissue. His swollen eyes flashed open. He looked furious, as if he wanted to kill me. While I worked, I could almost hear him: "Please let me die."

I cried as I struggled, against his will and mine, to keep him alive. "I'm sorry, Jeraldo," I sobbed. "I really don't want to do this, but I have to." Finally, the doctors issued the no code order. When I got off the bed, I apologized to Jeraldo. He closed his eyes, then opened them again and they seemed softer, as if he had forgiven me. I hope so.

Jeraldo's death was followed by more nightmares of Vietnam and more napalm-scented drinks. I felt like I couldn't go on anymore. My life was so desolate.

The next day, I was in the dialysis unit setting up the artificial kidney for another burn patient when I had a total breakdown. My entire body shook and I began sobbing hysterically. I looked at the machine and didn't recognize anything about it. My mind was blank. Everything I had learned in the past six years was gone. The room was out of proportion like a Peter Max poster, and if my life had depended on it, I could not have gone to dialyze that patient.

I collapsed into a chair. I couldn't move. I couldn't think. I couldn't talk. I couldn't do anything, except sit there and cry.

21

My Wife the Vet

I took an extended leave of absence from the hospital, but that was only a formality. I knew I could never return to nursing. At times I wasn't sure if I would even return to life. I went home and cried continuously for the next few days. Every night, when I'd fall into an exhausted sleep, I would be back in Vietnam trying to save Gene. *Gene and Katie, May 1968*.

I took another one of my semiannual nervous breakdown R&Rs in Santa Barbara and when the tears subsided, I spent a week driving aimlessly up and down the California coast between San Luis Obispo and Malibu while Bill waited back in Manhattan Beach. There were questions: What is wrong with me? Where is my life heading? What am I going to do with myself? What does all this mean? But there was only one answer: I don't know. The only thing I was sure of was that I felt desolate inside. The emptiness had finally triumphed.

When I returned to Manhattan Beach, I told Bill I had to get away to figure some things out. For how long? I didn't know. In early March, I flew to New York and stayed at his parents' apartment on East 52nd Street while they were on the road with a play. At a nephrology convention a year earlier, I had met a book editor who asked if I might be interested in working on a text about dialysis nursing. I contacted her shortly after my arrival and then attempted an outline. But each time I sat at the typewriter, I found myself writing about Vietnam, almost against my will. It's over, I kept saying. Vietnam is over! I threw the pages away and forced myself to write about dialysis. Yet Vietnam always ended up on the paper and in my conscious thoughts. When I walked the streets, I thought about Gene and thousands of other casualties. Sometimes a room would remind me of the surgical-T. Or I'd be in a crowded elevator and the people would make me remember slabs of bloody human meat.

I went to see the Jane Fonda movie *Coming Home*, thinking that it might help me fit the nightmares into perspective. It only made me hurt more. The first time I saw it, I sat in the theater crying until long after the last person had left. I kept going back, in spite of myself, like a child picking at a scab. I saw *Coming Home* seventeen times.

One weekend I visited an old friend, another dialysis nurse, who lived next to a volunteer fire department on Long Island. I was in the bathroom getting ready to go out to dinner when the siren went off. The sound was exactly the same as it had been in Pleiku. I dropped to the floor. Suddenly, I was back in Vietnam and we were under a rocket attack, except I realized I was safe on Long Island. I kept saying to myself that it was okay, yet I couldn't stop myself from low crawling to the living room to ask what had happened. I was met by four well-dressed women who thought I was playing some sort of silly joke. When they saw the sweat on my forehead, they realized there was no joke. An embarrassing silence followed while I got up from the floor. I was disoriented. "I'm sorry," I said to my host. "I feel silly, but that sound—"

"The siren?"

"Yes. That was our red alert in Pleiku."

They all looked at me as if I were crazy. I excused myself and freshened my makeup. Later that night, over dinner, one of the women said, "I didn't know you were in Vietnam."

"I was," I answered self-consciously.

"Was it anything like 'M*A*S*H'? "

"No, it was real."

I slept at my friend's house for two days. When I woke each morning, I was under the bed. The red alert siren must have gone off during the night.

I spent many weeks in New York thinking about the course that my marriage had taken. The doubts that I had been trying to deny for years would no longer stay hidden. There were so many things about the relationship that were wrong, and if I was truthful with myself, I had to admit that I was far from the ideal wife. I had put Bill through hell. He deserved a more stable life. Maybe we really were not meant to be together. Was it possible that the marriage existed merely because I had forced the issue? Was Bill really committed to me? Was I committed to him? I knew I loved him, but I also knew that love wasn't enough. Two people had to work at a marriage. A lot of times he wasn't willing anymore and I, as much as I tried, wasn't able to do whatever might be necessary to salvage our love. I began seriously considering divorce.

I discussed the possibility with another friend I had met through dialysis, Tony Kelly. Tony was a burly forty-five-year-old red-headed Irishman who was one of the most sensitive and caring people I'd ever known. He was also a dialysis patient and had been friends with Bill and me for almost five years. Sometimes when he knew I was down, he assembled a group of people and took me to a pub where everyone sang Irish songs until closing time. But mostly, he listened. I told him about all the problems Bill and I had been having and my thoughts about asking Bill for a divorce. When I was through talking, Tony advised me to go back and try again.

"Lynda, I was married for fifteen years to a woman I loved and who bore three children by me," he said. "We divorced because we thought the problems were overwhelming and that our love had died. Now I realize that the love was there. We were just blinded by so many other things. I miss her."

"Why don't you ask her to take you back?"

"Because now she has a new husband." Tony touched my shoulder, looked into my eyes, and told me the things he wished someone had said to him a few years earlier: "Lynda, do what you will. But before you end this marriage, please be sure you can look in a mirror and say honestly that you tried as hard as you could to make it work."

Bill came back to New York in May. While he was visiting, he made arrangements to do a radio documentary on an organization that had recently been formed: Vietnam Veterans of America. He invited me to the interview, where I met Bobby Muller, the group's executive director, and Joe Zengerle, a member of the executive council. Bobby was an intense man with speckles of gray in his dark brown hair. He was self-confident, sensitive, articulate, and charismatic. He was also a paraplegic. Bobby had been a Marine lieutenant when, in April 1969, he was wounded at Cam Lo, South Vietnam. He had formed the organization to bring more attention to the plight of the Vietnam veteran.

Joe Zengerle was a member of VVA's executive committee and he practiced law in Washington, D.C. Within a year of our meeting, he would be appointed as an undersecretary of the Air Force. A West Point graduate, Joe had been an Army officer for five years, serving in Vietnam as a company commander and as an advisor to General Westmoreland during the '68 Tet Offensive.

When I first met Joe and Bobby, I was introduced simply as Bill's wife and I remained in the background while Bill conducted the interview. Soon, Joe was telling this long, detailed story of his homecoming and the problems he faced in readjusting to the world. At the end of it, he glanced at me and saw tears. "Why are you crying?" he asked.

"You make me remember my own homecoming," I replied. "I haven't been able to recall it for a long time."

"What do you mean: your homecoming?" Bobby asked.

Bill answered, "My wife is also a Vietnam veteran."

"I was an Army surgical nurse in Pleiku," I said, "from '69 to '70, at the 71st Evac."

Bobby and Joe looked at each other across the table and then they both got big grins on their faces. "Holy shit," Bobby said. He backed his chair away from the table, rolled in a circle, and then popped a wheelie. "*Women veterans*! We forgot all about *women*!" For the next ten minutes, he kept looking at me and repeating, "Women veterans, of course."

Joe merely stared and shook his head. "My God," he kept saying. "The thought never crossed my mind."

They insisted that Bill include me in the documentary.

"I can't do that," Bill said. "It's not right for me to do a story about my wife."

"You've got different last names," Bobby said. "Nobody will know you're related."

"But—"

"Bill, if you don't use Lynda," Bobby argued, "we're not going to continue the interview. She's a veteran. She has a right to be heard."

Bill's documentary was called *Coming Home, Again*, and it featured quotes from Bobby, Joe, and me. Bobby talked about veterans' issues like unemployment, alcohol abuse, marital problems, and how much better the GI benefits had been for World War II vets. Joe talked about the shortage of Vietnam vets in policymaking positions, the lack of self-esteem among our peers, and the way our country was trying to deny the existence of the Vietnam war. I talked about getting off a plane in California and being taunted as I tried to hitch a ride to San Francisco International Airport.

When Bill returned to California, I began spending my days at the VVA headquarters in lower Manhattan, where I met dozens of other veterans—all men—who talked about the kinds of experiences that I had been having since my return from Vietnam. Suddenly, I didn't feel so alone anymore. These people were telling me that I could be proud of my service. The organization was trying to instill pride into all Vietnam vets. We had answered our country's call. It wasn't our fault that we were called for the wrong war.

In June, Bobby asked me if I would form the VVA Women Veterans Project. He felt the woman veteran was a very important issue and that nobody else was addressing her needs. He also said he was ashamed that he had not thought about women before. "If the leaders of VVA didn't know about women veterans," he said, "there probably aren't too many people out there who know. And they should."

Bobby's offer didn't come without a few words of caution. He warned me of all the pitfalls that were part of the job. Funding was unpredictable, paychecks were infrequent, the hours were long, and the pressure could be intense. I accepted on one condition: I needed a year to give my marriage one more chance and also to go back to college so I could have a background in psychology that would be strong enough to help me deal with the problems of other women.

By this time, I was back on a fairly even keel and didn't stop to think about my own personal troubles with Vietnam. There were other people who might need help. I didn't have time for my problems. Besides, I figured they were now behind me. I hadn't cried, smelled napalm, or had a nightmare in months. I was eating well, running several miles a day, and not drinking or smoking.

I returned to California in July of '79 and immediately went into marriage counseling with Bill. The next month, I began studying psychology under Antioch University's adult program "University Without Walls," in Los Angeles which granted degree credit for life experience. With my background, they told me I could get my diploma by attending full-time classes for only a year.

In conjunction with my courses, I began reading everything I could find about Vietnam veterans and trying to come up with a plan for the Women's Project that would bring the plight of women vets to national attention. I also wanted to offer those women a place where they could call for help, and to convince lawmakers that the issue of women veterans was a valid one.

I pored over every study I could find and became familiar with a syndrome called post-traumatic stress disorder, which had been identified in male veterans. PTSD was simply a delayed reaction to severe stress. The psychologists who had done the studies had found that it was common for victims of catastrophic experiences to suppress their feelings immediately after the event. Unfortunately, the feelings didn't remain suppressed. They would come out in a variety of physical, emotional, and interpersonal ways. Studies showed that Vietnam vets who were victims of PTSD had serious problems, which included inability to hold down a job, depression, rage, anxiety, sleep disturbances, recurring nightmares of combat, irritability, suicidal tendencies, flashbacks, feelings of alienation, low self-esteem, self-destructive behavior, and difficulty establishing or maintaining intimate relationships. The suicide rate for Vietnam veterans was 25 percent higher than that of their nonveteran peers. Unemployment and divorce statistics were worse. It sounded like I was reading my own psychological profile. The psychologists had not thought to include women in their studies, but I began thinking that if I had the same problems as the men, there must be plenty of other women in similar circumstances. There could be thousands of women vets experiencing PTSD who thought they were alone. My job would be to reach them before it was too late.

But PTSD wasn't the only hurdle facing the Women's Project. The more I investigated, the more I learned. For starters, neither the V.A. nor the Defense Department could give an accurate total of women who served in Vietnam, let alone who they were, where they lived, and what their physical and mental health might be. In fact, most V.A. hospitals didn't even have facilities for gynecological treatment, the most elemental health care need for a woman vet. Then there was the problem of chemical hazards left over from Vietnam. Agent Orange, which was manufactured by Dow Chemical Company, had been used to defoliate vast areas of the country until 1970. After that, it had been linked to cancer and birth defects. The V.A. had no provisions for providing medical care for former soldiers who might be suffering aftereffects.

Chloracne was one of the symptoms of Agent Orange exposure. I began to wonder if there wasn't some connection between rashes I had and the chemical defoliants that had been used near Pleiku. I knew then that until more Agent Orange research was done, it would be wise of me to avoid having children. I would not want sons or daughters to carry the curse of Vietnam for their lives, too.

While school and my VVA background work were proceeding well, my attempts at saving my failing marriage were meeting with little success. Bill and I had gone into counseling, and we attended a Marriage Encounter workshop after he did a documentary on the subject. For weeks afterward, it seemed like our relationship was improving, but then things went downhill again. It was frustrating for both of us. In many ways, we were best friends, but we didn't seem suited for marriage. And when we wanted to fix things, our timing was usually out of synch: When I would try to make things better, Bill would withdraw; when he would try, I would withdraw. As the rest of my life became fuller, it only served to underscore the emptiness that was overtaking our marriage.

During that year in school, I published an article about Gene in the *Los Angeles Times*. I began saving notes, poetry, and sketches about the war, and I started writing about it. When I returned to New York in the summer of 1980 to work for two months at VVA headquarters, I approached an editor with the idea of doing a book about women's experiences in Vietnam. "Nobody wants to read that kind of book," he said. He discouraged me enough so that I put the idea away—for a while.

Meanwhile, I was trying to find funding for the Women's Project and meeting with almost no success. One of the foremost women's groups in the country told me that women veterans were not enough of a cutting edge feminist issue. Another foundation promised the moon and delivered nothing. I kept hitting against brick walls. It was discouraging, but Bobby Muller and the other guys kept my spirits up.

I was due to return to California in August and was doing some last-minute work one Friday evening when a call came from an attorney's secretary in Louisiana. She said that her boss was searching for a woman who had written the article about "the young bleeder." He was putting together a defense for a guy who had killed a police officer in Shreveport during a Vietnam flashback. I was asked to testify. I had to leave for Louisiana at 5 A.M. Sunday. The trial had been running seven days a week.

The defendant was Wayne Robert Felde, a thirty-one-year-old combat veteran who had been with the 4th Infantry Division from March 1968 to March 1969, operating out of base camps in Pleiku and, later, Kontum provinces. As soon as he joined his unit, he experienced the worst side of war:

> "When we left the base camp we were flown out by chopper to a fire base," he said. "On the fire base is artillery units. Big guns. My new company was working patrols into the bush off this fire base. The big guns were shooting like crazy. There were planes flying and dropping napalm up in the mountains. We were told that was our new company out there in contact and they had been fighting for about eight hours already. There was choppers bringing in bodies to the LZ where we were waiting to be picked up. The chopper that took us out came in and set down. We had to drag four bodies off. They were all bloody and burned up from napalm. The bodies stunk. I got sick. We made a combat assault on the hill and joined the company. I saw my first firefight and I was scared. It lasted on and off that night and come daylight it was over. We had to pick up pieces of our guys to send home—arms, legs, three quarters of a whole person, burned up. You never got used to it. I was scared. I cried for guys I didn't even know."

Wayne stayed with his company for the entire tour. Although he got back to the world without serious physical wounds, he was mentally injured. He was tormented by flashbacks, paranoia, nightmares, irritability, frequent mood changes, arguments, alcohol abuse, and self-destructive tendencies. A brother-in-law summarized the difference: "Wayne was a changed person," he said. "He was very quiet and not as fun-loving, had nightmares, talking in his sleep, was nervous and twitchy, and started drinking."

Wayne's mother, a registered nurse, had repeatedly contacted his superiors, and on one occasion the Pentagon, to try to get psychiatric treatment for her son. She was unsuccessful. Wayne fought her attempts to convince him to seek help because he was afraid that if a shrink knew what he was going through, he might be committed to an institution. He quit five different jobs, dropped out of three technical schools, tried college briefly, was arrested numerous times for driving while intoxicated, and got married. That ended in divorce. During his married life, Wayne would go into unexplained violent fits of rage and would smash things. Then, in 1973, he got into a fight with an ex-convict. The man died. Wayne was convicted, but escaped from prison in 1976 after being denied parole.

He became a drifter for the next two years. He lived and worked in different parts of the country until 1978, when he was picked up by a police officer for public intoxication. Unfortunately, the officer, a rookie, had failed to search Wayne before putting him in the patrol car. Wayne had a .357 Magnum revolver. When the policeman later noticed it, there was a struggle. The officer was shot.

The head of Wayne's defense team, Graves Thomas, was not denying that his client had shot the officer; he was trying to have him found "not guilty by reason of insanity." He wanted Wayne committed to a psychiatric facility for treatment rather than warehoused in a prison.

Drs. John Wilson and Charles Figley, two leading experts in post-traumatic stress disorder, had diagnosed Wayne as suffering from PTSD. In addition, a psychologist and a psychiatrist from Louisiana corroborated that finding. I was asked to testify about the war, to help make the jury visualize the combat experience so they would be able to understand the kind of abnormal stresses that soldiers are under.

There was only one problem—I had never talked in public about what Vietnam was really like. I was petrified by the thought of sitting in a crowded courtroom filled with strangers and recounting incidents that I hadn't ever discussed with anyone. I didn't sleep much on Friday or Saturday nights. Instead, I paced the floor, drinking and smoking as a kaleidoscope of scenes from Vietnam unfolded before my eyes. It was all starting to come back to me. I recalled things that I hadn't remembered in years.

Sunday afternoon, I arrived in Alexandria, Louisiana, and was put up in the home of Graves's parents. That afternoon I took the stand. The session, however, was cut short by the objections of the prosecutor. As a result, the defense took me off the stand. They planned to recall me the following day after they laid more groundwork so my testimony could be admitted.

That night, while the lawyers and other expert witnesses held a planning session, I sat on the edge of the group, drinking double martinis to calm me and still remembering long-buried images of Vietnam. Before Dr. Figley returned to his hotel, he pulled me aside and asked, in private, "Is this the first time you've talked about it?"

"Yes."

"It must be very hard," he said.

I was obviously distraught. He put his hand on my shoulder to offer comfort. I jerked away. I didn't want anyone's comfort. I had to be strong.

The heat was stifling and there was no air-conditioning. Exhausted, I tried to sleep, but couldn't. Each time I began to fall asleep, I immediately jerked awake from a nightmare. When I attempted to read, I was unable to concentrate. I made myself another drink. It didn't help either.

By Monday, when I got on the stand again, I was totally drained. Mine was the last testimony of the day and I must have looked as bad as I felt. I was questioned about Gene, Napalm, the types of casualties we got, and what it was like to spend a year in a combat zone. I told the court how Napalm oozed down along the skin carrying flames with it, how bouncing Betty mines worked and the kind of wounds they created, and what it was like to spend day after day seeing kids dying. Before I was finished, almost everyone in the courtroom was crying. I was like a rock. *I've got to stay together*. I gripped the edge of my seat so tightly that my knuckles were white. When it was over, I walked out of the courtroom. Then I started shaking.

One of the defense lawyers, Wellbourne Jacks, had followed me out. He was big, about six foot, and he seemed so strong when he strode toward me and put his arms around me.

He didn't say a word, and despite my trying to push him away, he held on to me tightly. For the first time I allowed somebody else to be the strong one. I gave in and leaned against him and trembled uncontrollably. Finally everything overcame me, and the tears poured down my face. I sobbed in his arms and let him comfort me. It was something I had never let anyone do for me since that awful night with Coretta in Pleiku. Wellbourne will probably never know how much he did for me in those moments.

Court adjourned right after my testimony. I was still crying. As Wayne was being taken away by the sheriff, he approached me. He was wearing handcuffs. "I'm so sorry they put you through that," he said. "I told Graves I didn't want him to do it to you. I know how much it hurts."

My testimony didn't change things. Wayne was eventually convicted of first-degree murder and sentenced to death.

Monday night, I finally had had enough to drink so I could fall into an exhausted sleep. But the night was a troubled one. As soon as I put my head down, I was back in Vietnam. I was terrified by fire and explosions. There were thousands of burn patients, one right after the other. And Gene was a part of each dream. It was a time for every heinous nightmare possible. I woke up screaming at least once an hour. When I'd realize where I was, I'd pace the floor for a few minutes before collapsing back into another horrible dream.

The rest of my week was exactly the same. Every night I went through another hell.

I returned to New York on Tuesday and on Thursday I flew back to California. When Bill met me at the airport, he was worried. I looked like I wasn't going to make it. He wanted me to take some time to rest. But I had a speaking engagement in Anaheim the next day. It was to be my first formal presentation on the VVA Women's Project. My audience would be members of the Vietnam Veterans Counseling Program. It was my job to convince them that women had as much right to counseling and other benefits as did their male counterparts. The audience would be a tough one; I couldn't afford to make a mistake.

After I gave my speech, I got a very warm and positive reaction from the group. I had thought I was in control of myself until lunchtime when I sat next to Shad Meshad, a V.A. counselor who was one of the hardest working advocates for Vietnam veterans' rights in the country. Shad was a driving force behind the V.A.'s Outreach

Program—an attempt to make the V.A. more responsive to veterans through smaller, more personal storefront counseling centers. Initially, he had been offered the job of director of the Outreach Program, but he turned it down, preferring to work as a therapist rather than as an administrator.

Shortly after I started a conversation with him, he said, "How can you help other women when you need help yourself?"

I was taken back. "What do you mean?" I asked indignantly. "I'm okay."

"You look about as okay as a kamikaze pilot near the end of a mission," he said.

"But—"

"Lynda, you are in trouble," Shad insisted. "It's obvious. If you don't get help soon—*before* you try to help others—you are going to kill youself. I can guarantee it."

"I'm not—"

"Pay attention, lady. I'm talking about your life. From the moment you walked in here, I could see you were at the edge. How many times have you thought about suicide? When are you going to learn that the emptiness won't go away until you get the war out of your system? You think you can repress your feelings while you help others to deal with theirs?"

As much as I hated to admit it, I knew Shad was right. It was as if he could see inside of me and knew every bit of my anguish as well as I did.

In many ways, Shad saved my life.

We started on Saturday with a therapy he had been using called "Walking Through Vietnam." For the next week, Shad gave me his full attention. We spent the bulk of every day talking intensively about my year in 'Nam and about what I had gone through when I came home. As each day passed, things became clearer. Shad offered me a structured process for understanding the most difficult experience of my life. He also helped me to regain my sanity and gave me perspective. He showed me patterns that I had been repeating and offered methods for fixing the problems. He helped me to figure out what it all meant. The therapy was painful and, at times, frustrating. It was more intensive than the normal program, and I occasionally felt like it would kill me. But it didn't. I could see the progress. It was as if I were exorcising a ghost that had haunted me for a decade. Shad and I both knew it wouldn't all be gone in one week—there would be more counseling in my future—but this was a start. I no longer had to hold things inside. I no longer had to keep up a front. It was all right to hurt. It was all right to ask for help. I wasn't crazy.

Of all the things that Shad did for me, I was most touched by what he said when I told him how unappreciated I had felt. Shad had been a psych officer for II Corps in Vietnam and had known hundreds of nurses like me. He had enormous respect for each and every one of us. We were all doing something very positive, he reassured me. Our job was overwhelming, he said, but we nurses triumphed. And most importantly, we saved the lives of people who might otherwise have died.

"You were my heroes," Shad said.

When I heard his words, I knew he meant them. Hearing them made me believe in myself. I felt reborn. It was a beginning for which I owed Shad an enormous debt of gratitude.

My first interview, with the *South Bay Daily Breeze* in California, was arranged by Shad in September of 1980 to kick off a publicity blitz. In October, the Playboy Foundation gave the first grant to the Women's Project, and in November, I moved back East to work out of VVA's Washington office. Bill got a transfer and together we bought a house in Northern Virginia. I saw it as a chance to start fresh in my marriage. For a while, I was optimistic.

But it wasn't long before I realized that the marriage was already dead.

I asked Bill for a divorce in March of '81. I know I loved Bill, and probably always will in a very special way. He was there when I was drowning and he pulled me out. He gave me many memories that are precious. But I don't think we were meant to be husband and wife.

22

You Were My Heroes

Dear Ms. Van Devanter,

. . . I identified so much with you that I feel as if I know you. I was also a nurse in Vietnam and had experienced the same consequences you described in a recent radio interview. I managed to keep mine pretty much under control until last year. For some reason I still don't understand, I cracked up. I spent a couple of days in a civilian psychiatric ward, but left without telling anyone what my problem was. I did see a very nice female psychologist for six visits after getting out. I realized that something had to be done, so after the fourth visit, I decided to tell her one of my frequent nightmares. About halfway through, I looked up to see her reaction. She was crying. Needless to say, I haven't been back. These things are hard enough on me. I don't want to make somebody else miserable. . . .

Since November of 1980, the Vietnam Veterans of America Women's Project has been my entire life. I've done hundreds of interviews, spoken to thousands of people, and lobbied hard in Congress to get recognition for women who served in Vietnam. I also did everything I could to reach other women veterans. The response was slow at first, but soon it became overwhelming. As the phone calls and letters started coming in from other women who had been to Vietnam, I began to realize just how many were in the same position. I tried to answer every letter and to get the women together with counselors or other women vets so they could have a support system. That was important if they were going to get beyond the war.

> *Dear Lynda,*
> . . . I have not been able to get one particular GI out of my mind. He wrote me after he left our hospital, then the letters stopped. I cared for him special duty, twelve hours a day for twenty-one days. I would like to know if he's alive. Can you tell me how I might be able to find out. I need to know. . . .

At the end of the Iranian Crisis, when the hostages came home following their year in captivity, I found myself once again having nightmares. But this time I knew that I was not alone. I heard from hundreds of other veterans who were going through the same emotions. According to Dr. Charles Figley, post-traumatic stress disorder probably isn't ever totally cured, but it can be controlled. Knowing that made life easier. The nightmares lasted only for a short time and I knew if I waited and didn't try to destroy myself, they would soon be gone. I got back into therapy and eventually into a Vietnam veterans rap group, and continued to grow.

> *Dear Lynda,*
> . . . So far my life has been good, but I have my moments. I don't mind sitting on a one-to-one basis and discussing Vietnam, but last week I found out how explosive the subject can be for me. A university film series dedicated two weeks to Vietnam. They wanted a panel discussion after each film, but I couldn't do it. When I tried to talk about it in front of others, for absolutely no reason I began crying. After ten years, why? . . .

During 1982, I met a man who was the embodiment of Gene with one exception: This young bleeder had survived. He knew all about me from my media appearances, but I knew nothing of him until he greeted me at an airport in Airzona. Calvin Arnheim had been a helicopter door gunner in the Delta region in 1969 when a white phosphorous round exploded near him and destroyed most of his face.

I stayed with Calvin and his family for three days while I spoke at seminars. The first day we avoided the topic of Vietnam and I made a concerted effort to act like I didn't notice his face. But by the second evening, when Calvin and I were having dinner at a Phoenix restaurant after I had finished a college lecture, we finally mentioned the unmentionable. He told me what it had been like from his end on the day he was wounded when he tried to call for help and realized that the bottom of his jaw was gone. From my side, I could explain to him what was happening in the OR, why certain procedures had been necessary, and how we had felt for him.

When he came back from Vietnam, he had been angry with all the doctors and nurses. At one point, I had become the focus for that anger. "I wanted to know why you didn't just let me die," he said. "I didn't understand how you and the other medical people could sentence guys like me to lives like this."

"We never thought beyond tomorrow, Calvin. We never thought beyond the next casualties. We just cut them up, sewed them together, and sent them to Japan. Our job was to save lives. Tomorrow was for others to worry about."

For a year, Calvin had seen a psychiatrist. Once when the shrink had asked him about his sex life, Calvin came close to violence: "What the hell are you asking *me* that question for?" he demanded. "My sex life's fine. Why don't you ask my wife what it's like to make love to a monster?"

By the time Calvin and I met, he had put most of the anger behind him. He had been fortunate enough to have emotional support from his wife, family, and friends, along with good psychiatric help. He was working full-time, counseling other Vietnam vets. Not all were as lucky.

Calvin and I spent four hours in that restaurant freeing ourselves from our ghosts. When it was over, we each found some measure of peace. I knew that Gene wouldn't follow me anymore.

The next day, Calvin's wife drove me to the airport. She told me that he had had his first good night's sleep in a long time. "He slept like a baby," she said.

So did I.

Dear Lynda

. . . My family was proud of my tour in Vietnam and my small hometown supported me, although they avoided me after I returned. I was readjusting to civilization, carrying around a lot of bad memories and probably seemed aloof. To this day, when I meet people just sailing through life in ignorance of man's darker side, I get impatient and feel sorry for them. They have no idea what it's like to be hungry, homeless, or orphaned. I'm often scared for my kids. When I look at my eight-year-old daughter, I can see back to an eight-year-old Vietnamese girl who died of starvation. I saw ten- and twelve-year-old V.C. POWs wounded. They were so old for their years. . . .

Dear Lynda,

. . . I'm thirty-four years old and my marriage broke up after three years. I've lived alone with my seven-year-old daughter since then. I'm more afraid of thunder than she is. I can't take her to the fireworks. I scare her to death when I have a nightmare, although she has learned how to wake me up and comfort me. I have nasty moods and fits of depression that just spring up without notice. In short, my life is a mess and not getting any better. . . .

These days, in spite of my work with others who are in pain, I can say that I am no longer unhappy. Why? Because I can see, little by little, that progress is being made. I am optimistic. Other women vets are beginning to learn that they are not alone. They are forming groups, getting counseling and, in some small measure, being recognized for the contributions they have made. When each new woman tells me she's made her peace with Vietnam, I know I've helped in some small way.

We've been able to show the public that women deserve better treatment. Before we started the Women's Project, the V.A. had not, in more than half a century of existence, ever published anything that gave the least idea that women were entitled to veterans benefits, although the Armed Forces had been spending millions annually to bring women into the services. In 1981, the V.A. published its first booklet on a study of women's use of V.A. educational benefits. I began teaching counselors in the Vet Center training programs, and the centers began doing outreach to women vets. More and more of them came into the centers for counseling.

That's only a fraction of what's needed. But it's a start.

Dear Lynda,

. . . I felt ashamed of my feelings of depression, tension, and

> alienation because I didn't fire a gun. Vietnam was not a woman's place. My upbringing dictated that war was a man's job. I came from a very sheltered, structured, protected environment. But I hardened myself. . . .

Although most of the women who served in Vietnam were not standing in the boonies shooting someone's head off, we were close by, trying desperately to put that head back together again. And we weren't there in only medical capacities. Women were also intelligence officers, air traffic controllers, clerks, and security personnel. Yet even to talk about women in Vietnam is not the whole story. During World War II, hundreds of women were killed. There were more than sixty-five women who were POWs on Corregidor for years. Women were on the beachhead at Anzio, caring for the wounded while bombs exploded around them. In all of our wars, women have been killed, maimed, disabled, and psychologically injured. They deserve at least a thank you from their country.

> *Dear Lynda,*
> . . . You didn't have to spend your 365 days in a rice paddy to have been affected. I'm not sorry I went to Vietnam; I'm sorry no one ever understood when we came back. . . .

> *Dear Lynda*
> . . . I harbor a great deal of anger at being neglected and ignored. Only now, ten years since I left the war, do my colleagues even acknowledge I was there. Friends and coworkers want me to relate "funny stories." The pain is too great. . . .

> *Dear Lynda,*
> . . . It's about time the public is made aware of the forgotten veterans. . . .

About a year ago, I saw a PBS show with Tom Cottle, a psychologist who was interviewing a woman veteran. "Do you see any future for yourself," he asked. The woman said she didn't "give a damn" anymore. She didn't want to live to eighty and didn't care if she reached forty. "I figure if I make it to tomorrow," she said, "I'm ahead of the game."

Vietnam had robbed thousands of us of a future. Maybe the problem came from the day-to-day existence in the middle of destruction. Maybe it was because of the constant presence of death. Maybe it was the knowledge, in war, that tomorrow wasn't going to be any better than today. For years, I carried the emptiness with me. But the emptiness is gone now. Lately, although innocence is only a faint memory, I've regained a measure of the happiness I had before I left for Vietnam. I spend time at the mountain with my mother and father, know how to laugh during parties, and feel deep joy when I see a sunrise. I have finally started to believe once more in a future. And I know that, in time, other women veterans can reclaim their lost futures, too.

I'd be lying if I said there aren't still difficult times: the nightmares come occasionally. I often wonder what ever happened to Barbara. I get a twinge in my stomach when I hear helicopters, and I still can't answer that one nagging question that surrounds all war—"Why?"

But Vietnam doesn't own me anymore. I own it. Somewhere between the therapy with Shad, the work that I've done with the VVA, and my therapy and rap groups, I've reached the point where I can truthfully say that the war has lost its ability to destroy me. I'm back in control of my own life and I'm proud to call myself a veteran.

It has been a long, dark night, but I'm finally reaching home.

EPILOGUE

Going Back

As time passed and I gained a greater understanding of what Vietnam had done to me, I came to feel a desire, no, a need to return to the place that held the most painful and most important memories of my life. Since the U.S. has no relations with Vietnam, indeed does not even recognize it, the chances of my returning seemed slim. But in May of 1982, I was chosen to be part of a delegation of Vietnam Veterans of America to go back to Vietnam. There were nine of us, mostly Vietnam veterans, and our task was very different from the one we'd had so many years earlier. Then, we went as warriors. This time, we came in peace.

We were to continue the work that had been started six months earlier by Bobby Muller and three other members of the VVA Board of Directors. They had gone to Vietnam at Christmas of 1981 to try to open dialogue with the Vietnamese in the areas of the Americans who continue to be missing in action (MIA) from the war, the continuing questions about Agent Orange, and the problem of American-Vietnamese (Amerasian) children remaining in Vietnam since the war.

The Vietnamese had agreed to work with VVA to move toward a resolution of these issues, and our second delegation's task was to continue this work. The trip would be very much a working one, but I would also have the opportunity to again see some of the country that was so much a part of me.

During the weeks before the trip, as I prepared to leave, getting malaria pills and vaccinations from the health department this time instead of the Army, I thought often about how I'd felt the last time I went to Vietnam. This time I was probably as nervous as I had been the first time, but for different reasons. Then I was going toward something that was real and scary. This time I was going back to something that had been inside me for thirteen years, something nebulous, untouchable, unreal, but real all the same. How do I explain this? I had known Vietnam in my dreams for so many years. What would it be like now? I had known Vietnam at war for a year, and that war had raged inside me for years after. Could I finally make peace with it? In a way, I was afraid of coming back as different as the last time.

The leaders of our delegation were Tom Bird, a Vietnam combat vet who had founded and was director of the Veterans Ensemble Theater Company in New York, and Greg Kane, a Marine Corps veteran of Okinawa during the war, who was a member of VVA's Board of Directors. Tommy had been on the first delegation, so he would direct this one. There were also, besides me, Bob Holcomb, Scott Higgins, Dave Aldstadt, and Gary Beikirch, all of us Vietnam veterans. In addition, there were Leslie Platt, VVA's Special Counsel on Agent Orange, and Joseph Papp, a well-known producer, who had done some of the earliest theater works about Vietnam.

We flew together, this time from New York, taking the Eastern route instead of the Pacific route I'd flown in 1969. We left on the evening of May 25, all of us taking a van from Joe Papp's Public Theater in lower Manhattan out to JFK airport.

Greg played coach, handing out our tickets when we needed them, then collecting them again when we had boarded. He had a terrible fear that someone was going to lose one, and at times it felt like being on a school field trip.

We finally took off around 10 P.M. and my seat mate on the first leg of the flight was an older gentleman who was a noted orthopedic surgeon returning to Germany from a medical conference in New York. We talked much of the night, I being too nervous to sleep, and it turned out that he had spent the last year of the second world war as a seventeen-year-old POW in France. He had been wounded, and was captured and treated medically by American military medical teams. When they learned he spoke English and had an interest in medicine, they kept him at the hospital for the rest of his internment. There, he acted as an interpreter and medical orderly. As we talked, it became quite apparent that he'd had a positive experience as a POW, and I thought how strange it was that anyone could have a good experience under such circumstances. I wondered if that had all changed with Vietnam, and as I sat talking with this man who had once been our enemy, and was now teaching in American medical schools and conferences, I asked myself if any enemy remains so.

Dawn came quickly as we sped to the East, and soon we were in Frankfurt. Greg and Tom made a few pointed snickers as I took a minute to pack up my baggage on my wheels. I had refused to check my bags, having had the previous experience of an airline losing my luggage on the way home from Vietnam the first time. We headed for baggage claim, and a half-hour minimum wait for their bags to come. Greg had forgotten to check them all the way through to Bangkok. Since I already had mine, I breezed through customs, and headed upstairs to check us in for the next leg of the flight. So they could razz me all they wanted about not checking luggage, but I would always have mine.

The next legs of the flight, I sat with Scotty, and between eating, sleeping, and watching movies, *On Golden Pond* and *Absence of Malice*, the time flew as did we. I wrote in my journal a great deal, and while wandering through the darkened plane to stretch my legs, found Bob doing the same. We talked for a while about our need to remember everything of this trip, and Bob said he'd noticed everyone writing in journals. It seemed we all had that need.

As the second day and night wore on, I began to remember the confusion I'd had on my first flight to Vietnam thirteen years ago. I simply couldn't figure out what time and day it was at any given point, and when Scotty tried to explain it, I just got more confused and decided to stop trying. By the time we landed in Bangkok, I was grateful just to find out the local time and date. When the flight attendant told me, I realized that it was my birthday. How strange to be spending another birthday with Vietnam, I thought.

Bangkok was a blur of finding our hotel, sleeping for a while, eating, and shopping, this time buying a ring for myself, and a pair of emerald earrings for Mary to match the ring I'd gotten her so long ago. Late that night, we were in the hotel restaurant talking about the next few days and what they would hold. We were joined by Mike Wallace and his crew from *60 Minutes*. They were following us to do some stories on our return to Vietnam, what we would accomplish, and what Vietnam was like after the war.

They seemed nice enough, and asked for some information on all of us as background for their work. During the conversation, suddenly there was a light from behind me. I turned in time to see all of the restaurant's waiters bearing a birthday cake for me lit with thirty-five candles, and singing, haltingly, "Happy Birthday." I was totally surprised and touched that the guys had remembered. It had seemed until that moment that my birthday this year would fade by just as it had the last time I was in Vietnam.

Ironically, that night as I was drifting off to sleep, the television in the hotel was showing *A Rumor of War*, a movie about Vietnam. My dreams were filled that night with a mélange of memories of Vietnam, some good, and some not so good, but always there was the unanswered question, "*Why?*"

The next day, we returned to the airport for the final leg of our journey back to Vietnam. This time we would be taking Hang Khong Vietnam, the Vietnamese airline. As we checked in at the counter, I began getting nervous. I wandered off to buy a few small souvenirs, and suddenly found myself feeling weird, talking to myself, giggling; I couldn't even remember Bob's name. Joe was walking with me, and reassured me that I was only behaving normally for the situation, that is, off the wall. Strangely, that felt comforting.

There was a long wait for the plane, it was about two hours late taking off, and I found myself feeling more antsy. I just wanted Air Vietnam flight #832 to get on with it. I walked around looking at souvenirs. I wrote in my journal. I tape-recorded plane announcements. I talked with Dave and Gary. I paced the floor watching the TV monitor for departure announcements. And then, I saw people lining up at the gate. How anticlimactic. I hadn't even heard the announcement.

Once on the plane, an ancient 1950s model that hadn't seen much refurbishment since it was built, I was struck in the face by the memory of the heat of Vietnam. It was as though they were trying to prepare us. It must have been 120 or 130 degrees inside, and as I noticed the sweat beginning to pour from me, from all the usual places, then from the backs of my hands, and finally from under my fingernails, I knew. I was going back to Vietnam.

I sat with Gary, and we talked most of the way, straining always to catch the first glimpse of Vietnam. The *60 Minutes* crew was periodically shooting film, and occasionally, we turned our cameras on them as payback. I was wearing a white dress—my need to look like a woman this time as I arrived in Vietnam, in contrast to my last arrival—but the age of the plane included old dirt, and combined with my profuse sweating, I began to feel like a well-dressed dishrag.

An hour or so into the flight, they fed us some unfamiliar foods, most of them made from swine. I had long since been unable to eat meat, so I made do with the rice on the tray, until I had a momentary flash of fish heads and rice in somebody's wounded belly, and I put my tray aside. Finally, Gary and I recognized the terrain as Vietnam. He had also been stationed in the Central Highlands, as a Special Forces medic, and we were the first to recognize the mountains. We looked at each other, then back out the tiny window, and for the rest of the trip remained lost in our own thoughts. As we descended into Hanoi International Airport, I remembered the first time I had gone into Vietnam, and felt grateful for the peaceful easy descent this time.

We were greeted on the ground by about a half dozen Vietnamese men, well-dressed in short-sleeved shirts and slacks. A few Vietnamese Army soldiers were scattered around the terminal, and it gave me a start to see the familiar gold star on red background on their collars and hats. Tommy had been similarly startled when he had seen them on his previous trip, but he had warned us about it, and that eased things a bit.

The civilian men were to be our guides and translators. Most of them knew Tommy from his previous trip in December, so they had a very friendly reunion while the rest of us cleared the paperwork of customs. I was touched by another recollection as I filled in the declaration. The paper was thin slices of wood pulp, as was almost all paper we were to see for the rest of the trip, including the toilet paper. It struck home how poor was this country still.

I was startled from my writing by the overhead sound of Mig fighters flying by. I dropped my pen and ran outside to watch as they passed. It reminded me of the everpresent American jets during the war, and I silently wondered if this was a demonstration of pride or some sort of strange welcome. There were about six planes, and they made their screaming passes four or five times. Finally, I went back inside and finished my paperwork.

After collecting our luggage, we were directed to a line of black Russian-made limousines in front of the terminal, and we got into them for the long drive into Hanoi. Though I had never been in the north of Vietnam before, the land seemed very familiar. From the road as far as the eye could see were the rice paddies, just as I had remembered them. Men and women in black pajamas and conical hats were bending over working in the fields. We talked very little during the drive, each of us peering intently into the descending dusk for glimpses of the familiar and the unknown. We drove through villages that looked much like those around Pleiku, and when we got to the Long Binh Bridge at Hanoi, I was struck again by the legacy the war had left here. It was the only one of five bridges over the Red River still standing after the many American B-52 strikes, and as such, it took at least a half-hour to cross on its narrow lane, following unending lines of bicycles and pedestrians.

When we arrived at the Thang Loi Hotel, most of us were exhausted from the long day and flight. It would have been heaven just to go to sleep, but we were expected at the Government House to meet the Vietnamese Committees on MIAs and Agent Orange. I found my room down a long covered walkway, and took the time for a quick shower before racing back to the lobby to join the others.

The meeting was held in the main reception room in an old French colonial building. There were introductions all around, and since I had boned up on the Vietnamese language before the trip, I had my first chance here to practice. The men seemed very pleased that I spoke the language, and I learned that they understood that it was a very difficult language for most people to learn. They greatly appreciated it when foreigners made the effort to try. I spoke in Vietnamese with almost everyone I met during the trip, and it invariably produced a broad grin. It had been well worth the hours of study and practice.

The dinner we were served after the introductions exceeded any I'd had. It was a seven-course meal, consisting of crab and fish dishes, the wonderful clear Vietnamese soup I had remembered, crisp vegetables, the everpresent rice, and fruits for dessert. We drank a sweet sherrylike Vietnamese wine and tea, and I conversed at length with the men sitting on either side of and across from me, alternating between my halting Vietnamese and their rather fluent English. We spoke of many things, what we had done during the war, what I had remembered from my time here, the futility and destruction of war, what our lives were like now, our families and our work. I found myself liking these people, Luu, Khanh, Quang, Ngo Minh. They were becoming individuals to me now, not merely extensions of a war.

We returned to the Thang Loi about 11 P.M., and I fell into my low narrow bed immediately, forgetting even to pull down the mosquito netting. In the morning, I cursed myself for that. I awoke at 4 A.M., scratching the bumps left by the hungry fellows, hoping none of them were the females who leave malaria in their wake, and realized the sun was already rising. I decided to join it. I brushed my teeth and exercised, then put on my running shoes and went out for a few miles. Though I'd expected to be alone on the roads, I soon remembered how early the day begins in Vietnam. The dirt paths were filled with people on their way to work, to the fields, and to the market. For the first time, I realized that there was a middle-aged population here. I'd never seen anyone who wasn't very young or very old during the war, and here they were. Or perhaps those who were young when I'd last been here had finally had the chance to arrive at middle age. After all, that's what I was now, so many years later.

The people stared at me as I ran in my shorts, running shoes, and a T-shirt bearing writing in English. I smiled at all of them, and was rewarded by the same each time. I marveled. They were all the same as when I was here before, but I didn't have to worry that anyone had a knife or grenade behind the smile. We weren't at war, and I was safe. It was a revelation for me. I stopped a few times and spoke with people at village entrances and at kiosks selling fruit, cigarettes, and various and sundry machine parts. I greeted all of them in Vietnamese. *Cháo, Ông. Cháo, Bà. Cháo, Bác. Bác manh gioi không? Tèn tôi là* Lynda.

They responded with smiles and warm greetings. They asked where I was from, and when I said I was an American, the response was always friendly. I had expected the reverse, anything but friendship, but it was never so. They seemed happy to see me. Perhaps it had to do with the fact that I was an American woman, and not a man who might have been a soldier trying to destroy them during the war, but when Les and Dave went out later that day, they got the same kind of reception.

I didn't know what to make of it. I'd expected them to hate me, and I was finding friendship everywhere. I personified the most recent war they'd been victims of, and still they seemed to like me.

I headed back to the hotel, showered, then went to the lobby for the gathering of the group that would go to the first of the many meetings of the week, the MIA meeting. Tom, Greg, Scotty, Bob, Gary, Joe, and I were ushered off in the same collection of cars in which we'd arrived last night. We honked and weaved our way through the bicycles and pedestrians in a scene I'd always attributed to Italian drivers. Our drivers seemed to use only two parts of the car, the accelerator and the horn. We passed Ho Chi Minh's mausoleum, and I remembered how scared I'd felt when he died. Now I only wished that I could see this leader who'd had such an impact on my life and those I'd known during the war.

The meeting was long. There was the mandatory press period, while the *60 Minutes* crew filmed and the reporters from AP and *The New York Times* asked questions. Then they left, and we settled down to the real business. Tommy had asked me to take notes of the meeting, and I found myself writing furiously. Thank God they had to have everything translated. I don't know shorthand, and I invented one as I went along. The time for translation allowed me to get almost everything on paper. The Vietnamese talked of how difficult it was to find remains of our soldiers. As they spoke of the triple canopy jungle, the heat, the humidity, the insects, the wild beasts, I remembered how those things had affected me in Pleiku, and I began to understand how difficult it was for them to get out and search for MIAs. The people of the villages would have to cooperate in the searches, and I thought of how they would feel about trying to find American remains when they had hundreds of thousands of their own people still missing from the war.

I had little time for thought, only transcription, until Ngo Minh said that they had news of some MIAs that had been found since our previous delegation's visit. Goose bumps stood out on my arms as I recorded the names of people they had found. I thought of the families who would be getting notice of their loved ones, and I shivered. Would they see an Army green sedan roll up at their front doors like I'd imagined for Gene's family? Would they get a phone call from the State Department? Or would they just see it in the newspapers? I wanted to call each of them individually and tell them. I wanted them to hear it from someone personally, like I'd wished to be able to talk with the families of so many of those who had died under my care during the war. During a break, I asked Tom and Greg if there wasn't any way we could speak with or get word to the families of the people we'd been told about before the news people got to them, but there was no phone communication between Vietnam and the United States, and we had no way of notifying them.

The news people found access to telexes that could connect them to Europe, and thus to the United States, and the families found out through the news. I hope they knew that we had wanted it to be a better way for them. I hope they knew how much we were thinking of them, just as we had been thinking of families when their sons and daughters and fathers had died on our tables during the war. It was an emotional time for all of us, the Vietnamese as well as the VVA delegation.

During the rest of the time in Hanoi, we were kept very busy. We had meetings every day on the MIA, Agent Orange, the Amerasian children, and cultural exchange. I visited the History Museum, the Museum of Scientific and Technological Achievements, and the Hanoi Conservatory of Music. I saw art and history and music, and I began to get a sense of these people as I'd never understood them. There was no time during the war to go to history museums, and I had never known how many eons these people had faced war. America had been only the last in a long line of countries that had tried to overcome this nation by war for thousands of years.

I began to grasp a feeling for the people and the country that had never been available to me before. War destroys so many things, and one of the first to go is the ability to think of the enemy as human beings with a history and a future. If you do so, then it will not be possible to destroy them and their land. You must depersonalize someone to kill him, and that is what the war had done to all of us. We were now finally having the opportunity to see each other as humans. It was an important step for me.

Before we left for Ho Chi Minh City (formerly Saigon), we were received by the Foreign Minister, Nguyen Co Thach, and by the Deputy Foreign Minister, Ha Van Lau. Both meetings left us feeling very good about the chances for being able to resolve in a humanitarian manner the issues before us. But more than that, I found again a sense of friendship from these two men. Nguyen Co Thach was an instantly likable older gentleman, who was walking on a cane and had his left foot bandaged. I'd spoken with him in Vietnamese, and we learned that he had broken his foot while jogging. When I told him that I, too, was a runner, we had a long conversation that was like any I'd had with other joggers. The universal running subjects of daily mileage, knee problems, stretching exercises, and shoes dominated the discussion, and again I found myself realizing that these were people, just like us.

As I once more wondered about the friendly attitude being displayed toward us, Mr. Thach, and later that evening Ha Van Lau, expressed to us the belief they had that America's Vietnam veterans were as much victims as they were. They had no love lost for the U.S. government, but they understood that there was a difference between the warriors and the war. I was learning more all the time.

Monday morning we left Hanoi for Ho Chi Minh City, feeling as though we were leaving friends. Mr. Quang went along with us to continue interpreting for us, but there was a real sadness at leaving our other new acquaintances.

The flight down-country was marked by all of us peering constantly to catch glimpses of familiar locations. When we passed over the area that had been the DMZ, I half expected to see some kind of great wall or marker. Instead, it just melded into the landscape. We passed over the areas of Phu Bai, where I had visited Jack, and over An Khe. We missed the areas of Qui Nhon and Pleiku, but I had the feeling that I was somehow touching them from way above the ground.

As we came closer to the landing at Tan Son Nhut airport, I became very nervous. My muscles felt weak, my stomach was churning, and I was staring out the window of the plane trying to take it all in forever. Everything about the airport looked familiar, the terminal building, the camouflaged hangers, the sky, the fences and towers. I'd left Vietnam from this very airport, and until this moment, I'd remembered almost nothing of it and my last day in Vietnam.

We landed smoothly and taxied up to the terminal, and I was glued to my seat. I just couldn't get up yet. I was intent on memorizing everything I saw. After everyone else had left the plane, I rose and gathered my things, then walked down the steps of the plane to touch *my* Vietnam. Hanoi had been important, but this was the stuff of my time here. I stood on the flight line for several minutes, turning to look in all directions. Yes, there were the guard towers, and over there a few military planes painted in camouflage colors. I saw so many things I recognized, but what was more familiar were the feelings inside me. I was remembering everything of that last terrible day here. I walked toward the gate area, knowing exactly where I was going. Part of me wanted to stay glued to the spot I was standing on, and part of me was leading me, pushing me on to the rest of the memories.

I pushed through the swinging door I'd gone out of almost precisely twelve years ago. It was the same gate area, but something was missing. In my mind's eye, I saw a dozen or more benches here, with GIs sitting on them, the sadness of a lifetime in their eyes. Duffel bags were everywhere. Flak jackets and helmets were strewn on the floor. Flight announcements were being made constantly.

But now all those things were gone. The room was open and bare. The benches were missing. The only announcements were in Vietnamese. I walked over to a place where there should have been a bench and bent over to touch the holes in the floor where the benches had been bolted down. What happened to them, I wondered? It was as real as if it had been only yesterday.

I turned and walked back to the windows from which I'd stared out so long ago. The feelings of fear returned in a wave. I felt again the incredible sadness, the fear of all the Vietnamese around me, the longing for home, and the deep-rooted fear that I would never get out of here alive. "Vietnam sucks," I thought. "It sucks so bad that it can suck you back down from the sky. It sucks out your heart and your soul and your mind, and you can never get them back."

I was surprised to feel tears dropping on my folded arms. I began to realize that this was not twelve years ago, it was now. I had met and gotten to know Vietnamese this time, and they were people, just like me and my family and my friends. I didn't have to be afraid anymore. The tears came washing over me, this time, finally, in relief. It was over. The war was over for me.

As I stood there alone shaking and crying quietly, Colin Campbell, *The New York Times* reporter, came over and put his arm around my shoulders. "Are you all right, Lynda? Can I do anything," he asked?

"It's okay, Colin," I answered. "It's good this time. I needed this to happen. I just figured out that it wasn't Vietnam that sucked, it was the war. I wanted to come back here to find something I had left, and I just found it. It was my youth, my innocence. I know now that I can never get them back, but I've touched them, and it's okay. I know where they went. I even think I know what they are. It's so sad." I buried my head in his shoulder and let the tears wash away the war.

It was Memorial Day. Waiting until near sunset in Vietnam, sunrise in America, we nine gathered in a garden. Quietly, without real plans, we formed a circle on the grass, sitting cross-legged in heat, moisture, and mosquitoes. Such were our memories of the surroundings of the war.

I'd chosen a branch of a plumeria tree, flowers of a heady perfume and pure simple beauty. We placed it in the center of our circle and grew quiet. We held hands, and Gary began to speak, the soft gentle words of a minister. We remembered from his prayers our fallen friends; the 57,000 who lost their lives here, the many hundreds of thousands who gave, by their blood, to the war, the millions of our brothers and sisters who had fought here.

One could nearly touch, see what we thought and felt. All gazed at the grass, the plumeria, the blue of sky, but each saw the others' hearts in our own.

I reached for the branch of blossoms, and chose one for myself. Plucking it, I passed it to Dave who did the same, then it continued the circle around to Joe, who took the last one and returned it to me. I gently replaced the shorn branch in the center, and Gary asked for our silent prayers.

The voice of that silence could be heard in the drop of humid air upon a leaf, the wisp of a breeze in our ears, the chirp of a gecko in a bush, the song of a bird on the wing. I thought of my cousin, Steve, of Gene, of Sharon Lane, of so many who had passed through my life here. We sent our prayers for our warriors to the heavens, our prayers for their peace and respite, and our prayers for the world. They were the prayers of those who know dearly the cost of war, and know deeply the meaning of peace and freedom. Our silence was unbroken, like our circle.

A shared look for us all, and we returned from our private reverie. Gary intoned his and our heartfelt hopes for the rest of our brothers and sisters, alive and not, Americans all, who answered a call and gave of themselves. And we prayed for peace for ourselves as well.

So ended the sun for us on Memorial Day, 1982. Another Memorial Day for us, in Vietnam.

AFTERWORD, 2001

When the University of Massachusetts Press offered me the opportunity to write an update to this new edition of *Home Before Morning,* I jumped at the chance. Over the years, I've received thousands of letters from readers. I read every one when they first arrived, and I tried to answer each of them, but before I could even make a dent in the pile, the next day's mailbag would arrive. It became so overwhelming at times that finally I just chose ten letters from each day's mail and answered those. The rest I lovingly put back into the bag, hoping that someday I would be able to get to them. That enormous mailbag is still in my attic office in the old house in Virginia. If you didn't get a response from me all those years ago get ready, because I'm going to try to answer all of your questions now. Someday is here.

The most commonly asked question is "Did you ever find Barbara again?" Perhaps one of the saddest things about the war in Vietnam was that the way we went and returned—not in units but as individuals, one at a time—meant that most of us lost track of even the closest friends. So it was with me and Barbara, whose real name, by the way, is Cheryl. (I changed the names of most of the people portrayed in the book to protect their identities, sometimes disguising them or changing their characteristics, sometimes describing the characteristics of one real person I was with but giving them to another real person. Anyone who remembers the character of Carl will understand why I did that.) I searched for Cheryl for years. I had been in touch with her soon after we returned from the war, but then I withdrew from any identity as a Vietnam veteran and let too many years pass. When I sought her out again at the time that this book was first published, she was nowhere to be found. Professional "people-finders" tried to locate her but failed. I've spoken about her in nearly every public forum I've participated in and written about her in almost every newspaper and magazine article, but there's been no response. Cheryl, if you're reading this, please contact the publisher. I miss you.

Happily, I have been in touch with several of my former war buddies. Many of the men and women who were forged by the fire of war in Pleiku and Qui Nhon turned out to be real firebrands. Diane founded and doggedly pursued the eventual construction and dedication of the Vietnam Women's Memorial in Washington. Joanie rose to the top levels of the V.A. and has made permanent inroads for women veterans. Coretta (Marty) has become my dear friend once again, and I will always treasure that friendship. She has risen to the rank of colonel in the military reserve and now has the opportunity to teach young nurses what it is really like to practice combat medicine, and how to survive it with some semblance of sanity. She has also moved up in the V.A.'s nursing hierarchy and is a highly respected oncology nurse specialist.

Denise (Sam) is another dear friend restored to me. Her participation in the John Turkey movement didn't totally destroy her lifelong military career after all. She left the Army after Vietnam but returned later and stayed in for the full twenty years, making damn sure that no nurses were sent to war without being properly prepared. She even served in—and survived—combat again in Desert Storm. Her Army commanding officer father never quite forgave me for, as he put it, "turning [him] into a Squid Admiral" when I changed his description in the book, but he said it with his tongue in his cheek. He forgave Sam as well, knowing her actions came from deep conviction. Sam retired from the military as a colonel and moved on to the Peace Corps. It's so Sam.

All of these friends as well as Peaches, Lynn, Sue, Jude, Sara, and many others came back together for the first time at the dedication of the Vietnam Memorial in 1982 and again in 1984 at the dedication of the statue of the three infantry soldiers at the Wall. I had been one of the planners of the National Salute to Vietnam Veterans and made sure that women and men who had been in the medical fields were invited and properly represented at all of the functions. I still have and cherish the banner we carried proclaiming to all who saw it that we were "Women Vietnam Veterans . . . and Jude." Jude was the only male nurse we'd been stationed with whom we found, and he marched proudly with us to lay our wreath at the apex of the Wall following our parade down Constitution Avenue.

Jude had climbed the professional ranks as well, topping out as a colonel and a highly respected researcher at Walter Reed Medical Center. Then he was diagnosed with a brain tumor, something we all were convinced was the result of exposure to the insecticides and herbicides sprayed in Vietnam. Two other nurses who'd been at the 71st had been diagnosed with the same type of tumor, we learned. For years Jude faced it head on, courageously, with his brilliant humor intact. On one of our many visits with him and his wife, Jeanie, Joanie and I presented him with a replica of the key to the Bastille, something she had found on her many travels. A symbol of freedom and liberation, the original key had been sent to George Washington by the Marquis de Lafayette following the overthrow of the infamous prison at the start of the French Revolution. Reminded of our Bastille parties and Joni Mitchell's "Marat/Sade" and our morning parties reading e. e. cummings, we inscribed the card, "to jude for all the memories good bad glad and sad from that time in 1969 71st evac hospital the beginning of a lifetime friendship et cetera et cetera et cetera." Jude passed away a few months later.

For me, the years have been filled with making a life in peacetime, but I've never been able to leave Vietnam completely behind. It has been important to make sense, and good, come from it. As the national women's director of Vietnam Veterans of America from 1979 to 1985, I had the good fortune to collaborate with men and women who have dedicated themselves to working with Vietnam veterans, trying to improve their lives. I had the opportunity to participate in training the devoted counselors in the V.A.'s Vietnam Vet Center readjustment counseling program. I traveled all over the U.S. and to many foreign countries speaking at schools and public meetings about the Vietnam war, and about women who have served in wars throughout history. VVA provided me a forum for raising awareness of issues that had largely been ignored by Americans and our government. I hope that I left listeners with a new understanding of and appreciation for people they may never have thought about before.

In the course of this work, I forged friendships with people I would never have met otherwise, and some of them turned out to be unexpected supporters. After participating in a forum in 1981 with Country Joe McDonald, the renowned rock and roll singer who wrote and recorded "I Feel Like I'm Fixin' to Die Rag," he and I had the opportunity to talk for some hours about women and war. We went back to Florence Nightingale, the founder of the nursing profession and the first recognized woman veteran. She had been the head nurse of the hospital at Scutari during the Crimean War, caring for thousands of extensive war casualties. I'd never realized that Joe was a Vietnam era veteran himself, and he'd never realized that women had gone to war. Unlike most people, though, who would say, "Well, that's interesting" and not give it another thought, Joe delved further into the study of women and war. He has since become a leading authority on Nightingale's life, her participation in the Crimean War, and her extensive writings, which set the highest standards of care for the sick and injured. He has recorded songs and videos about her life, as well as about women who served in Vietnam. Now when he sings his most famous song, he begins it "Come on all of you women and men."

I was privileged to testify at many congressional hearings during my years with VVA and to participate in commissions addressing the needs of Vietnam veterans and women veterans of all wars. During these activities, I worked again with 71st Evac pals Joan Furey, Sara McVicker, and Diane Evans and met other women veterans—Rose Sandecki, Lily Adams, Donna Buechler, Jane Thomson, Linda Spoonster Schwartz—comrades who have become friends. Together we raised awareness, stimulated research, and achieved passage of laws and regulations that require the V.A. and federal and state governments to assist all women veterans, and those who served in Vietnam in particular. Today, every V.A. facility in the world has a women veterans' coordinator to help women obtain needed health care. Women can easily negotiate V.A. loans to purchase homes. They aren't met with disbelief or resistance when they apply for educational assistance through the GI Bill. There are now health care programs especially designed for women vets; today, women can obtain needed gender-specific care from the V.A., such as mammograms, pap smears, and counseling for sexual trauma. And, no small point—no one these days refers to "our boys" in the military and veterans population.

After I left VVA, the work was taken over by other dedicated people, including Mary Stout, who became the first woman president of a congressionally chartered national veteran's organization, and Linda Spoonster Schwartz and Rick Weidman, who continued the efforts of the Women Veterans Committee. One of the laws we and other hard-working VVA members helped to pass required the Secretary of Veterans' Affairs to establish an Advisory Committee on Women Veterans. Eventually, the V.A. created the Office of Women Veterans, now energetically headed by Joan Furey. Numerous national studies have finally been undertaken to ascertain women vets' status and needs for special assistance, and women are now being included in overall studies of veterans—for example, the comprehensive National Study of Readjustment of Vietnam Veterans published in 1989.

I spent many years in psychotherapy working to overcome PTSD. I put down my last drink of alcohol in May 1983, and, a day at a time, with lots of help from my friends, I have not had to pick up another. My marriage to Bill ended in divorce at the end of the book, but we remained close friends. Bill was one of the most courageous people I've ever known, and he faced great difficulties during his last years. He received another kidney transplant in the late 1980s, done by—of all people—one of the chief surgeons I'd worked with at the 71st Evac. Unfortunately, the transplant rejected, and Bill was seriously ill for many years after. He remained on dialysis, eventually becoming the longest-surviving dialysis patient in the world, thirty-six years. A talented radio news journalist, he worked the overnight shift on the Middle East and Asia desk at the Voice of America in Washington for many years before he finally retired. The director of VOA described him as the greatest radio news writer in the country. Bill remarried a couple of years ago, and I was very happy for him. Betsy, his wife, and Desirée, his stepdaughter, gave him the family life he had always wanted. Bill passed away a few weeks ago, and Betsy, Bill's sister, Jennie, and I were with him until the end. It was a strange sisterhood, but everyone who knew Bill understood it. He was the kind of person who inspired a generosity of spirit in all around him.

My dad never lost his pride in me. He passed away in 1996 at the age of eighty-one. We became quite close in his final years, and he frequently told me how much it meant to him that I had served, and how proud he was of the writing I had done. He often spoke of

Home Before Morning and what it was like to see in print his own words from all the tapes he had sent me during the war. He was thrilled when I completed another book during the Persian Gulf War. Joan Furey and I coedited *Visions of War, Dreams of Peace: Writings of Women in the Vietnam War,* a collection of poems by women who had served in Vietnam, on all sides. It was our personal protest against Desert Storm. North Vietnamese, South Vietnamese, and American women—all expressed in the book so many of the same feelings about war, no matter their background. Themes of motherhood abound in *Visions,* and the universality of spirit cannot be ignored.

In 1984, I married again. Tom has been my partner, my guide, my friend, my strength, my protector, my spiritual adviser, and the closest thing to the other face of me that I ever expect to find. We often say that together we make a whole person. His family adopted me as one of their own, and I treasure my relationships with them, his sisters especially. Along with my husband, I gained a beautiful, loving stepdaughter, Bridgid, who is now twenty-six. With characteristic humor, she has always delighted in calling me her "wicked stepmother." She has taught me so much about mothering. I have also learned from our treasured foster daughter, Jamie, also twenty-six. And, in 1985, I began to learn more, when I gave birth to our baby girl, Molly Eileen. She is an extraordinary young woman, and one of the greatest miracles of my life.

Molly was born with several heart and intestinal defects, and other problems have shown up over the years that are possibly connected with my chemical exposures in Vietnam. In June 2000, I testified with several other women vets at hearings held by U.S. Senator Arlen Specter of Pennsylvania. Together with the concerted efforts of Linda Spoonster Schwartz and VVA, the hearings resulted in the passage of legislation, recently signed into law, that requires the V.A. to provide assistance to Molly and other children who have birth defects associated with their mothers' exposure to chemicals in Vietnam.

I went back to nursing eventually in 1989, finding my niche as the night supervisor of a nearby hospital. Looking back, I am convinced that the night shift people at the 71st Evac Hospital in Pleiku were the most talented, independent, and intuitive group I have ever worked with. I found many of those same qualities in the gifted team of professionals working the "graveyard" shift here at Reston Hospital in Northern Virginia. Whatever happened on my watch (and it was always something)—blizzards, oil pipeline ruptures, or the occasional mass casualty situation—they took it in stride. I hadn't felt so fulfilled in my career since Vietnam.

In November 1994, however, the war returned for me in a way I had never anticipated. I became seriously ill, and everything about our lives was changed. For the first two years it was touch and go, and it seemed as though I spent more time as a patient in hospitals than not. I learned what it was to be on a ventilator, to be in ICU, to spend week after week seeing the same hospital walls. I was referred to hospitals all over the country. Finally, at the National Jewish Hospital for Respiratory and Immunological Disorders in Denver, I was diagnosed with an auto-immune, collagen-vascular disease, which the doctors concluded was the result of exposure to toxic chemicals. Vietnam was the only place I'd ever had such exposure. So I began the long, slow, grinding process of trying to get the V.A. to "service-connect" me for the illness so that I could get help from the government. My illness had devastated us physically, emotionally, and financially. After I was repeatedly denied assistance, my friends in the veterans movement suggested that I apply for service connection for PTSD, which had caused me such pain after I had returned from the war and which had reappeared to batter me again during the worst, life-threatening phases of my physical illness. The V.A. finally relented and accepted that connection, but as of this writing, it continues to deny me connection for the auto-immune disease. With the assistance of Rick Weidman and VVA, we will continue the fight, though, because we have learned that other nurses have developed similar illnesses. The connection must be made so that others may be helped too.

I have been unable to return to work because of my illness, and I miss it very much, but I'm grateful to the doctors and nurses, to Tom and my girls, and to loving friends who have helped me to survive. Early in 1997, about two years into my illness, Jeanie sent me the "key to the Bastille" that Joanie and I had given to Jude. She knew Jude would have wanted her to give it to me, she said, and reminded me that he's watching over me. Thanks, Jeanie. And keep watch, Jude. I need all the help I can get.

The disease has taken its toll on me. It has attacked most of my organs, connective tissues, joints, and bones. So far, at the tender age of fifty-three, I have had one total hip replacement and two total knee replacements. At this moment I'm preparing for shoulder surgery next week. I have one hip left to replace, but not the courage yet to do it. Joint replacement surgery takes so much out of me. I've had dozens of surgeries over the past six years to repair problems arising from this illness. I've had multiple spontaneous bone fractures and connective tissue ruptures. I acquire infections easily, and have become gravely ill with some of them. I've learned much about patience and acceptance, lessons that did not come easily to this "Type A," hard-charging lady. But I have my loving family and friends in the veterans community, and the many friends of Bill W. who have become the family we chose for ourselves. During some of the worst crises, I received letters and cards from Vietnam vets and other friends around the world. I will never be able to fully express my gratitude to them: they often gave me just the right spark to get through the next hour or moment or procedure.

Occasionally I can get out to an event with my Vietnam vet writer friends, such as the twenty-fifth anniversary commemoration of the end of the war last fall in Detroit. I had the opportunity to participate in a week-long gathering of writers from all sides of the war held at the University of Montana in June 1998. The conference staff rented a power scooter for me, and for the first time in years I had legs—and the first taste of freedom I'd had since the illness began. I could fly from one end of the campus to the other with the best of them. It was a week I'll never forget for another reason, too. I developed friendships with a number of the Vietnamese participants, my enemies thirty years ago, and I learned important lessons about how those enemies could feel the same about the war as I did. Going back to Vietnam in 1982 had been a major part of my healing, but that week in Missoula turned my enemies into human beings who could forgive as well as I could—the forgiveness of others and myself that is needed, finally, to make my healing meaningful.

We heard and shared poems of reconciliation by Americans and Vietnamese that deeply touched me, and I wrote a poem for a friend I met that week. It sums up where I am today emotionally and spiritually. It is dedicated to Bach Diep, the woman who had once been a V.C. and is now a filmmaker in Vietnam.

AN INTRODUCTION IN MANY LANGUAGES
for Bach Diep

You were the unknown soldier I feared in Pleiku
The subject of our searches and seizures
Our pat-down frisks
Our shameful cavity canvassing
Never, ever your own joyous, tender, funny storytelling self.

Tonight in Missoula you finally became you.
You with your arms and your hands racing through the air
Drawing with your funny, flying body
The pictures in your head
Once painted on celluloid canvas.

I understand the story you tell
The words not so important
As we dance with each other to the music of
My halting Vietnamese phrases
Your few English words
My not-much-better French
Your embarrassingly exquisite French.

But, together, our perfectly fluent tears
And laughter
And embraces
And New York Super Fudge Chunk
Create a new language
A bridge to connect us
That no bombs can destroy.

The tears from our separate souls of old pain
Mingle and become the same
As they roll from the eyes of our souls
Merging on our embracing cheekbones
Flowing over and under our lips and chins
Landing drop by measured drop
Upon our hearts
Watering our freeze-dried memories
And washing them clean.

Sharing stories and memories with you
Is breaking the Wall of Silence between us.
I'd like to meet you now, please.
May I introduce myself?
Ten toi la Lynda . . .
Et vous?

Before I leave this, I must express my deepest gratitude to W. D. Ehrhart, one of the purest, most persistent writers to come out of the Vietnam war. Bill and I have become fast friends over the years, sharing our good fortune to find in Annie and Tom understanding, loving spouses who have encouraged us when we were at our most difficult times. We have also shared our awe at the miracle of our daughters, Leela and Molly. Were it not for Bill, this book would still be languishing in the land of "out of stock," despite continued requests for it by individuals and schools, libraries, and bookstores all over the world. I thank him, and I hope you do as well. In addition, my thanks go to Paul Wright and Bruce Wilcox at the University of Massachusetts Press, who both kept faith when my latest surgeries kept me from finishing this afterword in a timely fashion as I'd planned, and Carol Betsch, for her careful, tender editing. Finally, I thank Penny Miller, my mentor for the past nearly twenty years; Joan, my first mentor; my fellow Friends of Bill; and most important, Tom and my girls. You have given me reason to live, one day at a time, and you have brought light and peace to my life and my soul. I cherish you.

GLOSSARY

anesthesiologist: specially trained doctor who administers anesthesia to patients while undergoing surgery.

anesthetist: specially trained registered nurse who administers anesthesia to patients while undergoing surgery.

aneurism: a bulge in the wall of an artery.

aorta: the main artery that brings blood from the left ventricle of the heart to the rest of the body.

APO: Army Post Office.

Article 15: a section of the Uniform Code of Military Justice; a form of nonjudicial punishment.

ARVN: Army of the Republic of Vietnam.

beans and dicks: slang term for military C ration hot dogs and beans.

boonies: backwoods, jungles, or swampy areas far from civilization.

Bouncing Betty: a land mine that shoots an explosive charge up to waist level before detonation.

butter bar: slang for the gold bar indicating the rank of a second lieutenant; also a slang term for a second lieutenant.

C-130: large propeller-driven Air Force planes that carry people and cargo.

catabolic: a destructive tendency by the diseased body to break down tissue faster than it can be replaced.

Charlie: the enemy.

chest cutter: a thoracic surgeon.

Chinooks: The Army's largest supply and transport helicopter.
chloracne: a rash characterized by boils, itching, and redness. It is caused by exposure to a toxic chemical called dioxin.
chopper: helicopter.
CIDG: Civilian Irregular Defense Group; manned by Montagnards.
C.O.: commanding officer.
Cobra: the U.S. Army's primary attack helicopter.
colostomy: an operation on the colon to reroute waste products from the bowel to an opening in the abdominal wall where they are collected in a bag attached to the side of the body.
crispy critters: burned patients.
D&I: debridement and irrigation; an operation to cut away dead skin, remove fragments, and clean a wound.
DEROS: Date of Expected Return from Overseas.
dialysis: a method of separating toxins from the blood by use of an artificial kidney machine.
dink: derogatory term for a Vietnamese person.
diverticulum: a sac or pouch in a body organ or cavity.
DMZ: demilitarized zone.
dopamine: intravenous medication to keep the blood pressure elevated.
DPC: delayed primary closure; a surgical technique in which the patient's wound is closed sometime after initial surgery.
dust-off: medical evacuation helicopters.
ER: emergency room.
ETS: estimated time of separation (from the Armed Forces).
expectants: casualties who are expected to die.
FAA: Federal Aviation Administration.
fire base: an artillery base set up to support combat ground troops.
flak jacket: a heavy fiber-filled vest designed to protect soldiers from shrapnel wounds.
FNG: fucking new guy.
frag: a piece of metal from an exploding rocket, bomb, or fragmentation grenade.
Freedom Bird: the plane that took soldiers from Vietnam back to the U.S.
Friendly Fire: accidental attacks on U.S. or allied soldiers by other U.S. or allied forces.
FUO: fever of unknown origin.

gas passer: anesthetist or anesthesiologist.
GI: an Army enlisted man; the term dates to World War II and originally stood for "government issue."
Glad bag: slang term for a bag used to wrap a dead body.
goiter: a non-cancerous tumor of the thyroid gland.
gook: a derogatory term for Vietnamese people.
gork: a slang expression for a patient who is brain-dead.
grunt: infantryman.
GSW: gunshot wound.
gurney: a wheeled stretcher.
hemodialysis: the process of cleansing impurities from the blood with an artificial kidney machine.
hooch: living quarters.
humped: marched or hiked.
ICU: intensive care unit.
ICU-itis: extreme disorientation experienced by some patients when they have no outside stimulus for a long time.
iliac artery: either of two large arteries that bring blood to the pelvis and the legs.
IV: intravenous.
jet jockey: Air Force fighter pilot.
lap pads: large sterile pads used to absorb blood when working in abdominal or chest areas.
lifer: a career soldier.
LM: lunar module.
LZ: landing zone.
M-16: standard semiautomatic rifle of the U.S. Army.
Mas-Cal: mass casualty.
MASH: Mobile Army Surgical Hospital.
Mayo stand: the wheeled working table on which the scrub nurse keeps the surgical instruments.
Medcaps: Medical Civil Action Patrols.
medevac: medical evacuation.
MFWs: multiple frag wounds.
Montagnards: a primitive people who live in Vietnam's Central Highlands.
MOS: military occupational specialty.
MP: military police.

napalm: a jellied petroleum substance used as a weapon against personnel.

NAPHT: National Association of Patients on Hemodialysis and Transplantation.

nephrology: the branch of medical science dealing with the kidneys.

NVA: North Vietnamese Army.

OR: operating room.

over the fence: in Cambodia or Laos.

peritoneum: the membrane lining the abdominal cavity.

POW: prisoner of war.

pseudomonas: a common bacterial infection among seriously burned patients that looks like a blue slime and has a revolting smell.

PTSD: posttraumatic stress disorder.

pungi pits: booby trap holes in the ground containing long sharpened sticks designed to pierce a soldier's body when he falls in.

PX: post exchange; a military base's department store.

R&R: rest and recuperation.

red alert: the most urgent form of warning; signals an imminent enemy attack.

REMF: rear echelon motherfucker.

renal: pertaining to the kidneys.

repo depot: replacement detachment.

retractors: surgical tools designed to draw back the edge of an incision.

RN: registered nurse.

roger: a radio communication term meaning "I understand."

ROKs: soldiers from the Republic of Korea.

sappers: Viet Cong soldiers who were specially trained to infiltrate heavily defended installations at night.

scrub nurse: a nurse who hands the surgeon his instruments during an operation.

scrub tech: a technician who hands the surgeon's instruments during an operation.

septic: infected.

shocky: slang term for a patient who is in shock.

shrapnel: metal fragments from an explosive device.

shunt: tubing outside the skin connecting to a vein and an artery to provide an access to the blood.

slant: derogatory term for a Vietnamese person.
slope: derogatory term for a Vietnamese person.
Sopwith Camels: light, fixed-wing reconnaissance aircraft.
Special Forces: Green Beret units.
spleenectomy: surgery to remove the spleen.
surgical field: the sterile area in which the surgeon and his assistants work.
T&T: through and through wound—one in which a bullet or fragment has entered and exited the body.
tapes: a rounded, curved surgical needle used for suturing.
Tet: the Vietnamese New Year.
tracers: ammunition containing a special chemical substance that causes it to leave a trail of smoke or fire, to make its path visible.
trach: tracheotomy—opening into a patient's windpipe to facilitate breathing.
triage: the procedure for deciding the order in which to treat casualties.
trip wires: fine wires stretched across trails and designed to set off booby traps.
turtles: new replacements; called turtles because it took them so long to arrive.
uremia: a condition in which the blood retains toxins normally excreted in urine.
V.A.: Veterans Administration.
V.C.: Viet Cong.
Victor Charlie: the phonetic alphabet for V.C.
VVA: Vietnam Veterans of America; not affiliated with the Veterans Administration.
Walter Wonderful: Walter Reed Army·Hospital.
the world: home.
zit: derogatory term for Vietnamese people.